LIBRARY IN A BOOK

ABORTION

THE FACTS ON FILE LIBRARY IN A BOOK SERIES

Each volume of the Facts On File Library in a Book series is carefully designed to be the best one-volume source for research on important current problems. Written clearly and carefully so that even the most complex aspects of the issue are easily understandable, the books give the reader the research tools to begin work, plus the information needed to delve more deeply into the topic. Each book includes a history of the subject, biographical information on important figures in the field, a complete annotated bibliography and a carefully designed index—everything the researcher needs to get down to work.

LIBRARY IN A BOOK

ABORTION

Carl N. Flanders

Bibliographic materials prepared by
Caroline M. Brown, M.L.S., Rutgers University

Facts On File
New York • Oxford

TITLE LIBRARY IN A BOOK: ABORTION

Copyright © 1991 by Carl N. Flanders

Facts On File, Inc.   Facts On File Limited
460 Park Avenue South   c/o Roundhouse Publishing Ltd.
New York NY 10016   P. O. Box 140
USA   Oxford OX2 7SF
                                    United Kingdom

Library of Congress Cataloging-in-Publication Data
Flanders, Carl N.
    Abortion / by Carl N. Flanders : bibliographic materials prepared by Caroline M. Brown.
        p. cm. — (Library in a book)
    Includes bibliographical references and index.
    Summary: Discusses abortion and court cases involving abortion.
    ISBN 0-8160-1908-8
    1. Abortion—United States—Juvenile literature. [1. Abortion.]
I. Brown, Caroline M.   II. Title.   III. Series.
HQ767.5.U5F62   1990
363.4'6'0973—dc20   90-42867

A British CIP catalogue record for this book is available from the British Library.

Facts on File books are available at special discounts when purchased in bulk quantities for businesses, associations, institutions or sales promotions. Please call our Special Sales Department in New York at 212/683-2244 (dial 800/322-8755 except in NY, AK or HI) or in Oxford at 865/728399.

Text design by Ron Monteleone
Jacket design by Nadja Furlan-Lorbeck
Composition by The Maple-Vail Book Manufacturing Group
Manufactured by The Maple-Vail Book Manufacturing Group
Printed in the United States of America

10 9 8 7 6 5 4 3

This book is printed on acid-free paper.

CONTENTS

Contents

ACKNOWLEDGMENTS

The author would like to thank the following organizations and individuals for their assistance: the American Civil Liberties Union's Reproductive Freedom Project; Planned Parenthood's Guttmacher Institute; the National Right to Life Committee; the Sprague Library at Montclair State College; and Eleanora von Dehsen and Nicholas Bakalar at Facts On File.

INTRODUCTION

The purpose of this book is to provide a one-stop source for information about abortion. The first part of the book is an overview of the topic. It is designed to give the reader a basic picture of the many issues involved with abortion. It includes a general introduction, chronology of major events, summary of important court cases, and biographical listing of key individuals.

Once acquainted with the subject of abortion, the reader can turn to the second part of the book for a comprehensive guide to reference materials on the subject. A broad spectrum of resources is identified for use in further research. Acronyms used throughout the text are listed at the end of the book. Also included are two appendixes that furnish information on the legal status of abortion.

The issue of abortion is neither legally nor politically settled. Litigation and legislation continue to take aim at this contentious issue. It is bound to remain a topic of intense debate for the foreseeable future. This book is current through December 31, 1989. Readers are encouraged to consult the reference sources in the second half of the book for developments subsequent to this date.

PART I

OVERVIEW OF THE TOPIC

CHAPTER 1

INTRODUCTION TO ABORTION

In the United States, about one of every three pregnancies never comes to term because the woman has an abortion. This translates into 1.5 million induced abortions a year. Include the rest of the world and the number rises to something on the order of 50 or 60 million. These statistics lead to an inescapable conclusion: Abortion is a fact of our times, a clinical procedure repeated daily and with great regularity. Moreover, it ranks among the most complex and controversial issues, inspiring contentious legal, political, and ethical debates and raising fundamental questions about human life and human liberty.

This introductory chapter is tailored to provide an overview of the abortion issue. It consists of six sections. "Historical Background" recounts the major developments and traces the evolution of societal attitudes since ancient times. "Abortion in the United States Today" summarizes the prevailing situation in this country: who has abortions, how they are performed, attitudes of the public, and the outlines of the abortion debate. "Abortion and the Law" addresses the main legal issues and reviews legislative activities and initiatives of the U.S. Congress. "Abortion and Religion" examines this important and controversial nexus. The international scope of the abortion issue is assessed in "Worldwide Perspective." The final section, "Future Trends," considers probable or possible developments in the years ahead. Court cases in bold print are reviewed separately in Chapter 3.

3

HISTORICAL BACKGROUND

Abortion has been practiced since the beginning of civilization. Throughout history, societies have employed a wide range of methods to force a pregnancy to an early and unnatural end. The documentary record suggests these were extremely painful, dangerous to the woman's health, and frequently fatal. Until the advent of modern medical practices and understanding, women were subject to primitive procedures, often improvised, including the common use of poisonous concoctions to induce abortion.

Abortion has been a social issue across recorded history. In ancient Assyria abortion was a crime under the Assyrian Code (12th century B.C.). Women who violated the code were tried and, if convicted, impaled on a stake and denied the dignity of burial. Earliest Jewish law strictly forbade abortion as a way of avoiding childbirth, except when necessary to save the mother's life.

During the classical era (6th–4th century B.C.), Greece allowed abortion. Practitioners either performed surgery or dispensed drugs. But tolerance had its social limits. An abortionist's failure to inform the father was criminally punishable. The philosophers Aristotle and Plato both advocated abortion as a way to control population. A minority of Greeks opposed abortion, notably Hippocrates (c.460–c.370 B.C.), who prohibited it in one of the versions of his renowned Hippocratic Oath on medical ethics and the physician's obligation to healing.

In ancient Rome the fetus generally was considered a part of the woman and abortion was legal. A husband who demanded his wife have an abortion was acting within the social norms. Moreover, he had the right to punish or divorce his wife if she had an abortion without his consent. Neither the Greeks nor Romans of antiquity were animated by concern for the life of the unborn. To the degree these and other ancient peoples proscribed abortion, they did so out of concern for the mother's health and life. Also, several millennia ago population control was rarely a factor. Women were not preoccupied with limiting family size. Instead, abortions were more likely sought to end pregnancies resulting from adultery or prostitution.

The first teachings of the Christian church scarcely mentioned abortion. However, by the end of the 1st century A.D. the church had proclaimed it a sin. In the 5th century a split developed between the Eastern and Western Catholic churches. While the Eastern church universally condemned abortion, Western Catholic theologians condoned procedures during early stages of pregnancy. The Western position stemmed from St. Augustine's belief that the unborn fetus lacked a soul prior to quickening. This is the point somewhere between the 4th and 6th months of pregnancy, when a woman first senses movement in the womb. After quickening, fetuses were said to be "formed" or "ensouled."

Throughout the Middle Ages and Renaissance in Europe, abortion was legal until the moment of quickening. Within the Catholic church there were conflicting opinions on abortion. In 1588 Pope Sixtus V called abortion the same as murder and thus subject to the same penalties. Within three years Pope Gregory XVI eliminated any penalties until ensoulment—which was then determined to be about 40 days after conception. In 1869 Pope Pius IX removed any distinction between formed and unformed fetuses and made the penalty for the sin of abortion excommunication regardless of the stage of fetal development. At about the same time abortion was banned in most of Europe. The decision of Pius IX was reaffirmed in 1917 with publication of the Code of Canon Law. Successive popes to the present day have firmly upheld this church canon.

Abortion laws and policies in the United States developed out of the Anglo-Saxon tradition. Great Britain actually had no abortion laws until the 14th century, at which time abortions performed after quickening were made illegal. These laws were based on the Christian view of ensoulment of the fetus at the time of quickening. For centuries abortion prior to quickening remained a private decision. Then in 1803 Parliament passed the first restrictive abortion statute, the Miscarriage of Women Act, which criminalized the practice regardless of the stage of pregnancy. However, abortions done after movement in the womb were punished more severely. The last major British abortion law of the 19th century, passed in 1861, made abortion a felony; this law remained in force for more than 100 years. In 1968 British lawmakers enacted the Abortion Act, which dramatically loosened legal restrictions. The measure permitted both eugenic abortion, meaning that of an abnormal or deformed fetus, and abortion when doctors determined that the pregnancy threatened the mental or physical health of the mother.

In the United States abortion prior to quickening was legal until the mid-1800s. In the nation's first court action on the issue, *Commonwealth v. Bangs*, the Massachusetts Supreme Court in 1812 ruled that abortion with the woman's consent was legal before fetal movement.

Despite the considerable health hazards of abortion in the 19th century, women continued to terminate unwanted pregnancies. Use of toxic substances and injurious methods made abortions exceedingly dangerous. Practices ranged from hot baths and bloodletting to ingestion of poisons and unsanitary surgery. Connecticut passed the first abortion statute in the United States in 1821, making it a crime to give a woman "quick with child" a poison meant to cause her to miscarry. In 1830 New York criminalized the performance of abortions after quickening but exempted those necessary to save the woman's life. New York in 1845 became the first state to place women under threat of prosecution for having an abortion.

This advance wave of stricter laws—what were in essence antipoisoning statutes—had a marginal effect. Abortion continued to be widespread, lucrative for its practitioners, and medically perilous for its subjects. The growing accessibility of abortion, and the concomitant health dangers to women, inspired more and more states to act to control the practice. Between 1821 and 1841, ten states enacted laws criminalizing abortion after quickening unless the mother's life was at stake. Other states soon followed suit, but the punishments were often lax and irregularly enforced. Abortionists were rarely prosecuted and almost never convicted.

At midcentury the antiabortion movement was driven by the American Medical Association (AMA). Founded in 1847 to establish professional standards, the AMA campaigned to halt unsafe abortions by medical charlatans and unlicensed practitioners. The organization mobilized to assert its authority and because many members were increasingly uncomfortable with the notion of quickening as the first sign of life. By then science had discovered that the union of sperm and egg initiated fetal development. This implied that to some extent life began at conception. In 1859 the AMA passed a resolution condemning abortion and urging states to make it illegal. The assault was directed not at the women having abortions but at the phony practitioners. In time each of the states changed its laws. By the end of the century abortion was a major crime nationwide. All but four states allowed therapeutic abortions to save the mother's life. In those four, even life-saving abortions were criminal.

The 19th-century movement to criminalize abortion was shadowed by a campaign to inform Americans about the availability of birth control. This sensitive issue became a subject of public policy when the U.S. Congress in 1873 passed the Comstock Law, banning the mailing of any material deemed obscene, including contraception and abortion-inducing drugs. Despite these regulations, women still had access to birth control and were therefore less dependent on abortion. While the abortion rate decreased overall, the practice continued on a large scale. An illegal abortion industry flourished and abortion remained a principal cause of maternal death. The situation drifted along unchanged through World War II.

Around 1950 the medical community, through the AMA, once again took the lead and mounted a drive to liberalize century-old state abortion

Introductio n t o Abortio n

laws. Increasingly, physicians were taking positions on abortion far more liberal than existing laws reflected. Many doctors were concerned about the thousands of women suffering complications or death from illegal abortions at a time when legal abortions had become safer than ever due to the rise of antibiotics, antiseptic surgery, and new abortion techniques.

In 1959, responding to the AMA's pleas, the American Law Institute (ALI) proposed a Model Penal Code (MPC) that advocated sweeping liberalization of state abortion laws. The ALI recommended that state lawmakers broaden the grounds for legal abortion to include the mental health of the mother, pregnancy due to rape or incest, and fetal deformity. Not one state legislature adopted the ALI suggestions.

By the 1960s public sentiment toward abortion had begun to shift. Growing numbers of Americans accepted criteria proposed under the MPC—which stopped short of a call for abortion on demand. Two factors spurred national interest in the debate over proposed statutory reform. One involved the drug thalidomide, a tranquilizer sold in Europe that caused serious birth defects. Many pregnant women who had used it feared the possible consequences and sought abortions. Americans became aware of the tragic potential of the drug through the case in 1962 of Sherri Finkbine, an Arizona woman who took thalidomide and whose doctor recommended an abortion for fear of possible fetal deformity. A storm of nationwide publicity prompted the Phoenix hospital where her abortion was to be performed to cancel out of fear of potential criminal liability. Arizona law at the time allowed abortion only to save the mother's life. Finkbine eventually flew to Sweden to have the abortion.

The second factor involved an outbreak of German measles in the United States in 1964. Concern about the possible impact that measles contracted early in pregnancy might have upon the fetus led many women to seek and have abortions. The thalidomide and rubella cases attracted significant national attention and tended to create empathy toward these women and the situations confronting them.

The 1960s was a period of great social change in the United States. A more open and frank discussion of abortion followed from the public's greater willingness to openly consider issues of human sexuality. The decade saw the emergence of the women's movement. One of its fundamental claims was that freedom and equality for women depended on their ability to control their reproductive lives. Abortion was cast as an issue bearing directly on their independence and liberty. By the end of the decade, the women's movement urged that the decision to have an abortion be recognized under law as a fundamental individual freedom—a protected privacy right.

This heightened focus on the issue led many states to turn to the MPC as a guide to reform their abortion laws. In 1967 Colorado, California, and North Carolina became the first states to liberalize their statutes. By 1973, 13 states had enacted similar measures. In the early 1970s four states took the further step of legalizing all abortions done by a doctor up to some legally designated time well into pregnancy. The most liberal law was New York's, which allowed abortion for any reason up to 24 weeks. In 1972 the American Bar Association (ABA) passed a Uniform Abortion Act, patterned on the New York statute, as a model for all state statutes. Also, the congressionally appointed Commission on Population Growth and the American Future released its final report recommending immediate and far-reaching liberalization of state abortion laws.

As legislatures continued to examine their laws, state and federal courts were beginning to consider various suits and actions challenging the constitutionality of existing statutes which prohibited abortion. In 1973, in the landmark case of **Roe v. Wade,** the Supreme Court moved to resolve the constitutional debate when it ruled that the privacy right encompassed a woman's decision to have an abortion. By extension, the Court held that states could not restrict abortions during the 1st trimester.

The impact of **Roe** on life and law in the United States was momentous. The decision legalized abortion in all 50 states and established women's choice as a fundamental right protected under the Constitution. Availability of the procedure rose dramatically as free-standing clinics sprang up around the country. Now a staple of the political and social lexicons, **Roe v. Wade** is virtually synonomous with the abortion issue for most Americans.

For the last 15 years the basic status of abortion under the law has not changed. The 1970s and 1980s saw determined pro-life forces in various state legislatures pass restrictive abortion statutes to test the scope and meaning of **Roe.** Invariably these laws were cut down on constitutional grounds in federal courts.

ABORTION IN THE UNITED STATES TODAY

This section fashions a picture of the abortion issue as it now stands in the United States. The first part explains the clinical side of abortion, focusing on the range of methods and procedures involved at various stages of pregnancy. Next comes a statistical and demographic profile of women who obtain abortions. This is followed by a summary look at public attitudes on the issue. Finally the competing views within the abortion debate in the nation are presented.

METHODS AND PROCEDURES

Whether spontaneous or induced, abortion is the ending of a pregnancy before natural birth. Once the woman's egg is fertilized by a sperm, the inseminated egg, or zygote, travels down her fallopian tube, enters the uterus, and implants in her uterine wall. For the next two months it is called an embryo. By this point, medical science refers to the developing life within the womb as a fetus. About half of all fertilized eggs fail to take hold and are, in course, discharged from the body. With some eggs that do implant in the uterine wall, the embryo or fetus fails to develop properly and is naturally expelled through spontaneous abortion. When this occurs after the 26th week of pregnancy, it is called a miscarriage. Most studies show 15 to 20% of all diagnosed pregnancies end in spontaneous abortion.

Induced abortion is the deliberate expelling from the womb of a fetus that has attached to the uterus and developed a placenta. Abortions induced for medical reasons, such as saving the mother's life or preserving her health, are generally called therapeutic. Those performed for nonmedical reasons are termed nontherapeutic or elective abortions. In the United States, all legal induced abortions must be sanctioned medical procedures performed by licensed physicians in medical settings.

Currently the vast majority of abortions take place in the first trimester of pregnancy—half, in fact, by the 8th week. Instrumental evacuation entails dilating the cervix, or opening of the uterus, and removing the fetus and placenta. The safest of all available methods, it is used in 98% of abortions. Second-trimester abortion is accomplished by either inducing premature labor or surgically removing the fetus and placenta. The first method accounts for about 80% of these later abortions. Surgery is rarely performed because it involves the greatest risk of any abortion procedure.

Early Abortion Procedures

Abortion is possible within the first weeks of pregnancy. However, at this stage the microscopically small embryo is so difficult to detect that performing a menstrual extraction, a technique for discharging the embryo from the uterus a few days after the first missed menstrual period, can end in an incomplete abortion. Another early method is the controversial new drug RU 486. Developed by French biochemist Dr. Etienne Baulieu, RU 486 blocks the fertilized egg from implanting in the uterine wall, causing the lining to break away and expel the zygote. When taken in the first weeks of pregnancy the drug is successful in from 90 to 95% of cases. It can be combined with the hormone prostaglandin to enhance its effectiveness, but the hormone causes unpleasant side effects. Despite its drawbacks, RU 486 appears to present women who in the past might have sought abortions with a new option. Dr. Baulieu goes so far as to predict his creation will lead to the eventual disappearance of abortion.

Probably the safest procedure, vacuum aspiration accounts for more than 90% of all abortions. In this method, the cervix is numbed, then gently dilated, using either dilators or rods called sterile lamanaria. With the latter, dilation may take as long as 24 hours, but it is far gentler and less traumatic. Once the cervix is dilated, a small tube, or cannula, is inserted in the uterus. The aspirator, which is connected to the cannula, is the vacuum device that creates suction to empty the uterus and complete the abortion. The whole process ordinarily takes place in less than half an hour. Some women experience only moderate cramping during vacuum aspiration, while others report intense pain and cramping.

Another evacuation method is dilation and curettage (D & C). With D & C the woman is anesthetized and her cervix is dilated. The physician then removes the fetus with a scraping instrument. While used extensively before the development of vacuum aspiration, curettage is rarely done any longer in the 1st trimester. Still, it remains the method of choice for abortions in the 12th or 13th weeks of pregnancy.

Late Procedures

Less than 10% of abortions take place after the 1st trimester. The figure declines to less than 1% after the 20th week. Determining exact fetal age is difficult; thus many doctors are apprehensive about performing abortions beyond the 20th week for fear they might expel a viable fetus.

Dilation and evacuation (D & E), similar to vacuum aspiration, is the preferred procedure between weeks 13 and 15. By the 2nd trimester, the fetus is too large to pass through the cannula and therefore must be dismembered with surgical instruments before suction removal. In contrast to other later procedures, D & E may be done on an outpatient basis and takes only 30 minutes to complete.

Medical induction or instillation is the most frequently used method after the 15th week. During this procedure, a chemical such as saline solution or prostaglandin is injected (or "instilled") into the woman's womb, inducing premature labor and causing her to expel the fetus and placenta. Typically labor lasts for hours, even days, and is often painful and emotionally taxing. With prostaglandin it is possible for the fetus to be born alive, though this happens very rarely. Unless the prostaglandin is given together with a toxic substance, or unless a shot is administered to stop the fetal heartbeat, there is no guarantee against a live birth. Under law, when a fetus is born alive, attending physicians must take full measures to protect its life.

In rare instances, women with uterine cancer or related medical problems have abortions. In these cases doctors employ one of two special surgical procedures. In a hysterotomy, both the fetus and placenta are surgically removed; in a hysterectomy, reproductive organs like the uterus and ovaries may be removed as well. Such abortions are especially hazardous and performed only in emergency situations.

Complications

Like all invasive medical procedures, abortion entails possible dangers. Statistically, it carries the same medical risks as childbirth. The medical community contends legalization of abortion in 1973 has contributed to a dramatic reduction in risk. The trend toward abortion earlier in a pregnancy, the use of vacuum aspiration, and the evolving expertise of physicians in performing abortions have all made the procedure less medically perilous to the woman.

The most common complications include infection, blood clots, excessive bleeding, and tears in the cervix or uterine wall. Very infrequently, and late in a pregnancy, women develop what is called amniotic fluid embolism. This potentially fatal condition occurs when amniotic fluid enters the bloodstream and travels to the heart.

About 2 to 3% of 1st-trimester abortions entail minor medical complications. Fewer than 1 in 100 involves a complication severe enough to warrant hospitalization or more surgery.

While many women experience no residual psychological or emotional difficulties, others may suffer from a condition identified as Post Abortion Syndrome, or PAS, a depression directly linked to having an abortion. The impact of abortion on a woman's emotional health is a controversial issue that remains under sharp debate. Abortion-rights groups claim there is no substantive evidence proving abortion is psychologically injurious. PAS is in no sense universally acknowledged by the mental health community. Still, support groups and counselors exist to help women who experience the symptoms associated with PAS.

Availability

Prior to **Roe v. Wade,** tens of thousands of women patronized an illegal abortion industry whose practitioners charged high, if not exorbitant, fees and observed no regulated health standards. Abortions were risky and expensive. Nationwide legalization wrought important changes. Even before **Roe,** certain states, such as New York and California, had eased their abortion laws. Clinics sprang up to satisfy the resulting demand. With the Supreme Court's historic ruling in 1973, hospitals no longer had a monopoly on abortion services. Physicians were free to perform them in private offices. Also, independent or "free-standing" abortion clinics emerged, making abortion both more accessible and affordable. For the last 16 years women have not confronted the medical hazards of substandard abortion mills. Clean and safe facilities stretch across the 50 states. A 1987 survey reported 2,680 abortion providers nationwide. Today a 1st trimester abortion costs on average a few hundred dollars, a figure that has remained relatively stable despite an overall rise in health care costs.

Almost nine in ten abortions are performed in the free-standing clinics, which have no hospital affiliation. While these clinics furnish other reproduction-related services, such as sterilization and contraception, they principally provide abortions. The remainder occur in hospitals or doctors' private offices. Free-standing clinics dominate the abortion industry for several reasons. They are readily accessible. Appointments are easy to make. They receive large numbers of referrals from doctors reluctant to perform abortions themselves in private offices. Perhaps the most significant factor is economic. These clinics provide abortions for one-third or even one-quarter the cost incurred at a hospital. Medical officers at free-standing clinics earn much less per abortion than hospital doctors, who charge several hundred dollars. Moreover, hospitals ordinarily require an overnight stay. Clinics render services on an outpatient basis.

About one-half the independent clinics are members of a professional organization called the National Abortion Federation, or NAF, which has drawn up and issued industry standards. The NAF sponsors courses for doctors and other health care professionals, conducts research, and educates the public on the safety and availability of abortion services.

STATISTICS AND DEMOGRAPHICS

One in three women who get pregnant each year chooses to have an abortion. Surveys and studies furnish an annual flood of figures on the composition of these abortion recipients. Researchers gather data on various demographic characteristics—for instance, a woman's age, race, religion, and economic status—and use this material to put together a statistical profile of women who have abortions. In the United States, two leading organizations compile and monitor abortion statistics. The Centers for Disease Control, part of the federal government's Public Health Service, accumulates and publishes information furnished by the states. The private Alan Guttmacher Institute (AGI), the research branch of Planned Parenthood Federation, comprehensively surveys all the abortion facilities nationwide.

Introduction to Abortion

Abortion rates and ratios are key statistical concepts. They provide researchers with distinct yet complementary information. Both of these figures are based on women of childbearing age, which is defined as 15 to 44 years old. What distinguishes a rate from a ratio is the way each is calculated. To determine a rate, all women of childbearing age are counted and the number is expressed in terms of 1,000 such women. For example, in a given year a rate of 30 would mean that for every 1,000 women in the United States aged 15 to 44, there were 30 who had abortions. But to figure a ratio, only pregnant women are counted. A ratio of 300 in a given year would indicate that for every 1,000 pregnant women, 300 aborted. Rates and ratios help researchers to detect patterns and trends in a population—for example, a decline or increase in abortions from year to year. These two statistics are also frequently used to compare abortion patterns across various demographic traits.

Every year some 6 million of the approximately 55 million women of childbearing age in the United States get pregnant. Half of the pregnancies are planned or intended. Of the total number of pregnancies, about 3.5 million are brought to term, another 1 million end in miscarriage, and the remaining 1.5 to 1.6 million are aborted. It is estimated that after World War II perhaps 1 million illegal abortions were performed annually in the United States. Greater accessibility of reliable birth control methods through the 1950s and 1960s contributed to a drop in the practice. The decline was attributable to better contraception and to the high cost and riskiness of abortions. As states began to liberalize their abortion laws in the late 1960s, legal abortion expanded in a significant way. By 1973 about 750,000 legal abortions were performed. After 1973 and nationwide legalization, the numbers rose steadily, finally doubling to roughly 1.5 million and then leveling off.

The majority of American women obtaining abortions are single, young, and white. Most have 1st-trimester abortions by vacuum aspiration. The highest abortion ratios are found among unmarried women, women over 40, teenagers, and nonwhite women. Recall that in calculating abortion ratios, only pregnant women are counted.

Generally, abortion is the recourse for women faced with unwanted pregnancies. According to researchers, between 50 and 60% of all pregnancies in a given year are unintended. Estimates are that half of all abortions could be avoided through consistent use of contraceptives. Some forms of birth control are more reliable than others, but 15% of women will get pregnant despite using contraception. At least a quarter of abortions are done on women whose birth control has failed.

Young women have the greatest number of pregnancies and the greatest number of abortions. Yet in fact they are statistically less likely than older women to abort rather than give birth. Of all women of childbearing age, those 25 to 29 are least likely to have an abortion. Only 22% do. Meanwhile, women over 40 get pregnant the least but are most likely to end the pregnancy. One in two has an abortion. With about 45% of their pregnancies ending in abortion, teenagers as a group have the highest ratio. Each year more than 1 million American teens get pregnant; and 1 out of every 20 American women 18 and 19 years old undergoes abortion.

An estimated four out of five abortions are performed on single women. Among teens seeking the procedure, more than 95% are unwed. Single women have almost double the number of abortions as births. By contrast, married women get pregnant more frequently, have more babies, and choose abortion less than their single counterparts. Married women have almost ten times as many births as abortions.

Prior to legalization, women generally were reluctant to admit they had obtained an abortion. As a result, researchers continue to have difficulties determining precisely how many women are having abortions for the first time. It is generally conceded that the number of women who have multiple abortions has increased substantially, from about 20% in 1975 to close to 40% today.

Black women comprise only about 13 percent of the U.S. female population, yet they account for approximately one-third of the abortions. It follows that blacks have both higher abortion rates and ratios than whites. However, for each of the races the highest percentage of abortions by far tends to occur among women aged 15 to 24.

Half of all abortions are performed within the first six weeks of pregnancy. The figure is over 90% for the first 12 weeks. Less than 2% of abortions take place past the 5th month.

Historically, maternal mortality was a distinct and everpresent possibility. In the 20 years preceding legalization of abortion, estimates of the number of annual deaths of women ranged from 200 to 500. Today mortality statistics have declined precipitously in the wake of safer procedures, earlier abortions, and increased numbers of skilled practitioners. Currently, there is 1 maternal death for every 250,000 abortions performed.

The preponderance of abortions take place in cities and suburbs. About 90% of the licensed facilities nationwide are located in metropolitan areas, and these account for about 98% of the country's abortions. Interestingly, eight of every ten counties in the United States have no abortion facility. Almost one-third of the childbearing age women live in these counties. While abortion rates vary dramatically by state, the general pattern is that rural states have a much lower incidence than their urban counterparts.

14

By most accounts, the average abortion costs roughly $200, although prices may range from $75 to $900, with clinics generally the cheapest and doctors' offices the most expensive. The price escalates the longer the woman waits. The jump is dramatic after the 1st trimester. An abortion done in the 10th week is likely to cost half of one done in the 16th week. Expenses appear to vary by state. As a rule, abortion is likely to cost more in a rural area than in an urban area.

A small number of private insurers issue policies that cover abortion expenses. With the cutoff of federal money since 1977 under the Hyde Amendment, virtually all public-funded abortions are financed by state governments. Currently 28 states have laws permitting abortion funding only to save the mother's life. Fourteen states authorize Medicaid payments for abortion regardless of the reason for the procedure.

PUBLIC ATTITUDES

Abortion remains a fractious social and political issue in the United States. The gulf between opponents suggests an America polarized: on one side, the right-to-life movement, prepared to amend the Constitution and banish the practice. On the other, pro-choice advocates insisting that abortion on demand is a woman's fundamental right. But opinion polls and surveys indicate that only a minority of Americans fall under one or the other of these extreme positions. Fewer than one in five persons believe abortion is morally wrong in all instances irrespective of the circumstances. Between a fifth and a quarter believe a woman is entitled to choose an abortion in all cases. These positions stake out the extremes. The majority of Americans occupy the area between these stances. Most believe abortion should be legal, at least for compelling reasons.

Research suggests that a majority of Americans support women's abortion rights for these compelling, or so-called hard, reasons: to save the mother's life or to protect her health; if the woman is a rape or incest victim; or if the fetus is abnormal. Fewer condone abortion for "soft" reasons: an unwanted child might prove economically burdensome or inconveniently clash with a woman's professional plans.

Public acceptance appears to be linked to the stage of development of the fetus. People are more inclined to support an early, 1st-trimester abortion than a 2nd-trimester procedure. Support for 3rd-trimester abortion declines dramatically, except where the abortion is an emergency procedure done to save the woman's life. Not surprisingly, persons who consider abortion moral believe it should be legal. However, not all who deem it immoral think it should be legally banished.

Factors influencing attitudes include people's religious tenets, whether they have had an abortion, and their education, income level, and lifestyle. Conservative and Reform Jews tend to have the most liberal views, overwhelmingly supporting the idea that abortion should be a private decision between a woman and her physician free of state interference. Catholics are the most likely to oppose abortion—although Catholic women statistically are as likely to have abortions as Protestant women.

A higher level of education is connected directly to greater support for abortion. High school dropouts are far more inclined to oppose abortion than high school or college graduates. The more income a person earns— and this is especially so with women—the more likely he or she is to support abortion. Urban residents are more apt to support abortion rights than small-town or rural residents. Inhabitants of either the East or West Coast are more likely to support a woman's abortion choice than those living in the Midwest or South.

While differences are narrowing, the fact remains that white Americans have expressed more tolerance for abortion than blacks. Historically, many blacks looked on abortion as a practice being advanced partly to stem their population growth. Also, the relative prevalence of single parenthood in the black community apparently has made its members less inclined to view abortion as a way to deal with out-of-wedlock pregnancies. Meanwhile, white middle- and upper-class teens see abortion as an expedient means to deal with an illegitimate pregnancy.

THE ABORTION DEBATE

A debate implies competing sides, adversarial positions, views in counterpoint. The often contentious abortion debate is waged between members of the pro-choice and pro-life movements. These two groups set the terms of the discussion and establish its tone. What follow are synopses of the views of, respectively, abortion supporters and abortion opponents.

Supporters of Abortion

People who count themselves supporters of abortion do not share a uniform view on the issue. For some, the support is adamant and unconditional. For others, it is qualified or dictated by circumstances. Nonetheless, most individuals condoning a woman's right of choice subscribe to a fundamentally similar outlook, drawing on the same basic fund of attitudes. Over time these ideas and convictions collectively have been joined under the label of pro-choice.

The pro-choice position generally dismisses the idea that a fetus is a biological or legal "person." Adherents argue against efforts to equate abortion with the taking of a life. They believe pregnant women should be free to choose whether or not to end their pregnancies as the special circumstances of their lives may dictate. As the legal debate has so amply illustrated, supporters of choice view abortion as a matter of privacy and basic individual liberty. A woman's capacity to decide whether or not to have a child is a fundamental test of whether she controls her own body. Without such control, the pro-choice argument goes, women are powerless to govern their lives and futures. Nor may they achieve true equal rights or aspire to real equal opportunity so long as their reproductive choices are abridged.

Choosing an abortion is seen as a woman's fundamental right under the Constitution and one that ought to be shielded from state interference. Governments should not be empowered to force women to bear children the women themselves do not care to have. Ardent pro-choice advocates say the abortion decision ought to be a woman's alone to make and that the procedure should be available on demand until well into the pregnancy.

Supporters of choice do not accept the notion that a fetus at all stages of development is a meaningful human life and therefore entitled to civil and legal rights equal to those of the mother. Use of language is indicative. The pro-choice lexicon avoids even the suggestion of a potential person, favoring such terms as "uterine contents" or "fetal matter" and avoiding the expressions "baby" or "unborn child."

Abortion-rights advocates say the antiabortion claim that human life begins at conception is an article of Christian doctrine and cannot be made the basis for establishing public policy in a pluralist and religiously mixed society such as the United States. Calling them irresponsible and hypocritical, proponents of choice regularly criticize pro-life forces for focusing all their energies on the unborn out of professed concern for the sanctity of life, but then withdrawing such concern when these pregnancies are brought to term by poor women or single mothers who lack the resources to provide for a new baby.

Advocates of legal abortion may diverge on when the practice is acceptable. Support is virtually unanimous for serious medical reasons and in cases of rape or incest. However, the great majority of abortions are done for economic or social reasons, under what could be termed elective circumstances. These reasons include poverty, illegitimacy, poor timing, and inconvenience. Generally, pro-choice supporters say these factors arise in situations where only the pregnant woman can judge whether or not the abortion is appropriate for her at the time.

Those who support abortion for these so-called soft reasons feel the prospective quality of life for the child is an important factor to consider. Some even contend that it is morally wrong to bring an unwanted child into the world. They point to compelling evidence showing that such children are often abused or abandoned, or end up leading lives of poverty and limited opportunity.

There are people personally opposed to abortion for moral or ethical reasons who nevertheless support legal abortion on the grounds that women will have them irrespective of the practice's status under the law. Such persons are troubled both by the prospect of illicit and medically unsafe procedures and by the implications for the American social fabric of criminalizing an activity that so many citizens will continue to engage in on a regular basis.

Groups that support choice do not see adoption as a solution or even a viable alternative. They point out that the overwhelming majority of women—on the order of 95%—when confronted with an unexpected pregnancy consider only two options: keeping the child or aborting.

Like the 19th-century movement to reform abortion, the 20th-century campaign to repeal laws against abortion was driven largely by the medical community. During the 1960s physicians were joined by thousands of women active in the movement for equal rights. These were women who defined reproductive freedom as a key precondition of equality.

The first single-issue group dedicated to the reform of antiabortion legislation was established in 1969. Called the National Association for the Repeal of Abortion Laws and later rechristened the National Abortion Rights Action League (NARAL), it has endured as one of the most influential organizations in the movement and remains the largest and most formidable pro-choice group, claiming more than 150,000 members nationwide.

Other groups, such as the National Organization for Women (NOW), the Ms. Foundation, and the Women's Political Caucus, have incorporated the issue of abortion as a cornerstone of their larger political agendas. Liberal religious groups, mostly from established Protestant and Reformed Jewish congregations, joined to form the Religious Coalition for Abortion Rights, a national organization comprised of more than 30 groups advocating a woman's right to choose. A faction within the Catholic church, Catholics for a Free Choice, defends a woman's right to have an abortion.

The Reproductive Freedom Project, a special branch of the American Civil Liberties Union (ACLU), has furnished much of the legal counsel for pro-choice litigants in cases that have gone before the Supreme Court subsequent to **Roe v. Wade.** The Planned Parenthood Federation of America, a self-described family planning agency, has become increasingly involved in mainstream abortion politics. Its research arm, the Alan Guttmacher Institute, is perhaps the nation's preeminent resource center for statistics on abortion.

18

Introduction to Abortion

Opponents of Abortion

In the United States the people who flatly oppose legal abortion are in a minority that hovers around 22% of the populace. These are the constituents of the right-to-life movement, and, in the accepted parlance of this issue, they espouse the "pro-life" position. (The pro-choice camp prefers to call its adversaries "antiabortion" or "antichoice.") Simply put, pro-life partisans oppose abortion because they believe a fetus is a person and that forcing it from the womb and disposing of it is murder. Abortion, in their judgment, is inescapably an issue of public morality. They peg the beginning of human life to the moment of conception or, at the very least, to the point at which the inseminated egg implants in the uterine wall.

As noted earlier, pro-choice supporters claim that a culturally and religiously diverse nation lacks wide public consensus on when life starts. Therefore, no single religious view should be made the basis for deciding public policy on what, to abortion-rights advocates, is appropriately an issue of private morality. Opponents of abortion respond by saying that it is exactly the role of the people in a democracy to make collective moral judgments on affairs that affect the moral or ethical sensibilities of citizens. In their view abortion is killing. A woman's choice to obtain one, then, is not a private moral exercise that deserves to be out of reach of the public realm.

Abortion opponents maintain that, as a person, the fetus is entitled to full rights under the Constitution, to include, most fundamentally, the right to life. The unborn's right to life is said to outweigh whatever prerogative a woman might claim when deciding whether or not to have a child. Indeed, since **Roe v. Wade,** pro-life forces have assailed the privacy right that is the foundation for legal abortion as a fabrication of liberal activist justices legislating from the Supreme Court bench.

Antiabortionists say preservation of long-standing family values and promotion of a fundamental regard for human life are important aims of their movement. Wanton murder of 1.5 million fetuses yearly in the United States is said to desensitize the public to the sacredness of life or potential life. By its very expedience, opponents claim, abortion depreciates the value society as a whole places on motherhood. They criticize the feminist rhetoric about abortion being the symbol of a woman's empowerment and her hedge against male oppression, calling this idea an indictment of other women who choose to assume traditional roles of housewife and homemaker. They contend the high incidence of abortions for out-of-wedlock pregnancies suggests a strong link between irresponsible sexual activity and the pro-choice advocacy.

19

There are those within the pro-life movement who are less decisive when it comes to abortions necessary to save the mother's life. In fact, some actually support the practice under this extreme circumstance. Eugenic abortion, condemned on moral and ethical grounds, is portrayed basically as women and their doctors playing God with abnormal fetuses by deciding what constitutes a life worth living.

Unlike the pro-choice movement, the organized pro-life campaign has received only marginal backing from doctors and the medical community. The movement's following has a strong religious complexion. Most of its active members belong to one of the Christian denominations, and their opposition to abortion is inseparably bound up in their religious convictions. While Mormons, American Orthodox Jews, and Southern Baptists oppose abortion, the Roman Catholic Church has been most politically influential in abortion politics. However, since 1981, when President-elect and pro-life advocate Ronald Reagan assumed office promising to pursue a conservative social agenda, a number of evangelical and fundamentalist Protestant denominations have arisen as major sources of antiabortion political activism.

Troubled by the Court's legalization of abortion, in June 1973 a group of American Catholic bishops and laity established an organization called the National Right to Life Committee (NRL). This single-issue group is committed to ending legal abortion in the United States. While its membership remains largely Catholic, the NRL also has a sizable fundamentalist constituency. The group has endured as perhaps the most influential pro-life organization, with more than 2,500 chapters nationwide. Its activities include political lobbying, research and education, public demonstrations, and providing resources and counsel to pro-life litigants in key legal battles and court cases.

Two other groups active in the antiabortion campaign are Catholics United for Life (CUL), which originated the pro-life tactic of "sidewalk counseling" of women outside of abortion clinics, and Birthright, a national network of crisis pregnancy counseling centers offering women abortion alternatives. Multiissue groups such as the Eagle Forum, Concerned Women of America, and the Moral Majority are all sources of abortion opposition. Women Exploited by Abortion (WEBA) was founded to assist women suffering from Post Abortion Syndrome. Most recently, the ultra-religious group Operation Rescue has garnered national headlines for staging peaceful demonstrations that have disrupted the normal functioning of abortion clinics across the country.

The right-to-life movement has benefited from its close ties with the conservative Republican leadership in the United States. The New Right's political emergence in the early 1980s was achieved in part through its espousal of traditional family values and conservative social policies. Opposition to abortion became an important plank in the Republican right's social platform. Pro-life forces have supported candidates who share its abortion views, and a number of these have gone on to form a right-to-life advocacy inside the government at both the state and federal levels.

The nation's free-standing clinics have been favored targets of the right-to-life protest. Pro-life tactics range from peaceful distribution of anti-abortion literature and picketing to staging waiting room sit-ins or physically blocking patients from entering. Extremists have resorted to more violent means, including arson and bombings. According to the National Abortion Federation, between 1977 and 1987 there were more than 700 separate acts of serious physical destruction against clinics, amounting to several million dollars' worth of damage. The mainstream of the pro-life movement, responding to criticism of its initial relative silence, has since renounced such extremist acts as the work of terrorists. The perpetrators themselves have justified their actions as necessary civil disobedience, undertaken to block the wholesale murder of defenseless fetuses.

ABORTION AND THE LAW

In the past quarter century abortion has been indivisibly bound up with the law. State and federal courts have adjudicated a constant current of litigation on a broad range of issues related to abortion. Meanwhile, legislatures have labored to craft and enact public policy. This section contains two parts. The first, "Legal Issues," discusses the pivotal questions of law that have dominated the debate over abortion. "Legislation" then details what have been the key congressional initiatives on abortion.

LEGAL ISSUES

To a large extent the abortion debate has been waged in the courts. The principal legal issues that have defined the line between partisans and shaped the debate include: the right of privacy and its extension to abortion; the contest between individual liberties and state interests; whether abortion is a matter for the courts or the legislatures; the constitutionality of laws regulating or restricting abortion in light of **Roe v. Wade**; and public funding of abortion.

Much of the legal debate over abortion turns on the question of its constitutionality. The federal Constitution includes a Bill of Rights—the first ten amendments—that sets forth the basic rights of citizens. These amendments outline the individual liberties enjoyed by the people. These rights, ranked as fundamental, cannot be withdrawn or even limited by government except through due process of law. Historically, the Bill of Rights applied only to federal law. State legislatures were exempt from its reach. The amendments shielded core liberties and rights from actions of the national government. The 5th Amendment, with its due process and equal protection guarantees, all along has been the mechanism for applying the rights enumerated in the remaining amendments to federal law.

Passed in 1868, the 14th Amendment changed the complexion of constitutional law. It places states under the same obligation as the federal government to guarantee due process and equal protection of laws. This amendment has become so vitally important because it is the vehicle that courts use to access the federal Bill of Rights and apply it to state legislation. The amendment figures greatly in the abortion issue. Much of the litigation has entailed challenges by individuals to state laws regulating abortion. These actions overwhelmingly have involved claims that legislation violated due process or denied equal protection of the laws.

The United States has a dual system of courts that parcels out legal actions between federal and state jurisdictions. State courts have authority over virtually all civil and criminal cases pertaining to people and property within their territory. If a federal question is involved at this level, a decision of a state supreme court may be appealed to the U.S. Supreme Court. Federal courts have limited jurisdiction: They may hear cases only if the power to do so has been granted them by a federal statute or the U.S. Constitution. Primarily, federal courts deal with actions based on federal law or the federal Constitution. Abortion mainly has been litigated in federal court because the legal contests have involved challenges to the constitutionality of state laws.

The federal courts are organized into three tiers. The district courts are trial courts, or courts of original jurisdiction. Each state has at least one federal district court. Cases brought in district court present both issues of fact, which deal with the events disputed in the case at hand, and issues of law, which deal with application and interpretation of the laws to the facts of the case.

The second level, the U.S. Courts of Appeals, hears appeals of decisions of the district courts. The United States is divided into 12 circuits, each of which takes appeals from several districts. The focus in the appeals court is on whether the trial court correctly interpreted the law. Findings of fact ordinarily are presumed complete and thus not reviewed at the appellate level.

The U.S. Supreme Court is the court of last resort for the nation. It hears limited appeals from the circuit courts, the district courts, and the highest state courts where a federal question is presented. The Supreme

Court, through judicial review, may strike down legislation it deems unconstitutional. This power historically has been used rather sparingly, as Courts have attempted to respect the legislative arena and not trespass on expressions of the democratic will.

How is it abortion became a major issue before the Supreme Court? Until the mid-1800s the practice was legal in the United States. By the end of the 19th century, states nationwide had passed criminal abortion statutes, which were actually antipoisoning laws intended to protect women's health and punish medical quacks dispensing dangerous, toxic substances to induce abortion. By the 1960s improved procedures and medical advances had made early abortion as safe or even safer than childbearing. The country's attitudes toward birth control in general were becoming more liberal. Significantly, the feminist movement was coalescing and women's rights groups were emerging as an important political force. Feminism claimed that in order for women to achieve equal rights and opportunity with men, they had to have power over their own bodies and control over their reproductive choices.

The Supreme Court in 1965 in a momentous decision **(Griswold v. Connecticut)** established a fundamental right of privacy. The Court said the right was inherent in the context of the Constitution and implicit in various guarantees of the Bill of Rights. The privacy right was said to shield the intimate lives and personal affairs of individuals from government intrusion. The **Griswold** ruling, which extended the privacy right to adults' sale and use of birth control, became the key to the constitutionalization of the abortion issue.

In the late 1960s those challenging the constitutionality of antiabortion statutes argued that a woman's decision to have an abortion was encompassed by the fundamental privacy right. Whether to have a child was characterized as an intensely personal deliberation involving physical, emotional, and financial consequences. The 14th Amendment's concept of liberty was said to protect a woman's fundamental right to choose to end an unwanted pregnancy. In **Roe v. Wade,** The Supreme Court endorsed this idea that the privacy right included a woman's decision to terminate her pregnancy.

This establishment of the abortion choice as a core liberty explains why subsequent challenges to laws restricting the procedure have been pursued in the courts rather than the state houses. A constitutionally shielded right is insulated from simple legislative action or majority politics. A fundamental right is a right that cannot be deprived or rescinded without due process of law. Antiabortion laws have been contested on grounds they denied a fundamental right through legislative plebiscite and therefore were in violation of due process guarantees.

The rebuttal stance claims that nothing in the language of the Constitution guarantees women a right to have an abortion. It is suggested that the Supreme Court simply fabricated a new liberty, stamped it "fundamental," and extended it to pregnant women.

The debate has turned on a doctrinal question: whether the Constitution protects fundamental interests beyond those explicitly set out in its text. The affirmative view says the abortion right is located in the "shadows" of other guarantees of the Bill of Rights. It is implicit in the 14th Amendment's liberty concept. It is found among the unenumerated rights reserved to citizens under the 9th Amendment. Adversaries of these stands reply that construing rights is a form of legislation from the bench and therefore a function beyond the Court's duty. When Justices liberally interpret the text, they are roaming in the territory of policy and moral judgments. Opponents of an activist judiciary say such territory is appropriate to the elected representatives of the people—not to the courts.

The issue of competing state interests is linked inextricably to the discussion of privacy rights. The abortion decision, courts hold, is a fundamental liberty that may be exercised by women in the first three months without government interference. But under the law the right is not absolute. Women cannot have abortions on demand. As a pregnancy advances, competing state interests in protecting both maternal health and potential human life arise to circumscribe the woman's choice. Over gestation, the state's interests become so "compelling" that government is empowered to regulate abortion. When the fetus is capable of surviving outside the womb, the state may forbid abortion.

The seesaw contest between women's individual liberties and competing state prerogatives is further complicated by the core conviction of the right-to-life movement that the fetus is a human being from the moment of conception. This belief involves a clear and profound legal claim that the unborn are persons within the scope and meaning of the Constitution and are therefore entitled to a fundamental right to life. Abortion, then, becomes the deliberate taking of a human life—in other words, murder. Courts have rejected this position, saying legislatures may not define the fetus as a legal human being prior to viability and then erect criminal codes based on such a definition. Pursuing its aim through the political process, the pro-life movement has campaigned for a constitutional amendment that would guarantee the unborn full liberties and protections under the Bill of Rights.

The Supreme Court issued trimester guidelines that, up to the present, have been the law on balancing competing, shifting individual and state claims. The legal contest since **Roe** has been waged over the trimester framework and has entailed challenges to state or city laws regulating abortion. The task of courts has been to strike the proper balance and, ultimately, to decide what is permissible public regulation of abortion within the broader context of **Roe.**

State and local governments have defended statutory efforts as valid measures taken to protect legitimate public interests in the health of the mother and potential life of the unborn. Pro-choice proponents have countered that these legislative efforts at regulation, far from serving legitimate public concerns, too often have been intentionally and unconstitutionally fashioned to discourage women from having abortions. Rather than safeguarding state interests, regulatory schemes have placed unjustified obstacles in the way of women exercising a fundamental right. These laws, the argument goes, have been unduly burdensome and hence in violation of due process.

Legislation since **Roe** has sought to regulate abortion through measures that fall under several basic categories:

Performance requirements have regulated where abortions could be performed, when, and by whom. Five states have tried at different times to mandate that even 1st-trimester abortions be done in hospitals. Others have required that abortions after viability be performed only if two doctors agreed the procedure necessary to save maternal life. But courts consistently have overturned unduly restrictive regulation of early abortions. Rules singling out free-standing clinics for special controls have been found unconstitutional. Yet federal courts have upheld state laws making it illegal for unlicensed personnel to perform abortions. Generally, states have been allowed to enact only those regulations on 2nd-trimester abortions that are reasonably related to protection of the mother's health. This hardly has resolved the controversy. Critics of **Roe** claim the Supreme Court more recently has undermined its own trimester framework by consistently disallowing virtually any regulation of abortion in the 2nd trimester—in effect placing the first six months of pregnancy beyond the scope of lawmakers.

Consent requirements have been at the crux of the legal debate. Some statutes required informed written consent of the woman before an abortion could be performed, purportedly to ensure the woman's decision was made freely and knowledgeably. Within limits, these provisions were upheld as valid. Yet other variations requiring women be informed of the hazards of abortion and of the methods to be used were struck down as unduly burdensome because they served no clear, legally recognized interest.

Other laws included spousal and parental consent requirements. These forbade performance of abortions unless the husband consented or, when the woman was underage and unmarried, unless the parent or guardian consented. Spousal consent laws have been uniformly invalidated as courts have ruled a husband may not exercise a veto power over his wife's constitutionally protected, fundamental right to choose an abortion. Parental consent provisions have been defended by states as steps taken to safeguard the welfare of minor girls. The pro-choice movement has claimed these rules failed to distinguish between immature and mature minors and therefore denied women under 18 their constitutional rights. Siding with the pro-choice position on minors' rights and abortion, the Supreme Court has said that a parental consent law is permissible only as long as it also provides an alternative source of consent, such as a judge, in cases in which the girl does not want to apprise her parents.

Reporting standards, requiring doctors or hospitals to maintain records and report all abortions, have been challenged as an invasion of privacy and intrusion on the confidentiality of the doctor-patient relationship. These regulations have been upheld when they ensure the woman's anonymity and guarantee the information will remain confidential.

Conscience clauses have allowed doctors and institutions to refuse to perform abortions if doing so violates their moral or religious principles. Initially such laws were thought to be constitutional only as they related to private hospitals or individual medical professionals. Since 1977 the Supreme Court has held that public hospitals and personnel as well may refuse to participate in nontherapeutic abortions.

Fetal protection has been one of the most taxing and fiercely disputed elements of the abortion legal debate. States and municipalities continue to adopt laws requiring doctors to take concerted—even extraordinary—steps to save the life of a fetus that is or may be viable. Usually these measures have placed doctors under threat of criminal charges for failing to follow the requirements. Legislatures enacting these provisions have maintained the rules conformed with the state's valid interest in protecting the unborn. Opponents contend these provisions place unreasonable burdens on physicians attempting to make difficult, discretionary medical judgments at the inherently ambiguous point of viability or near viability. The federal courts consistently have struck down strict standard-of-care provisions aimed at the period just approaching viability. But the Supreme Court's decision in **Webster v. Reproductive Health Services** (1989) suggested the Court might be prepared to give states more leeway to regulate abortion toward the end of the 2nd trimester.

The *legal battle over public funding of abortion* has revolved around the question of whether the states or federal government should have to pay for abortions for indigent women under Medicaid programs. Since **Roe** (1973), a good many states have elected to fund legal abortions without restrictions. Others either have barred state payments totally or severely restricted financing for all but lifesaving procedures. In the mid-1970s five states were ordered to fund abortions by federal courts. Appeals from some of these decisions eventually reached the Supreme Court. In key decisions in 1977 and 1980, the Court ruled that neither the Social Security Act nor the equal protection clauses of the Constitution required state or federal financing of abortions on the same basis as payment for medical expenses of childbirth.

LEGISLATION

After the Supreme Court's ruling in 1973 legalizing abortion in all 50 states, the politically sensitive issue became a major topic before Congress. Both pro-life and pro-choice activists descended on Washington, D.C., to pursue their agendas. The right-to-life movement immediately took the offensive with a range of anti-abortion initiatives. The same year as **Roe v. Wade,** Congress passed legislation blocking American foreign aid monies to programs overseas that performed or promoted abortions. In addition, the nation's lawmakers tacked a "conscience clause" on a bill funding a number of federal health programs. This measure barred institutions receiving federal financing from forcing personnel in any way to perform abortions in violation of their personal religious or moral beliefs.

In the aftermath of **Roe,** pro-life forces targeted federal funding of abortion for political battle. Most federal financing was done through Medicaid, a program established under the Social Security Act to subsidize medical care for the nation's needy. In 1976 freshman Representative Henry J. Hyde (R-IL), staunchly antiabortion, attached a rider to a huge domestic appropriations bill. In final form, the Hyde Amendment declared that no federal money could be allocated to pay for abortions unless the life of the mother was endangered by carrying the fetus to term. Essentially the amendment allowed the federal government to finance only those therapeutic abortions required to save the mother's life. All elective abortions, along with those sought in cases of rape or incest, were excluded. It should be noted that initially the Hyde rider only affected federal money. It did not prevent the states from continuing to spend their own Medicaid funds.

Pro-choice groups challenged the constitutionality of the Hyde Amendment in federal courts, delaying its implementation by a year. In two cases decided in 1977, **Beal v. Doe** and **Maher v. Roe,** the Supreme Court upheld the rider and it immediately went into effect. The Court ruled that nothing in the Constitution or in federal law required that public tax dollars be spent on abortion. In 1980 the Supreme Court returned to the issue in **Harris v. McRae,** reaffirming that both federal and state governments could refuse to fund all but life-saving abortions.

Once the Hyde Amendment took effect in June 1977, federally funded abortions dropped from about 300,000 per year to about 2,500. By 1985 the yearly number had dipped to less than 500. Individual states likewise were no longer under any compulsion to pay for other than life-saving procedures. By 1980 40 states had moved to restrict Medicaid-funded abortion. As of 1988, 14 states were providing public financing for abortions on request for indigent women.

Still federal law, the Hyde Amendment has been renewed every year since 1977. Some earlier versions allowed payments for pregnancies arising from rape or incest. More recently the bills have cut off Medicaid payments for all but life-saving reasons.

Beyond its ongoing and successful campaign to restrict government-funded abortion in the United States, pro-life proponents have labored to stop American payments to international agencies earmarked for abortion services in foreign nations. Beginning in the early 1980s, the Reagan administration withdrew U.S. funding from family planning organizations operating abroad that either performed or promoted abortion. Despite vocal objections from domestic supporters of international family planning efforts, this has remained U.S. policy to the present.

Efforts in Congress since the early 1970s to abolish legal abortion or overturn **Roe** have included the attempted passage of any number of proposed amendments to the U.S. Constitution. In 1973 Senator James Buckley (R-NY) introduced the first of the Human Life Amendments (HLA) to be submitted over the course of the coming years. These HLAs typically granted the fetus the status of a "person" from the moment of conception and entitled the unborn to a right to life under the Constitution. Any of the Human Life Amendments would have made abortion illegal. None of the 25 or so that have gone before Congress has come close to enactment.

Failure of the HLAs led pro-life advocates to fashion an alternative approach: a states' rights amendment to the Constitution. This was written in such a way as to restore to the state legislatures the power to pass laws governing abortion—in other words, to give back to the states the legislative powers they enjoyed prior to **Roe v. Wade.** No states' right measures has ever made it out of Senate Judiciary subcommittees.

Attempts to overturn **Roe** took a new turn in 1981 when Senator Orrin Hatch (R-UT) introduced a Human Life Federalism Amendment (HLFA), which gave both Congress and the states the power to regulate or restrict abortion and asserted that a right to an abortion was not guaranteed by the Constitution. The Hatch proposal would have effectively overturned **Roe** and meant a return to individual state laws. But as with the HLAs and states' rights proposals, the HLFA failed to pass. In 1983 Hatch introduced another version. This one actually made it out of committee to the floor, and for the first time the whole Senate voted on an antiabortion amendment. It was rejected, falling 18 votes short of the necessary two-thirds majority to pass.

Because amending the U.S. Constitution demands overwhelming support and involves a lengthy parliamentary process, right-to-life legislators switched tactics, introducing so-called human life bills. A proposed statute is far easier to have enacted than a constitutional amendment. Senator Jesse Helms (R-NC) in 1981 introduced a bill which stated that human life begins at conception and that a fetus is guaranteed full rights and protections under the Constitution. Opponents of the bill argued that it unconstitutionally sought to limit a woman's fundamental right to choose an abortion. The measure was defeated, as was a second such bill Helms introduced a year later.

In session after session since the early 1980s, Congress has revisited these same issues and reprised legislative proposals similar to those mentioned here. However, Congress in recent years has not advanced any noteworthy or significant new initiatives.

ABORTION AND RELIGION

The intersection of religion and abortion since **Roe v. Wade** has shaped the terms of the debate as much as any other factor. The religious connection has ensured that abortion remains a deeply contested moral issue in the United States. Various Christian denominations have driven the religious response. In particular, the Roman Catholic Church has exerted the dominant presence and influence. Its hierarchy has been at the forefront of the antiabortion movement.

Catholic doctrine states that abortion is a mortal sin. But, as noted in the "Historical Background," the church did not always consider the practice a grave transgression. Throughout much of its 2,000-year history, Roman Catholicism viewed abortions performed prior to the point when the fetus first moves as tolerable and permissible. Official church doctrine since 1869 has been to condemn abortion on the grounds that what begins at conception as a human life is morally entitled to the right to life. In 1968 Pope Paul VI reiterated Roman Catholic concern for the sanctity of life. He forbade all abortions, therapeutic or otherwise, for church faithful. His successors have uniformly upheld this position.

While a number of Catholic theologians and clerics have argued in favor of allowing therapeutic procedures, the official position remains that all abortions be condemned. Only a medical procedure that indirectly takes the life of a fetus, such as surgery for an ectopic pregnancy performed to save the mother's life, is morally sanctioned. Procedures that directly take the life of the fetus, however, are immoral in all instances. Liberal voices within the church have called the Vatican's position rigid and out of step with many of the contemporary social and economic realities that underlie abortion. They suggest that the Catholic church's intransigence ultimately threatens to alienate lay Catholic women and drive them from the fold.

The Roman Catholic Church's political involvement and investment of resources in the organized pro-life movement have made it a target of charges about jeopardizing the historical separation of church and state. Critics have gone after the church for actively campaigning to influence the political process and shape government policy to reflect its own moral tenets. Unbowed, America's Catholic bishops in November 1989 announced a renewed offensive against legalized abortion, at the same time warning Catholic politicians about the irreconcilability of pro-choice support with church doctrine. The Roman Catholic Church has the right to instruct its members neither to have abortions nor to support a woman's right of choice. Whether it should be permitted to exercise political influence so as to deny abortion rights to others who might have a different moral view is a key question.

The debate over separation of church and state raises a related question: to what degree should nonprofit religious organizations, such as the Roman Catholic Church, be restricted from influencing legislation and public policy? As a charitable organization, the Catholic church enjoys tax-exempt status. Courts may revoke this status when any such designated organization seeks to influence lawmaking or functions as a political interest group. Facing the threat of legal action in 1974 by the pro-choice Women's Lobby, the National Conference of Catholic Bishops (NCCB) was forced to register as a political action committee for its lobbying activities in Washington, D.C.

Regardless of whether abortion is appropriately a public or private moral issue, the Roman Catholic Church opposes the practice on grounds it is the murder of innocents. The church believes it is defending the lives of millions of powerless fetuses—moreover, that it is morally compelled to connect this belief with social action.

In recent years fundamentalist Protestant churches and interdenominational groups, such as the Moral Majority, have been similarly active in opposing abortion and have engaged in the same methods of opposition as the Catholic church.

WORLDWIDE PERSPECTIVE

From advanced industrialized nations to underdeveloped countries, women the world over practice abortion. The global trend is toward liberal policies. Seventy-five percent of the world's population lives in nations where abortion, at the least, is legal to preserve the woman's health. Half reside where abortions are available on demand. In the last 20 years countries for the most part have moved to loosen rather than toughen their abortion laws. The United States is among a small number of industrialized states where abortion remains such a controversial public issue.

While most of the world's governments permit some form of abortion, nearly 1 billion people, primarily from sub-Saharan Africa, Latin America, and fundamentalist Moslem Arab states, inhabit countries where women have no access to safe or legal abortion. Because illegal abortions go unreported, it is impossible to pinpoint the exact number of abortions globally. However, researchers estimate that the annual number of women worldwide who have abortions is between 50 and 60 million. China's reported 14 million yearly abortions and the Soviet Union's 11 million lead the world figures.

Great Britain liberalized abortion in 1967 when Parliament passed a law permitting the procedure in order to safeguard the woman's mental or physical health and for eugenic purposes. Among the factors leading to the legislative reform were high numbers of illegal abortions and resulting medical complications and maternal deaths. With the new law's enactment, annual legal abortions doubled in Great Britain, putting a strain on the British socialized medical system, or National Health Service.

While laws vary considerably, most European countries now allow some legal abortions. France and Greece permit them on request up to viability, while West Germany and Austria allow abortions for a range of medical and social reasons. Abortion is fairly common even in nations with large Catholic majorities. Since 1978 Italy has allowed women 18 years or older to have 1st-trimester abortions to protect their own health, when the pregnancy results from rape, or when the fetus is deformed. In 1981 Italian voters rejected a measure to establish more restrictive abortion policies. In 1986 Spain enacted abortion legislation patterned closely on Italy's.

Generally, the Scandinavian countries have Europe's most liberal abortion laws. Currently abortion on request is allowed in Denmark, Norway, and Sweden. The practice is permitted for a broad array of medical and social factors in Finland, Iceland, and Luxembourg.

The Communist countries of Eastern Europe likewise have liberal abortion policies. Two factors contribute to this situation. First, birth control information and materials continue to be scarce. As a result, contraceptives generally are not available. Second, chronic economic problems have led these governments either to encourage or mandate limits on family size.

The Soviet Union revamped its laws in 1955, and neighboring Communist countries followed suit. Today the Soviet Union and Yugoslavia make abortion available on demand. Lack of birth control remains characteristic and is illustrated by the estimate that, on average, a Soviet woman has six abortions in her lifetime. In Czechoslovakia, East Germany, and Hungary, women need the approval of a medical commission to have an abortion, but such approvals are routine and readily obtained. Polish women need only go to a family doctor. After liberalizing laws in the late 1950s, both Romania and Bulgaria reversed themselves a decade later and tightened policies in response to dramatically declining birth rates.

Since 1952 Israel essentially has countenanced abortion on request provided the procedure is done under proper medical conditions by a licensed physician. In light of increased Jewish emigration from Israel, a decline in the birth rate of Jewish Israelis, and a dramatic rise in the birth rate of Arab Israelis, the government in the last decade has attempted informally to encourage childbearing and discourage abortion. Some Middle East countries, such as Iran and Iraq, have strict antiabortion laws. Still, the practice is not uncommon. For women in the Moslem Arab world who can afford the high fees, obtaining an abortion reportedly is not difficult.

Abortion and infanticide were common and culturally tolerated in Japan until the end of the 1800s. Abortion again proliferated after World War II when the government made the practice accessible in order to control population growth in the wake of economic devastation. Since 1972 the annual number of legal abortions in Japan has hovered around 1.5 million. These are obtained for various social, economic, and medical reasons. Interestingly, the major religions of Japan—Buddhism, Confucianism, and Shinto—place no doctrinal constraints on the practice. Despite reportedly mixed emotions of some Japanese women, the number of abortions has been consistently rising in proportion to live births since the 1950s.

Despite tremendous overpopulation, India until recently had tough, proscriptive abortion laws. Now the country allows abortion for medical and social reasons. Conditions of overcrowding and extreme poverty would seem to make credible those estimates that up to 4 million illegal abortions per year took place in the late 1960s and early 1970s.

Faced with overpopulation problems as it seeks to modernize, China allows abortions and encourages its women to have them. Despite the Communist government's denials, there are widespread and continuing reports from international family planning agencies that Chinese women are pressured into obtaining abortions once they have had one child. Since 1981 an incentive program to control the number of births has been in place. Couples pledging to have only one child are provided greater benefits by the government. Some 60% of Chinese couples reportedly have taken the vow. Those reneging on the pledge apparently have had to repay the benefits.

Generally, African countries have restrictive abortion laws. Thus illegal abortions are frequent and often self-induced. Injuries and deaths from the complications of illegal abortions are substantial, especially among the very poor who lack medical supplies and sanitary conditions. Exceptions exist, such as Ghana, Zimbabwe, and Liberia, which allow abortions when the pregnancy threatens the woman's life or health and in instances of rape or when the fetus is abnormal.

The nations of Latin America, with characteristically large Catholic populations, have the world's most restrictive abortion laws. This situation reflects the powerful antiabortion position of the Roman Catholic Church. Still, illegal abortions occur in significant numbers, and the health complications are considerable because most of the procedures are self-induced and accomplished with crude methods. Anywhere from one-quarter to one-half of all pregnancies in Central and South America end in induced abortions.

FUTURE TRENDS

The emotionally charged issue of abortion promises to remain controversial on several fronts. It is possible the debate will grow more contentious in years to come, as advances in medical science generate new, or intensify old, moral and ethical problems.

Improved medical technology and prenatal care could shift the point at which a fetus is able to survive outside the womb back to an earlier stage of a pregnancy. Such a development would have serious legal implications. The concept of viability is at the heart of abortion law. **Roe**

---

v. Wade established the point of viability at the start of the 3rd trimester and forbade states from barring abortion prior to it. Earlier viability seemingly would undermine **Roe**'s trimester framework and raise the possibility of earlier government restriction. Much of the medical community contends that dramatic progress in prenatal survivability is infeasible for the forseeable future. They point out that a fetus's lungs simply do not develop sufficiently to sustain life before the 23rd week of pregnancy. But others predict bold advances in medical technology that will lead to development of an artificial womb that can keep alive a fetus removed from its mother prior to viability.

Use of donated human fetal tissue in medical research and therapy raises hard questions for the future. Such tissue has proved valuable for physicians treating numbers of chronic adult diseases, most notably Parkinson's and Alzheimer's. Wary critics see ominous possibilities should this practice continue or proliferate: women purposely becoming pregnant with the sole intent of aborting the fetus in order to provide tissue for medical treatment for a loved one; or, perhaps, the emergence of an industry based on selling aborted fetal remains for profit.

The new French drug RU 486 doubtlessly will inspire debate and controversy in the United States. This pill, taken early in pregnancy, induces abortion. According to its developer, RU 486 will make ending an unwanted pregnancy as easy as a visit to the pharmacy. The drug is now being marketed in France, but the pro-life movement in the United States has condemned the product and vowed to fight its legal introduction here.

The abortion issue will continue to be debated and contested in the courts. The Supreme Court's decision in **Webster v. Reproductive Health Services** suggested that the Justices are poised to narrow or abandon **Roe v. Wade** and throw the issue back to the states and their elected lawmakers. Either of two cases scheduled to come before the Court for argument in its 1990 term could present the Justices with the opportunity to overrule the landmark 1973 ruling.

In the fall of 1989 the United States appeared to be entering a period of even greater political ferment over abortion. The **Webster** ruling, generally seen as granting states more power to limit access to abortion, has persuaded the leadership of the pro-choice movement to mobilize politically across the country to campaign for preservation of women's full abortion rights. Advocates of each side promised in the aftermath of **Webster** to make abortion a critical issue in future elections and before legislatures at every level of government nationwide. Not surprisingly, the turbulent issue figured importantly in the key 1989 political races—to the clear advantage of victorious pro-choice Democrat gubernatorial

34

candidates in New Jersey and Virginia. Following November's string of ballot-box losses, a concerned Republican leadership, its eyes on the 1990 and 1992 national elections, suggested the party moderate its strict antiabortion stance and accommodate pro-choice views within its ranks. By year's end numbers of Democrat and Republican pro-life politicians, fearing for their political futures and sensing themselves increasingly out of step with the majority of the American electorate, had begun to move away from—or even abandon outright—their opposition to abortion rights.

In the wake of **Webster,** the abortion battle surfaced in several state legislatures. Pennsylvania and Florida lawmakers were first to consider tough new antiabortion measures. In October 1989 Florida legislators roundly defeated Republican Governor Bob Martinez's proposals to restrict abortion. A month later the Pennsylvania House and Senate voted through a law imposing the nation's strictest curbs on abortion. Pro-choice forces immediately announced their plan to legally challenge the statute.

At the federal level, Congress approved a series of 1990 appropriations bills to loosen restrictions on federal financing of abortion. After President Bush vetoed these measures, abortion-rights advocates in the House and Senate vowed to revisit the question in 1990 and to make abortion a central issue in future nationwide elections.

Any change in the makeup of the Supreme Court will excite great interest. During the Reagan presidency, majority votes in decisions upholding abortion rights and reaffirming **Roe** gradually narrowed. Pro-choice observers suggest that Reagan's three appointments to the top bench have tipped the ideological balance and given the Court a conservative complexion. Many legal commentators believe the makings of a narrow five-to-four margin to abandon **Roe** are already in place. With three liberal justices more than 80 years old, the prospect of an imminent vacancy is strong. Anyone selected as a replacement undoubtedly will face intense examination of his or her views and past pronouncements on abortion during the Senate confirmation process. If the recent past is a fair gauge, the success or failure of a nomination might ultimately hinge on the abortion issue.

CHAPTER 2

————■————

CHRONOLOGY

This chronology recounts the significant developments and benchmark events of the past 25 years concerning the abortion issue. The chapter includes material drawn from government, politics, and the law; science, health, and medicine; and religion and culture. Emphasis is largely but not exclusively on the American experience of the last quarter century. Key developments worldwide that warrant attention are included.

The chronology is organized into yearly segments. Individual entries are preceded by the month and day on which they took place. Entries feature two cross-referencing techniques: (1) a legal action or court case that appears in bold print is covered in depth in Chapter 3; and (2) dates in parentheses following an entry—for example, (Jun. 5, '85)—indicate directly related items within the chronology.

While abortion has become in recent times a wrenching legal and moral question, it was not always so troubling and divisive a public issue. As discussed under "Historical Background" in Chapter 1, abortion was legal in the United States until the mid-1800s. Initial efforts to criminalize the practice in the 1830s and 1840s accelerated after midcentury, driven mainly by concerns about maternal health and medical professionalism. By 1880 state legislatures across the nation had made abortion illegal. Criminal statutes, directed at the abortionists, imposed penalties of fines and imprisonment. This body of legislation would regulate abortion in the United States until the 1960s. Although the practice had been outlawed by the turn of the century, abortions did not stop; women in subsequent decades obtained them illicitly and illegally.

In 1959 the American Law Institute issued its Model Penal Code, which provided state legislatures with recommended guidelines for liberalizing their abortion laws. The code foreshadowed the pending emergence of abortion as a major social issue.

Over the next several years the growing controversy over abortion centered on the availability of eugenic procedures. The well-publicized case in 1962 of Phoenix mother Sherri Finkbine drew national attention. Finkbine sought an abortion after learning that the drug thalidomide, which she had taken during pregnancy, was known to cause severe birth defects. An Arizona hospital, sensitive to public objections and wary of the possible legal consequences, refused to allow the procedure, and Finkbine eventually traveled to Sweden to have a legal abortion. There she discovered that the fetus in fact was severely deformed. An outbreak of German measles in the United States in 1964 led many women to seek similar therapeutic procedures.

By 1965 the entire issue of abortion had become a matter of widespread public debate. The chronology begins the same year with the U.S. Supreme Court's historic ruling in **Griswold v. Connecticut** establishing a constitutional right to privacy. The right became the foundation for the landmark 1973 **Roe v. Wade** decision legalizing abortion.

1965

June 7: In **Griswold v. Connecticut,** the U.S. Supreme Court broadens the meaning of the due process clause of the 14th Amendment to include the right of privacy in the marital relationship. The Court, in striking down Connecticut's 1879 law barring the use of contraceptives, rules that married couples are protected under the Constitution by a right of privacy. The privacy right becomes the fulcrum of the **Roe v. Wade** decision legalizing abortion. (Jan. 22, '73)

December 31: The Church of England issues a report calling abortion justified if the health of the mother is threatened by bringing the pregnancy to term.

1966

March 6: Findings of a survey by the National Opinion Research Center reveal that some 64% of Americans favor more liberal state abortion laws.

December 21: In an end-of-the-year address, Republican Governor of New York Nelson A. Rockefeller calls for an easing of the state's abortion law and directs the state assembly to study the issue in its next session. (Mar. 30, '68; Apr. 11, '70)

1967

April 12: A study conducted by the International Planned Parenthood Federation reports that between 15 and 20 million women worldwide undergo abortions each year.

April 25: Colorado becomes the first state to liberalize its abortion law after Republican Governor John A. Love signs a bill permitting abortion (contingent on the approval of three doctors) when either the child or mother would suffer permanent mental or physical disability or when pregnancy is the result of rape or incest. The law does not bar Colorado nonresidents.

June 15: Republican Governor Ronald W. Reagan signs into law a measure relaxing most curbs on abortion in California. The law, which establishes no residency requirement, permits abortions when the mother's health is gravely threatened by the pregnancy or when the pregnancy is the result of rape or incest.

June 21: The American Medical Association (AMA) House of Delegates endorses less restrictive state abortion laws in its first policy change on the subject since 1871.

July 14: The British Parliament passes landmark legislation legalizing abortion in instances where it is judged necessary to prevent severe physical or mental injury to the mother or when there is substantial risk the child will be born with serious physical defects. The measure provides for such abortions to be performed free under the country's National Health Service program.

1968

February 14: The California Medical Examiner's Board reprimands and disciplines several Sacramento physicians who, prior to the 1967 changes in the state law, performed eugenic abortions on women exposed to German measles. The doctors defended the practice as necessary to safeguard the mental health of the mothers. The board ruled the abortions violated the intent and spirit of state guidelines.

March 24: In a major policy statement, the American Civil Liberties Union (ACLU) calls for the abolition of all laws nationwide that impose criminal penalties for abortions done by licensed doctors, no matter the reason. The organization says existing state laws illegally restrict women's rights and are unconstitutionally vague.

March 30: New York Governor Nelson A. Rockefeller endorses proposals issued by his Commission on Abortion Reform to revise and liberalize the state laws. Rockefeller concurs with the commission's claim that broad changes are needed to cut the number of illegal abortions and to make it easier for poor women to gain access to safe services. (Dec. 21, '66; Apr. 11, '70)

July 12: A presidential advisory council headed by former U.S. Senator Maurine Neuberger (D-Oregon) issues its suggestions on ways to improve the status of American women. The panel recommends the repeal of laws making abortion a crime and the recognition of the full legal rights of illegitimate children.

1969

February 16: The National Association for the Repeal of Abortion Laws (NARAL) is established in Chicago. Its organizers commit to a campaign to have all voluntary abortions performed by licensed doctors legalized nationwide.

November 1: For the first time the Planned Parenthood Federation of America urges that abortion be removed from all state criminal codes and be made available as a lawful, sanctioned medical procedure.

November 29: The findings of a Gallup Poll survey reveal that 40% of U.S. adults would support legislation permitting abortion on demand in the 1st trimester of pregnancy.

1970

March 11: With its adoption of a new statute, Hawaii becomes the first state to eliminate criminal penalties for abortion.

April 11: New York Governor Nelson A. Rockefeller signs into law the bill repealing the state's 1830 statute, thus making abortion a matter between a woman and her physician up to the 24th week of pregnancy. Enactment of the measure culminates a four-year battle in the New York state assembly to liberalize abortion. (Dec. 21, '66; Mar. 30, '68)

June 25: Following bitter debate, the AMA House of Delegates votes to permit doctors to perform abortions for other than strictly medical reasons. The decision leaves to the physician's judgment whether social and economic circumstances warrant ending a pregnancy.

October 12: Pope Paul VI compares abortion to infanticide and calls its legalization a return to barbarism and paganism. The remarks are delivered in a message to a convention of Roman Catholic doctors in Washington, D.C.

The U.S. Supreme Court, in *McCann v. Babbitz*, lets stand a lower court ruling that Wisconsin's antiabortion law is unconstitutional because it infringes on women's "constitutional rights to have abortions in the early stages of pregnancy."

December 26: President Richard M. Nixon signs into law an expansion of family planning services that authorizes creation of a federal office to coordinate ways to control population growth. The measure bars use of public monies where abortion is advanced as a method of birth control.

1971

April 3: Governor Nelson A. Rockefeller of New York temporarily suspends state Medicaid payments for abortions while the legislature considers whether to bar such funding permanently. The governor orders interim exceptions made in cases where the woman's health is endangered. (Feb. 10, '72; Aug. 24, '72)

President Richard M. Nixon orders the armed services to abandon liberalized abortion rules adopted in 1970. He directs all military personnel and dependents to follow the laws of the states in which they are posted. Nixon calls abortion an unacceptable form of birth control and says he cannot reconcile unrestricted abortion policies with his personal belief in the "sanctity of human life."

April 21: The U.S. Supreme Court, in its first major decision on the issue, upholds a Washington, D.C., law barring doctors from performing abortions except when the mother's life or health is at stake. In **U.S. v. Vuitch** the Court contends that the statute is not unconstitutionally vague. The majority opinion does not answer the further question of whether all antiabortion laws violate a woman's constitutional right of privacy by limiting her ability to choose to end an unwanted pregnancy.

June 28: New York Governor Nelson A. Rockefeller signs the first state statute anywhere in the country outlawing commercial abortion referral services.

1972

February 7: The American Bar Association (ABA) endorses a uniform federal statute to allow women to have abortions "upon demand" in the first 20 weeks of pregnancy.

February 10: The New York State Court of Appeals upholds a recent decision by the state's social services commission to bar the use of Medicaid funds for abortions that are not medically necessary. The court rules that the directive does not discriminate against poor women in violation of constitutional guarantees of equal protection and due process. (Apr. 3, '71; Aug. 24, '72)

March 16: The Commission on Population Growth and the American Future, headed by John D. Rockefeller III, sends its controversial report to President Richard M. Nixon. The panel recommends all states dramatically ease their antiabortion restrictions. The report calls on all levels of government to fund abortion services and urges also that private health insurance cover abortion costs. On May 5 Nixon publicly rejects the commission's major proposals.

May 13: New York Governor Nelson A. Rockefeller vetoes the legislature's attempted repeal of the state's 1970 law liberalizing abortion.

July 12: The Democratic National Convention ends with a rejection by delegates of efforts to include in the party platform a constitutional right to abortion.

July 29: The People's Party chooses pediatrician and antiwar activist Dr. Benjamin Spock as its presidential candidate. The party's platform includes a pledge to fight for the legalization of elective abortion.

August 24: A three-judge federal panel invalidates the 1971 decision of the New York State social services commission that prohibited Medicaid payments for elective abortions. The panel rules that the order denies poor women their constitutional entitlement to equal protection of the laws. (Apr. 3, '71; Feb. 10, '72)

September 4: Democratic presidential candidate Senator George McGovern (D-SD) reiterates his position on abortion, saying the issue should remain a matter for state regulation.

November 30: Pennsylvania Governor Milton J. Shapp vetoes a tough antiabortion bill passed by the state legislature, calling it "so restrictive as to be unenforceable." The legislature subsequently overrides the veto and eventually the Supreme Court finds the law unconstitutional. (Jan. 9, '79)

December 22: The American Public Health Association sets out a new policy position when it proposes the elimination of all state laws that restrict abortion.

1973

January 22: The U.S. Supreme Court, in the companion cases of **Roe v. Wade** and *Doe v. Bolton*, overrules all state laws that bar or restrict a woman's right to obtain an abortion during the first three months of pregnancy. In its historic resolution of the controversial abortion issue, the Court drafts new guidelines that result in broadly liberalized state laws. However, the majority opinion does not grant women an absolute right to an abortion.

February 14: The National Conference of Catholic Bishops, calling the **Roe v. Wade** ruling contrary to moral principles, warns American Catholics they risk excommunication if they either have or perform an abortion.

April 17: The National Institutes of Health (NIH) announces a ban on research involving live aborted human fetuses. The ruling is aimed at stopping researchers' practice of keeping fetuses alive for several hours under laboratory conditions in order to conduct experiments.

May 31: U.S. Senator James L. Buckley (R-NY) and six cosponsors introduce a constitutional amendment that would ban all abortions except those medically necessary to save the life of the mother. The proposal, directed at overturning the effects of the U.S. Supreme Court's landmark 1973 ruling legalizing abortion, dies in a Senate subcommittee.

1974

May 20: The pro-choice Women's Lobby brings suit against the U.S. Catholic Conference, challenging the antiabortion activities of the tax-exempt Roman Catholic organization. The Women's Lobby seeks to pressure the conference either to drop efforts to influence legislation or to formally register with Congress as a lobbying group. On May 24 a federal district judge dismisses the suit, claiming the plaintiff failed to show that the main purpose of the conference is to shape legislation.

September 5: President Gerald Ford in a televised news conference says the federal Congress should not be involved in abortion legislation. He pledges his support for a constitutional amendment that would make the issue an exclusive responsibility of state lawmakers.

November 26: A U.S. congressional conference committee agrees to drop a Senate amendment to a key funding measure that would have banished the use of federal monies to pay for abortions. The committee action clears the one remaining obstacle to passage of the appropriations bill for the Departments of Labor and Health, Education and Welfare (HEW).

December 14: The Department of HEW excludes abortion from the list of family planning services for which the federal government will pay 90% of the cost under Medicaid. The ruling draws strong objections when it is revealed that the department will allow government subsidies for sterilizations.

December 15: France's national congress approves a bill legalizing abortion. The measure permits any woman to obtain an abortion during the first ten weeks of pregnancy.

Chronology

1975

January 22: A reported 25,000 antiabortion demonstrators converge on the Capitol steps in Washington, D.C., on the second anniversary of the Supreme Court's **Roe v. Wade** decision making abortion legal. The protestors call on Congress to pass a constitutional amendment to ban abortion.

February 15: Boston obstetrician Kenneth C. Edelin is convicted of manslaughter in the death of a human fetus he legally aborted. The case drew national headlines and raised hard ethical questions about the practice of temporarily sustaining fetal life under laboratory conditions for purposes of medical experimentation. (Dec. 17, '76)

March 10: U.S. Senators James L. Buckley (R-NY) and Jesse Helms (R-NC) introduce a constitutional amendment that would outlaw abortions except in cases where the pregnancy threatens the life of the mother. (Sep. 17, '75)

April 14: The U.S. Civil Rights Commission announces its opposition to the measure proposed by Senators Buckley and Helms that would sharply curb abortion in the United States. The commission argues that any such amendment would undercut protections secured by the 1st, 9th, and 14th Amendments of the Constitution.

June 16: In the case of *Bigelow v. Virginia*, the U.S. Supreme Court strikes down a Virginia statute that prohibited publication of advertisements for legal out-of-state abortion services. The Court rules that such ads are protected by press freedoms under the 1st Amendment.

July 26: The U.S. Senate overrides President Gerald Ford's veto of a major health bill allocating funds for family planning programs. The measure sanctions fines and imprisonment for persons in charge of federally funded programs who coerce women to undergo abortions by threatening them with a loss of other government health services.

September 17: A Senate judiciary subcommittee rejects all efforts to overturn the Supreme Court's 1973 **Roe v. Wade** decision establishing a constitutional right to abortion. The subcommittee move ends the abortion controversy for the current congressional term.

December 1: In *Greco v. Orange Memorial Hospital Corporation*, the U.S. Supreme Court upholds a lower court ruling that allowed a private hospital receiving public funds to forbid a doctor to perform abortions there.

1976

April 28: The U.S. Senate blocks a proposed constitutional amendment sponsored by member Jesse Helms (R-NC) that would guarantee unborn children a "right to life." The vote is the first time since the **Roe v. Wade** (1973) ruling that either chamber of Congress has given even procedural consideration to an antiabortion amendment to the Constitution.

July 1: In **Planned Parenthood v. Danforth,** the U.S. Supreme Court rules that a state may not require the written permission of a husband or, in the case of a dependent minor, the prior consent of a parent in order for an abortion to be performed.

September 17: The U.S. Congress approves the Hyde Amendment, which prohibits the use of federal Medicaid funds to pay for abortions except to save the life of the mother. Wrangling over the antiabortion measure sponsored by Representative Henry Hyde (R-IL) had delayed final congressional approval of the appropriations bill for the Departments of Labor and HEW for three months. (Sep. 30, '76)

September 30: Congress overrides President Gerald Ford's veto of the funding bill for Labor and HEW. The Hyde Amendment becomes federal law. (Sep. 17, '76)

October 22: U.S. Federal District Judge John F. Dooling rules unconstitutional the Hyde Amendment curbs on Medicaid payments for abortions. His decision blocks implementation of the new provision in all 50 states. (Aug. 4, '77)

November 29: The U.S. Supreme Court, in *Sendak v. Arnold*, upholds a lower federal court ruling that struck down an Indiana law requiring 1st-trimester abortions be done in a hospital or licensed health facility.

December 17: The Massachusetts Superior Judicial Court unanimously overturns the manslaughter conviction of Dr. Kenneth C. Edelin in one of the nation's most famous abortion cases. The court rules that doctors performing legal abortions commit manslaughter only if they end the life of a fetus that is definitely alive outside the mother's body. (Feb. 15, '75)

1977

January 13: In confirmation hearings before the U.S. Senate, the nominee for Secretary of HEW, Joseph A. Califano, Jr., says he will work to restrict or even bar abortions under all federal health programs, including Medicaid.

January 22: An estimated 30,000 pro-life marchers descend on the White House on the 4th anniversary of the Supreme Court's **Roe v. Wade** ruling easing legal restrictions on abortion. March for Life organization president Nellie J. Gray urges President Jimmy Carter to cut off all federal funding of abortions.

Chronology

May 24: The U.S. Senate blocks a resolution calling for a constitutional convention to draft an antiabortion amendment.

June 20: The U.S. Supreme Court rules that nothing in federal law or the Constitution requires states and cities to spend Medicaid funds on elective abortions. The Court holds that women do not have a constitutional right to an abortion at public expense. The ruling comes in three cases entitled **Beal v. Doe, Maher v. Roe,** and **Poelker v. Doe.**

July 9: The Planned Parenthood Federation of America, responding to recent Supreme Court and congressional actions limiting the availability of abortions, announces a $3 million fund-raising drive to campaign against any further restrictions.

August 4: Federal District Judge John F. Dooling lifts his order blocking the Hyde Amendment. He says attorneys for pro-abortion groups failed to show that the congressional act curbing federal funding of abortions was "unconstitutionally vague." The U.S. department of HEW immediately bars all federal subsidies for abortion services except in cases where the mother's life is endangered. (Oct. 22, '76)

August 16: National Conference of Catholic Bishops president Joseph L. Bernardin reveals the most sweeping antiabortion plan ever proposed by the American Catholic hierarchy. The five-point proposal marks the start of a major new church drive against abortion.

November 26: Connie J. Downey, head of a Carter administration study group on alternatives to abortion, disbands the panel after concluding that the only real options are "suicide, motherhood and, some would add, madness." In a memo to HEW Secretary Joseph A. Califano, Downey says the group lacked the direction, scope, authorization, and money needed to attack the problems underlying unwanted pregnancies.

December 7: A five-month battle over federal funding of abortion ends when the House and Senate agree on a compromise position, enabling final passage of the $60 billion appropriations bill for the Departments of Labor and HEW. This modified version of the Hyde Amendment eases restrictions on federal Medicaid payments for abortions for low-income women in cases of rape, incest, and severe physical illness.

1978

May 18: The Italian parliament legalizes abortion on demand in the 1st trimester of pregnancy.

June 13: The U.S. House of Representatives votes to tighten curbs on federal funding of abortion. Antiabortion members reject the compromise language of the year before. Instead they try to limit payment of public monies only to those procedures necessary to save the mother's life. (Oct. 14, '78)

October 10: The U.S. Congress approves an appropriations bill for the Department of Defense that restricts use of military funds for abortions by armed forces personnel or their family members.

October 14: The U.S. House of Representatives reverses an earlier vote and approves a compromise with the Senate on antiabortion legislation. Thus Congress agrees to continue in effect its 1977 arrangement permitting Medicaid funding for abortions: (1) to save the mother's life; (2) to end pregnancies that would result in severe and long-term damage to the mother's physical health; and (3) in cases of rape or incest when the crimes are promptly reported to authorities. (Jun. 13, '78)

November 30: Leaders in the national antiabortion movement announce plans to campaign for the defeat in 1980 national elections of five "liberal" senators who support public funding of elective abortions. The announcement signals adoption of a new tactic by organized pro-life forces to further politicize abortion and make it a litmus test issue in elections.

1979

January 9: The U.S. Supreme Court strikes down as unconstitutional a Pennsylvania law requiring doctors performing legal abortions to choose the method most likely to save the life of a fetus that might be viable. The court rules in **Colautti v. Franklin** that the statute is too vague and too restrictive on the professional judgment of physicians. (Nov. 30, '72)

June 7: Antiabortion activist Sean Downey announces his candidacy for the Democratic party's 1980 presidential nomination.

July 2: In **Bellotti v. Baird,** the U.S. Supreme Court judges unconstitutional a Massachusetts law requiring parental consent or approval of a judge before an unmarried minor may obtain a legal abortion. The court calls the statute an undue burden on the individual's right to an abortion as established in **Roe v. Wade.**

November 10: Findings of a New York Times/CBS poll reveal that 64% of American Roman Catholics and 69% of Protestants support abortion in at least some cases.

November 16: A House-Senate deadlock over the federal funding of abortions stalls the appropriations bill for several key executive departments of the U.S. government. Congress instead passes an emergency spending bill after reaching a compromise on the use of public financing of abortions. The agreement permits Medicaid funding of abortion when the mother's life is threatened and in cases of rape and incest.

December 10: Nobel Peace Prize recipient Mother Teresa denounces abortion as the "greatest destroyer of peace" in remarks upon receiving the award in Stockholm, Sweden.

1980

January 15: U.S. District Judge John F. Dooling declares the Hyde Amendment unconstitutional, a ruling the U.S. government immediately appeals to the U.S. Supreme Court. The amendment, passed by Congress in 1976, restricts federal financing of abortions for poor women. Dooling orders the Carter administration to resume federal Medicaid payments for medically necessary abortions. (Jun. 30, '80)

January 22: The National Abortion Rights Action League (NARAL) launches Impact '80, a program intended to counteract the political activities of antiabortion groups in the presidential-election year.

June 30: In the case of **Harris v. McRae,** the U.S. Supreme Court, reversing District Judge Dooling's January judgment, upholds the Hyde Amendment barring the use of federal funds for most abortions for indigent women. The court rules that poor women have no constitutional right to abortions at public expense. The majority opinion states that Congress did not infringe on basic constitutional guarantees of due process and equal protection when it passed the measure in 1976. (Jan. 15, '80)

July 8: At the Republican National Convention, the party's platform committee adopts a plank endorsing a constitutional ban on abortion.

August 12: The Democratic National Convention adopts a minority report of its platform committee opposing curbs on public financing of abortion.

September 21: Republican presidential candidate Ronald W. Reagan and independent nominee John B. Anderson clash on the abortion issue during a nationwide televised debate. Anderson says Reagan's support of a constitutional ban on abortion threatens a woman's "freedom of choice."

October 1: Congress breaks its deadlock over federal financing of abortion when House and Senate conferees approve a stopgap spending bill for several government departments. The two chambers agree to a compromise that further tightens eligibility rules for Medicaid payments. It is the second year in a row that the abortion funding dispute has blocked enactment of a major appropriations bill.

October 31: For the third consecutive year Congress includes the antiabortion language of the Hyde Amendment in the Department of Defense appropriations bill.

The Senate approves an amendment to a continuing resolution that gives the states the right to refuse their share of Medicaid-funded abortions even under the limited circumstances allowed by federal law.

1981

March 23: In the case of **H.L. v. Matheson,** the U.S. Supreme Court decides that a state may require a doctor to notify the parents of a minor girl upon whom the doctor is about to perform an abortion, at least in cases when a girl is still living at home and is dependent on the parents. The Court says a Utah law does not violate a minor's privacy right because the statute does not allow the parents to veto the abortion decision.

May 18: In a national referendum, Italian voters overwhelmingly reject a proposal to repeal that country's liberalized abortion law.

June 3: U.S. Senator Jake Garn (R-UT) and Representative Henry J. Hyde (R-IL) resign in protest from the advisory board of the National Pro-Life Political Action Committee after it names nine incumbent congressmen who favor abortion rights as targets for defeat in the 1982 elections.

June 4: Congress approves the strictest Hyde Amendment limits ever imposed on federal funding of abortion. The measure bans Medicaid payments unless the mother's life is at risk.

July 9: A U.S. Senate subcommittee approves a controversial bill sponsored by Jesse Helms that is designed to overturn the U.S. Supreme court's **Roe v. Wade** decision legalizing abortion. The measure declares that human life begins at conception and that the unborn are protected under the 14th Amendment. Moreover, the bill bars federal district and appeals courts from considering cases that challenge any new state abortion statutes. The measure eventually dies in full committee.

September 9: Supreme Court Associate Justice–designate Sandra Day O'Connor testifies in confirmation hearings that she considers abortion a valid target of legislative action.

December 16: A Senate subcommittee approves a constitutional amendment proposed by Orrin G. Hatch (R-UT) declaring that the Constitution secures no right to an abortion. The Hatch Amendment gives the states and Congress joint authority to regulate abortion. It says that in any conflict between state and federal law, the more restrictive of the two governs. (Mar. 10, '82; Sep. 15, '82)

1982

March 10: The Senate Judiciary Committee approves the proposed Hatch Amendment to the Constitution. It is the first time since the U.S.

Supreme Court's 1973 **Roe v. Wade** decision legalizing abortion that a full committee of Congress has endorsed an antiabortion amendment. (Dec. 16, '81; Sep. 15, '82)

July 29: The U.S. Justice Department files a friend-of-the-court brief urging the Supreme Court, in a series of pending cases, to defer to state and local laws restricting abortion rights.

September 15: The Senate votes 47 to 46 to block a measure sponsored by Jesse Helms (R-NC) that would impose severe restrictions on abortion rights and public funding of abortion. Since August 16 a group of senators had filibustered the amendment, which Helms had tried to attach to an unrelated bill raising the government's debt ceiling.

Senator Orrin G. Hatch (R-UT) withdraws his proposed constitutional amendment to give Congress and the states joint authority to restrict abortion. He cites insufficient time left in the session to fully consider the measure. (Dec. 16; '81; Mar. 10, '82)

1983

January 27: Antiabortion activist Dan B. Anderson is sentenced to 30 years in prison for the kidnapping of Dr. Henry Zevalos, who performed abortions as part of his Granite City, Illinois, practice. The case drew national attention when Anderson threatened to kill Zevalos if President Ronald Reagan failed to end legal abortion.

May 11: Roman Catholic Sister Agnes Mary Mansour, director of Michigan's welfare agency responsible for funding abortions, gives up her religious vows rather than risk expulsion from her order by the Vatican.

June 15: In **Akron Center for Reproductive Health v. City of Akron,** the U.S. Supreme Court reaffirms a woman's constitutional right to obtain an abortion. The majority strikes down as unconstitutional a city ordinance that places numbers of restrictions on access to abortion services. In another case, *Planned Parenthood v. Ashcroft*, the high court upholds key provisions of a Missouri law requiring teenage girls to obtain prior parental consent or the approval of a judge.

June 28: The U.S. Senate rejects a newly introduced Eagleton-Hatch Amendment, which states that "a right to abortion is not secured by the Constitution." The vote marks the first time either chamber of Congress has acted on an amendment designed to overturn the **Roe v. Wade** (1973) decision legalizing abortion.

November 12: The U.S. Congress approves a catchall spending bill that has a provision barring use of federal employee health benefits to pay for abortions. The one exception to the restriction is when the mother's life is endangered by the pregnancy.

1984

January 30: In a speech renewing his call for a constitutional ban on abortion, President Ronald Reagan compares the national pro-life movement with the Civil War struggle to end slavery.

June 17: The Reagan administration announces it will withhold American aid from international population control programs that either practice or advocate abortion as a family planning method.

July 5: Democratic Governor of New York Mario Cuomo speaks at Harvard's JFK School on the need for elected public officials to respect the historic separation of church and state. Cuomo says politicians cannot make personal moral and religious views the basis for shaping and enacting public policy on the difficult, sensitive issue of abortion.

August 11: The UN International Conference on Population adopts a U.S.-backed recommendation that abortion in no way should be promoted as a legitimate family planning alternative.

September 9: Roman Catholic Archbishop of New York John J. O'Connor charges Democratic vice-presidential candidate Geraldine Ferraro with misrepresenting the church's stand on abortion. O'Connor says Ferraro has created the mistaken impression that Roman Catholic teaching is flexible and open to interpretation. She denies the archbishop's claim.

September 13: New York Governor Mario Cuomo delivers a widely publicized speech at Notre Dame University on religious belief and public morality. He says that elected officials in a diverse society such as the United States who object to abortion on moral grounds should nonetheless resist attempts to outlaw the practice if it is supported by most citizens.

September 16: Episcopal Bishop of New York Paul Moore, Jr., says that while he does not favor abortion, he regards it as a "decision of conscience" to be made by women individually and that it should not be something the state may restrict.

October 7: President Ronald Reagan and Democratic nominee Walter Mondale clash over the abortion issue in the first televised debate of the presidential campaign. Reagan repeats his support for the objectives of the pro-life movement. Mondale contends the choice to end a pregnancy in the 1st trimester should be a woman's alone to make.

December 4: FBI Director William Webster draws criticism from women's rights groups when he announces his agency does not classify recent abortion clinic bombings as acts of terrorism.

1985

January 3: President Ronald Reagan condemns the recent wave of abortion clinic bombings around the United States as "violent, anarchist activities" and pledges to see the perpetrators brought to justice.

February 6: U.S. Agency for International Development (AID) administrator Peter McPherson suspends payment of $23 million to the UN Fund for Population Activities because of Reagan administration concerns the money might support forced abortions in China. (Aug. 28, '86; Aug. 14, '87)

March 12: An Alan Guttmacher Institute Study reveals that American teenagers become pregnant, give birth, and have abortions at much higher rates than teens of other industrialized nations.

June 27: The Spanish national parliament approves legislation legalizing abortion, ending a 40-year ban on the procedure.

July 2: Lutheran lay pastor Michael D. Bray is sentenced to ten years in federal prison for conspiring to bomb ten abortion clinics in three states and Washington, D.C.

July 15: The U.S. Justice Department, in a friend-of-the-court brief, asks the Supreme Court to return the abortion issue to the state legislatures by overturning its **Roe v. Wade** decision. The brief comes in a case before the high court concerning the constitutionality of a Pennsylvania antiabortion law. (Jun. 12, '86)

September 8: Pope John Paul II issues his strongest condemnation of abortion to date. He says an unborn human being's "right to live is one of the inalienable human rights."

October 8: The three-year legal dispute over how to dispose of 17,000 aborted fetuses discarded by a California medical laboratory ends as the fetuses are provided a nonreligious burial with a eulogy written by President Ronald Reagan. The case attracted national focus when key anti-abortion groups sought legal custody of the fetuses.

November 14: America's Roman Catholic bishops approve a plan to discourage abortions that links the effort to other human rights issues collectively called "ethics of life."

1986

March 10: A reported 80,000 marchers supporting abortion rights gather at the Capitol in Washington, D.C. National Organization for Women (NOW) organizers call it a sign of the "rejuvenation of the women's movement."

June 12: In the case of **Thornburgh v. American College of Obstetricians and Gynecologists,** the U.S. Supreme Court reaffirms its **Roe v. Wade** (1973) decision establishing a constitutional right to abortion. The ruling holds key provisions of a Pennsylvania law are unconstitutional because they are intended to deter women from having abortions, (Jul. 15, '85)

August 19: The Vatican revokes the authorization of the Reverend Charles E. Curran to teach theology at Catholic University of America because of his views on a number of sexual issues. The liberal Curran argues the church's opposition to abortion should not be absolute. The case marks the first time censure has been imposed on an American Roman Catholic theologian.

August 28: The U.S. AID withdraws a $25 million contribution to the UN Fund for Population Activities because of its involvement in China's compulsory abortion program. (Feb. 6, '85; Aug. 14, '87)

December 16: The U.S. Supreme Court declares a congressional ban on direct corporate spending in political campaigns unconstitutional as applied to a Massachusetts antiabortion group organized as a corporation.

1987

February 25: Fireworks expert Dennis Malvasi, top suspect in a series of abortion clinic bombings in New York City, surrenders to federal agents one day after a televised appeal by Roman Catholic Archbishop John J. O'Connor. Malvasi pleads guilty on June 13 and is sentenced in September to seven years in prison.

July 31: President Ronald Reagan announces new regulations that will bar family planning clinics that receive federal money from counseling clients about abortion. He reveals the updated guidelines at a White House meeting of pro-life activists. (Dec. 18, '87; Jul. 2, '88)

August 14: Despite pressures from Congress, the U.S. AID again withholds money from the UN Fund for Population Activities over its support of China's population control program. (Feb. 6, '85; Aug. 28, '86)

August 25:   President Ronald Reagan names a federal task force to encourage adoption as an alternative to abortion.

September 20:   Pope John Paul II sternly condemns the legal practice of abortion in the United States. The pontiff delivers the message on the last leg of his trip to this country.

September 22:   Senator Robert Packwood (R-OR) is the first Republican senator to oppose Robert Bork's nomination to the U.S. Supreme Court. Packwood says he fears Bork will overturn the **Roe v. Wade** decision.

October 23:   The U.S. Senate votes 58 to 42 against Judge Bork's nomination to the Supreme Court. The margin of defeat is the greatest in American history for an appointee to the nation's highest court. Bork's legal conservatism, his frank critique of the constitutional reasoning behind the landmark Supreme Court decisions in **Griswold v. Connecticut** and **Roe v. Wade,** and his expressed view that the abortion issue should reside with the states all contributed to the successful opposition to his nomination by abortion-rights advocates.

December 14:   In **Zbaraz v. Hartigan,** the U.S. Supreme Court upholds a Federal District Court ruling that struck down as unconstitutional a 1983 law requiring girls under age 18 who wanted abortions to wait 24 hours after both parents had been formally notified.

December 18:   Congressional leaders reveal they will not resist a Reagan administration plan to proceed with new abortion restrictions on family planning groups getting federal funding. (Jul. 31, '87; Jul. 2, '88)

1988

January 23:   A reported 50,000 antiabortion protestors march in Washington, D.C., on the 15th anniversary of the U.S. Supreme Court's decision in **Roe v. Wade** legalizing abortion.

July 2:   A U.S. District Court upholds the constitutionality of new Reagan administration regulations that deny federal payments to family planning clinics which provide abortion counseling. (Jul. 31, '87)

July 20:   Police arrest 134 pro-life protestors outside the site of the Democratic National Convention in Atlanta. The demonstrators are members of the national antiabortion organization Operation Rescue.

July 28:   The U.S. Senate approves Medicaid funding of abortions in cases of rape or incest. Its action marks the first time since 1981 either chamber of Congress approved a measure to expand the use of federal money for abortions. On September 14 the Senate drops its attempt to broaden public funding when it accepts the tougher restrictions advocated by the House.

August 13: Moral Majority leader the Reverend Jerry Falwell hails ongoing protests in Atlanta staged by the ardent antiabortion group Operation Rescue. The demonstrations outside various abortion clinics have resulted in hundreds of arrests. Falwell endorses a national campaign of "civil disobedience" to change abortion law in the United States.

September 17: An advisory committee of the National Institutes of Health concludes that use of fetal tissue obtained in legal abortions for medical research and therapy is morally acceptable.

September 24: The French government approves marketing of the new drug RU 486, which induces abortion in the earliest stage of pregnancy. (Oct. 27, '88)

September 27: Vice President George Bush, the Republican nominee for President, retracts a controversial remark made the night before in his televised debate with Democratic candidate Michael Dukakis. Bush says that while he supports efforts to have abortion barred under the Constitution, he does not believe women should suffer criminal penalties. He suggests that whatever criminal liability is involved should reside with the attending doctor.

October 27: Under mounting pressure from pro-life advocacy groups, the French company Groupe Roussel Uclaf suspends sales of its new abortion-inducing drug RU 486. Two days later the French government orders distribution of RU 486 resumed immediately, and the company announces it will comply. In defending the government's intervention, French Minister of Health Claude Levin calls the controversial new drug the "moral property of women." (Sep. 24, '88)

November 1: Democratic presidential candidate Michael Dukakis declares his strong support of a woman's right to choose whether to have an abortion. The remarks are made during a last round of campaigning in California before the general election.

November 6: President Ronald Reagan signs into law a federal measure banning commercial sales of human fetal organs and tissues.

November 15: The U.S. Supreme Court refuses to reopen the question of whether a man may have any legal right to interfere with a woman's decision to end her pregnancy. In 1976 the Court ruled that a state cannot make a woman's right to abortion contingent on a husband's permission.

November 26: The Pan American Health Organization reports a sharp rise in clandestine abortions in Latin America, many of which end in death for the woman.

1989

January 10: Surgeon General C. Everett Koop reports that his study yielded no conclusive scientific evidence on the psychological effect of abortion on women.

The U.S. Supreme Court agrees to rule on the constitutionality of a Missouri law intended to limit abortion access. The Justice Department says the case of **Webster v. Reproductive Health Services** offers the Court an appropriate opportunity to override **Roe v. Wade.** (Jul. 3, '89)

January 14: In a speech President Ronald Reagan says that he will continue his efforts to shape and influence federal policy on abortion even after he leaves office.

February 10: Both the New York State Appeals Court and the U.S. Supreme Court refuse to hear the appeal of antiabortionists Lawrence Washburn and John Short, who seek to stop a Long Island man, Martin Klein, from ordering an abortion for his pregnant, comatose wife, Nancy. Days earlier the state supreme court had made Klein legal guardian and empowered him to authorize the abortion he says will save his wife's life.

February 11: Doctors perform the abortion on Nancy Klein, comatose following a car accident, ending the remarkable two-week court battle between her family and abortion foes.

February 24: The Senate Finance Committee votes to approve Dr. Louis H. Sullivan as Secretary of the Department of HHS after the nominee assures antiabortion members his views on the issue conform with those of President George Bush. Sullivan's nomination almost was derailed when rumors emerged that he supported a woman's right of choice and opposed attempts to have **Roe v. Wade** overturned.

March 26: Fifty career lawyers with the Justice Department release a petition protesting the Bush administration's request of the Supreme Court that it use a pending Missouri case as the vehicle to overturn the 1973 **Roe v. Wade** ruling.

April 9: An estimated 300,000 pro-choice advocates march in Washington, D.C., in support of abortion rights. The protestors carry coat hangers to evoke the days of illegal abortions, and wave banners that urge the U.S. Supreme Court to keep abortion legal and safe.

May 15: NBC airs the television movie **Roe v. Wade** about the U.S. Supreme Court's landmark 1973 decision legalizing abortion. Afterward the network presents an hour-long news special on the issue, providing equal time to pro-life spokespersons who claim the movie had a pro-choice bias.

July 3: In **Webster v. Reproductive Health Services,** the U.S. Supreme Court upholds the main provisions of a Missouri law prohibiting public funding of abortion and requiring tests for fetal viability after the 20th week.

July 6: New York Governor Mario Cuomo, in the wake of the **Webster** ruling, pledges to veto any state law restricting abortion. Cuomo says nothing in the Supreme Court's decision altered his view about abortion rights and the right of poor women to Medicaid funding for abortion. Addressing the issue again on September 10, Cuomo declares that abortion "must be a matter of the woman's conscience."

July 25: Republican Governor Bob Martinez, suggesting the U.S. Supreme Court's recent **Webster** decision cleared the way for stricter state anti-abortion measures, calls a special session of the Florida legislature to consider a slate of strict abortion limitations. (Oct. 11, '89)

August 3 Under increasing pressure to clarify his abortion views, New York Republican mayoral candidate Rudolph Giuliani says he totally accepts a woman's "right of choice" on abortion. His Democratic opponents, observing how Giuliani earlier in the campaign had advocated that the Supreme Court overturn **Roe v. Wade,** claim the Republican hopeful has flipflopped on the issue to dodge harmful political consequences of an antiabortion stance.

September 27: French medical researcher Dr. Etienne-Emile Baulieu, who developed the abortion-inducing drug RU 486, is named winner of the Lasker Award, among the most prestigious medical research prizes. Antiabortion groups criticize Baulieu's recognition.

October 6: The Florida Supreme Court rules that state legislation requiring teenage girls to get a parent's consent for an abortion violates the clause of the Florida constitution guaranteeing its citizens a right to be "free from governmental intrusion in their private lives." The court strikes down the law.

October 11: A special session of the Florida legislature draws to a close after lawmakers defeat all of Governor Bob Martinez's proposals for tighter restrictions on abortion. Legislators across the political spectrum admit they responded to strong constituent pressures to reject the new abortion limitations. (Jul. 25, '89)

October 25: The U.S. House of Representatives sustains President Bush's October 21 veto of a congressional measure to permit federal funding of abortions for victims of rape and incest. Bush's rejection of the legislation was one of four 1989 presidential vetoes of bills seeking to relax longstanding bans on federal financing of abortions and abortion-related activities.

November 1: The Bush administration extends a 19-month-old ban on federal funding of research on fetal tissue. The decision is made over the objections of two federal panels that say fetal tissue experiments hold promise for treating diabetes and Parkinson's disease. Administration officials claim such research is unethical because it encourages women to undergo abortions to provide a supply of tissue.

November 3: New York Roman Catholic Cardinal John O'Connor proposes the establishment of an order of nuns, the Sisters of Life, dedicated to ending abortion and euthanasia.

November 7: Pro-choice Democratic gubernatorial candidates Jim Florio and Doug Wilder win their respective races in New Jersey and Virginia. The governors-elect, supporters of women's abortion rights, benefited by the abortion issue, which was injected into the fall campaign following the U.S. Supreme Court's **Webster** decision giving states greater leeway to regulate abortion. Florio and Wilder alike drew strong support from politically mobilized pro-choice groups. Abortion was an election-year liability for pro-life Republican gubernatorial hopefuls Jim Courter of New Jersey and Marshall Coleman of Virginia. Courter's reversal on the issue late in the race was described by state Democrats as a calculated concession to political realities in order to save his sinking candidacy.

America's Catholic bishops, addressing Roman Catholic politicians who personally oppose abortion but do not want to limit the choice of others, warn that Catholics cannot invoke the idea of choice to defend legal abortion. The bishops' statement, delivered at the National Conference of Bishops in Baltimore, is part of a new push to rally antiabortion forces in the aftermath of the July U.S. Supreme Court ruling that cleared the way for states to further restrict the practice.

November 10: Three prominent Republican women fund-raisers declare they will not support antiabortion candidates in 1990 and intend to establish a political action committee to assist Republicans who endorse abortion rights. The trio warns the party that an unyielding opposition to abortion will lead to losses nationwide in next year's elections.

November 14: The Pennsylvania legislature overwhelmingly passes a bill imposing the nation's toughest abortion curbs. Democratic Governor

Robert P. Casey, who helped draft the legislation, signs the measure into law four days later.

November 23: An Illinois abortion case, seen by legal experts as the Supreme Court's most likely opportunity in 1990 to overturn or narrow its 1973 **Roe v. Wade** decision legalizing abortion, is settled out of court. Two remaining cases on the docket offer the justices the chance to review the **Roe** ruling.

December 5: Democrat Lucy Killea, barred by Roman Catholic bishop Leo T. Maher from receiving communion because of her support for abortion rights, is elected to the California Senate. Her victory tips the balance in the legislature in favor of upholding abortion rights.

December 10: As thousands demonstrate outside New York's St. Patrick's Cathedral, several dozen extremist activists disrupt mass to protest Roman Catholic Cardinal John O'Connor's recent statements deploring abortion. Police arrest 43 demonstrators, who also express their displeasure with O'Connor's views on AIDS and homosexuality.

CHAPTER 3

COURT CASES

Since the U.S. Supreme Court's historic 1973 ruling in **Roe v. Wade,** the issue of abortion in the United States has resided squarely in the judicial system. A sequence of legal actions in state and federal courts has shaped the debate and ultimately set the bounds on public policy. This chapter provides summaries of what are generally acknowledged as the most significant court cases on abortion to date. These cases have addressed the pivotal legal issues surrounding this complex and often divisive matter: a right of privacy and its extension to a woman's decision to have an abortion; the balance between a fundamental individual right and competing state interests; a right to life of the unborn; consent requirements; a minor girl's constitutional rights; medical performance standards; and public funding of abortion.

Actions presented here raised issues of constitutional significance, and all ultimately were decided by the Supreme Court. Each case is presented in the same format: "Background," "Legal Issues," "Decisions," and "Impact." Court cases in bold print are discussed separately within the chapter.

GRISWOLD V. CONNECTICUT (1965)

Background

A Connecticut law prohibited the use of birth control devices and made it a crime for anyone to provide information or instructions concerning contraceptive use or practice. In November 1961 Estelle Griswold and Dr. C. Lee Buxton, officers of a Planned Parenthood league, were arrested for dispensing birth control information to married couples. The two subsequently were convicted in state circuit court and fined $100. When efforts to have the convictions overturned in state appellate courts failed, Griswold and Buxton appealed to the Supreme Court.

Legal Issues

Lawyers for Griswold and Buxton called on the Court to set aside the convictions on grounds the Connecticut criminal statute unconstitutionally invaded a right of privacy of married persons by intruding in the very personal matter of birth control. Attorneys argued that while nowhere in the text of the Bill of Rights was privacy explicitly mentioned, the Court basically had recognized personal privacy as a fundamental right shielded from government interference in a series of cases dating back to 1923.

Decision

In a seven-to-two ruling announced on June 7, 1965, the Court invalidated the law and declared the Planned Parenthood officers could not be punished for aiding its violation. The seven Justices in the majority were split on the proper constitutional provision to use in striking down the statute, but they agreed that married couples had privacy rights that could not be curbed in the manner of the Connecticut law.

Justice William O. Douglas, writing for the Court, held that the right of privacy was an independent right implicit in the 1st, 3rd, 4th, 5th, and 9th amendments. He declared: "Specific guarantees in the Bill of Rights have penumbras, formed by emanations from these guarantees that help give them life and substance. Various guarantees create zones of privacy." The Court declared that marriage was within a protected zone of privacy and that Connecticut had intruded upon the zone by barring married couples from using contraceptives. Expressing the majority view, Douglas concluded: "Would we allow the police to search the sacred precincts of marital bedrooms for telltale signs of the use of contraceptives? The very idea is repulsive to the notions of privacy surrounding the marriage relationship."

In a concurring opinion, Justice Arthur Goldberg wrote that the right to personal privacy was one of those enjoyed by the people under the 9th Amendment, which states that "enumeration in the Constitution of certain rights shall not be construed to deny or disparage others retained by the people." He said the amendment showed that the Constitution's authors believed fundamental rights existed that were not expressly listed in the first eight amendments of the Bill of Rights.

The two dissenters, Justices Potter Stewart and Hugo Black, found no right of privacy either expressed or implied in the Constitution. They rebuked the majority for relying on vague concepts of "fundamental rights" or liberty to strike down a law it found unreasonable or repugnant. Black cautioned the Court against acting as a "superlegislature" passing its judgment on the social desirability of legislation. He said the only appropriate remedy would be for Connecticut lawmakers to repeal the state's birth control statute.

Impact

In terms of the development of constitutional doctrine, **Griswold** is among the most influential Supreme Court decisions of the last 20 years. For the first time, the Court established a fundamental right of privacy anchored in the Constitution. The ruling revealed a readiness to locate, or construe, fundamental rights in the Bill of Rights beyond those specifically mentioned in the text. In 1972 in *Eisenstadt v. Baird* the Court extended the privacy right to the "intimate association" of unmarried persons.

Griswold paved the way for the "constitutionalization" of abortion. The 1965 decision served as the outstanding precedent in 1973 when the Court ruled in **Roe v. Wade** that the new constitutionally protected right of privacy was broad enough to encompass a woman's choice of whether or not to have an abortion.

UNITED STATES V. VUITCH (1971)

Background

Dr. Milan Vuitch, a surgeon, regularly performed abortions as part of his Washington, D.C., practice. In May 1968 police arrested Vuitch in his office and charged him with performing illegal abortions in violation of the District of Columbia statute, which permitted only those necessary to save the mother's life or to preserve her health. The law at issue had been enacted by Congress and applied only to the district. Therefore Vuitch's purported violation of a federal law led to indictment in federal court. The government alleged Vuitch had performed nontherapeutic and ultimately unnecessary abortions. He countered that the abortions in question had been done to protect the mental well-being of the women involved and thus were justified within the meaning of the D.C. law's provision about safeguarding maternal "health." Vuitch cited the case of the patient with whom he was consulting at the time of his arrest. Caught in a troubled marriage, victim of psychological abuse, she faced an unwanted pregnancy by a husband she feared and detested. The prospect of bearing the child, Vuitch suggested, would only contribute to the woman's "mental suffering."

The case was scheduled for Federal District Court. Before the trial began, the district judge dismissed the government's charges on grounds that the D.C. statute was unconstitutionally vague and also that the burden of proof had been improperly placed on the defendant. The United States appealed the judgment directly to the U.S. Supreme Court.

Legal Issues

In their brief, Vuitch's lawyers challenged the D.C. law on several counts. Echoing the district judge, they attacked the statute as unconstitutionally vague because it failed to make clear whether the maternal health exception encompassed mental health. Nor did it exactly indicate what degree of health threat would justify an abortion. Counsel also contended that the D.C. law abridged Vuitch's 1st Amendment right to carry out his professional responsibilities. Finally they argued the measure unconstitutionally interfered with a woman's right to choose to end an unwanted pregnancy. On this point, Vuitch asked the Court to make a broad ruling by extending the fundamental privacy right established in the landmark case of **Griswold v. Connecticut** to a woman's decision whether or not to have an abortion. No federal court had yet confronted this emerging claim. However, in 1967 the California Supreme Court had taken a major step in this direction when it ruled in the criminal abortion case of Dr. Leon Belous that a woman had a "fundamental right to choose whether to end her pregnancy."

Decision

On April 21, 1971, the Supreme Court announced its decision. It upheld the D.C. law by a five-to-two vote, saying the language regarding preservation of "life or health" was not so vague as to violate the due process clause of the 14th Amendment. Writing for the majority, Justice Hugo Black held that a reasonable reading of the law revealed that it permitted abortions for both physical and mental health reasons. At the same time, the majority ruled the statute had been wrongly interpreted and applied by the government when it required Vuitch himself to prove the abortions he performed were necessary. Black said shifting the burden of proof from the state to the defendant was contrary to established criminal procedure. The Court ruled that for the government to convict a doctor under the D.C. measure, it should have to establish in court that the abortion was not necessary to preserve the woman's health or life. The case was remanded to the Federal District Court, at which point the Justice Department decided not to pursue the charges against Vuitch.

Impact

U.S. v. Vuitch was historically noteworthy because it was the first abortion case the Supreme Court had considered. When the Court affirmed that protection of the mother's mental welfare was a legitimate reason for authorizing an abortion, it granted greater leeway to women and their physicians in determining whether to bring a pregnancy to term.

The Court handled its first abortion ruling cautiously, deciding the case on a narrow basis. By ruling that the government had erred in interpreting the law, the majority was able to uphold the D.C. statute while avoiding a possible dispute over the proper roles of respective branches of government. The Court shielded itself from potential charges that the judiciary was impinging on the legislature's traditional powers and responsibilities. Importantly, the Court chose not to rule on the constitutional claims based on the privacy right. The Supreme Court would not take on the issue of whether a woman had a constitutionally protected right to choose an abortion until **Roe v. Wade.**

ROE V. WADE (1973)

Background

Norma McCorvey, 21, was unmarried and working as a waitress in August 1969 when she became pregnant following an alleged rape. (In 1987 McCorvey revealed publicly she had fabricated the rape story.) She wished to end the pregnancy by abortion, but a Texas law made procuring an abortion a crime except to save the life of the mother. Rape was not recognized as an exception under the strict state code. Several Texas lawyers who believed this 1857 statute unconstitutional and who wanted to see abortion legalized became aware of McCorvey's situation. Recognizing the elements for a test case, they persuaded her to bring a legal challenge to the existing law. In March 1970 McCorvey, under the pseudonym "Jane Roe," filed a class action suit in Federal District Court in Dallas, seeking a judgment that the state's abortion statute unconstitutionally abridged her right of personal privacy and violated due process guarantees by denying her access to a safe abortion performed by a competent doctor. She asked the district court officially to block local district attorney Henry Wade from enforcing the Texas abortion prohibition.

After both sides filed motions, the district court ruled the Texas law was unconstitutionally vague and overbroad. The three-judge panel held that the state's abortion restrictions infringed women's "fundamental right to choose whether to have children." The court entered a declaratory judgment on Jane Roe's behalf but denied her request for an injunction barring continued enforcement of the law. Both sides immediately appealed aspects of the lower court's judgment to the Supreme Court. Before the Justices were able to reach a decision, McCorvey had the child and put the baby girl up for adoption.

Legal Issues

In accepting the *Roe* case for argument, the Court agreed to confront for the first time the complex questions of whether state antiabortion laws like the one in Texas violated a constitutionally protected right of privacy and whether an unborn fetus is a human being under the Constitution.

Jane Roe challenged the Texas law on two basic grounds. Her attorneys argued the statute on its face was too broad and therefore in violation of due process protections. The law made no distinction between abortions performed early in a pregnancy and those performed later. Also, its sweeping restriction took no account of complicating circumstances, such as rape or dangers to the mother's health presented by pregnancy. Second, Roe claimed the law infringed her fundamental right to choose whether or not to have a child. This basic right, her lawyers argued, was implicit in the concept of personal liberty embodied in the due process clause of the 14th Amendment. She maintained that a woman's decision to have an abortion was shielded from government interference by the same fundamental right of privacy which the Court had recognized in **Griswold v. Connecticut.**

The state of Texas asked the Court to reverse the lower federal court's ruling on all key points. Attorneys argued that since the late 19th century the regulation of abortion had been a legitimate public policy concern and a matter for the state legislatures, not the courts. They criticized attempts to "constitutionalize" the issue of abortion and called the purported privacy right largely a judicial invention. Texas called on the judiciary to refrain from trespassing on the historical domain of the states.

The state contended it was within its proper powers in restricting abortion because it had compelling interests in watching out for the mother's health during pregnancy and in protecting the potential life of the unborn. This issue of "potential life" figured pivotally in the state's claim. A number of groups opposed to abortion, including the Roman Catholic Church, filed friend-of-the-court briefs on behalf of district attorney Wade and Texas advancing the idea that a fetus becomes a human being at conception and is therefore entitled to full constitutional rights, to include, most important, a right to life.

Decision

On January 22, 1973, the Supreme Court delivered its historic decision. By a vote of seven to two the Court ruled that the Texas law barring abortion except to save the mother's life was unconstitutional. Writing for the majority, Justice Harry Blackmun began with a statement explaining that abortion had not always been a crime under American law and was, in fact, legally and socially tolerated until the second half of the 19th century.

The majority ruled a constitutionally guaranteed right of privacy protects a woman's decision to have an abortion, at least in the early weeks of pregnancy. The opinion cited a line of earlier Court decisions that had recognized an emerging, fundamental privacy right and concluded: "This right is broad enough to encompass a woman's decision whether or not to terminate her pregnancy." The Court said that while the right to choose an abortion is fundamental, it is not absolute and so must be balanced against competing state interests in ensuring the pregnant woman's health and protecting potential human life. Each of these interests, the Court asserted, increases and becomes more "compelling" as the pregnancy advances.

Justice Blackmun drafted a set of detailed guidelines to describe the relative legal rights of pregnant women and the states. The so-called trimester analysis declared:

- For the first three months of pregnancy, or 1st trimester, the decision is left entirely to the woman and her doctor. The state's interest in her welfare at this stage is not compelling enough to justify interference because 1st-trimester abortions are as safe as childbirth or even safer.
- During the 2nd trimester a state may regulate abortion in ways reasonably related to maternal health, such as licensing the doctors involved or regulating clinics.
- In the 3rd trimester (after the 24th week), the period during which the fetus is judged to be "viable," or capable of surviving outside the mother's womb, a state may forbid abortion in the interest of protecting potential life—except where it may be necessary to preserve the life or health of the mother.

The majority rejected the notion that a fetus is a person upon conception and therefore enjoys a constitutionally protected right to life. Blackmun looked at various uses of the word "person" in the Constitution and concluded that, as employed in the 14th Amendment, the word did not include the unborn.

Two members of the Court filed strong dissents. Justice Byron White wrote that "nothing in the language or history of the Constitution" supported the majority's judgment. He suggested that the Court, through an exercise of "raw judicial power," had simply made up and declared a new constitutional right for pregnant women. He argued the issue should be left to the state legislatures and the expression of the democratic will of the people.

Justice William Rehnquist called the majority's trimester guidelines "judicial legislation" and claimed the whole issue of abortion was better left to a judgment by elected lawmakers. Noting that a majority of states had had abortion laws for more than 100 years, he suggested that a right to an abortion was not "so rooted in traditions of the people as to be ranked 'fundamental.' "

In the companion case to Roe, *Doe v. Bolton*, the Court upheld a lower federal court's declaration that Georgia's abortion law was unconstitutional. The statute had been revised in 1968 to conform with liberalized guidelines recommended by the American Law Institute in its 1959 Model Penal Code. The Georgia law, like the Texas one, allowed abortions to save the mother's life. It also permitted the procedure when pregnancy resulted from rape, when the fetus was likely to be born seriously deformed, or when pregnancy endangered the mother's health. Nonetheless, the statute made qualifying for an abortion difficult even in the presence of these conditions. The law outlined a series of restrictive regulations, consultations, court actions, and review boards. Moreover, it required abortions to be performed in accredited hospitals.

In overturning the Georgia law, the Court repeated its finding in *Roe*: that a woman's fundamental right to choose an abortion is not absolute, but must be balanced against competing, valid state concerns as the pregnancy progresses. The majority agreed with the lower court that the accredited-hospital requirement, mandatory medical consultations, and residency rules were unconstitutionally burdensome because they applied throughout pregnancy and were not justified by any compelling state interest.

Impact

Roe v. Wade has become a fixture of the American social, political, and legal lexicons. The immediate practical consequence was clear: The rulings effectively overturned existing abortion laws in all 50 states. Not only were laws that allowed abortion only when a woman's life was endangered found unconstitutional; but laws, such as Georgia's, based on the liberal approach of the Model Penal Code, were effectively struck down because of burdensome rules and unwarranted regulations that served no compelling government interest.

Also significant has been the effect on evolving abortion law and constitutional doctrine. *Roe* changed the respective roles of the legislature and the judiciary in dealing with abortion. Historically, the issue had resided with the states and their elected representatives. By establishing the abortion decision as a constitutionally protected, fundamental right, the Court made state legislation subject to a strict standard of judicial review by federal courts. Ultimately, responsibility for regulation shifted from the legislative branches of the states to the judicial branch of the national government.

In *Roe*, the Court extended and expanded the right of privacy established in its prior decision in **Griswold.** For women's rights activists and supporters of the pro-choice movement, Roe signaled a historic victory in their efforts to have all matters related to a woman's reproductive life shielded from government interference. Abortion opponents have attacked the decision as judicial activism, an emblem of the permissive attitudes of the Court, and an unwarranted judicial infringement on the traditional powers of the states. The pro-life movement consistently has sought to have *Roe* overturned.

Despite its far-reaching ruling legalizing abortion in the first trimester, the 1973 decision was, in an important respect, a compromise action that negotiated a path between competing individual rights and state interests. The ruling marked out a shifting balance between the state's interest in potential life and a woman's right to terminate an unwanted pregnancy. Before the point of fetal viability, the Court said, the woman's right outweighs the state's interests. Once the fetus is able to live outside the womb, the balance shifts and the state may ban abortions that are not necessary to preserve the woman's life or health.

Roe did not mark the end of the abortion law battle. Abortion as a shielded privacy right has been the subject of extensive litigation since 1973. In the face of numerous legal challenges, the Court consistently has reaffirmed the landmark decision.

PLANNED PARENTHOOD V. DANFORTH (1976)

Background

After the Supreme Court's historic ruling in **Roe v. Wade** making abortion a matter between a woman and her doctor in the first three months of pregnancy, the Missouri legislature in June 1974 drafted a comprehensive abortion law. The statute spelled out a broad range of regulations and restrictions. Importantly, it introduced such matters as medical performance guidelines, consent requirements, and mandatory record keeping that the Court had not addressed in **Roe**. Governor Christopher Bond signed the measure into law on July 17, 1975. Three days later two Missouri-licensed physicians, David Hall and Michael Freiman, and a branch of Planned Parenthood in central Missouri together filed suit in Federal District Court against the state. Their class action challenged parts of the law setting forth various limits and restrictions on abortion. The provisions they contested included ones:

- prohibiting abortion if the fetus could be judged viable "with reasonable medical certainty" (except to save the life or health of the mother).
- requiring, in the first 12 weeks, the woman's informed consent in writing to the abortion and her guarantee it was given free of coercion.
- requiring, in the first 12 weeks, the spouse's consent to the abortion (unless the abortion was necessary to save the mother's life).
- requiring consent of the parent or guardian for unmarried women under age 18 (unless the abortion was necessary to save the mother's life).
- prohibiting a doctor's use of saline amniocentesis as an abortion method after the first 12 weeks of pregnancy.
- requiring physicians to keep complete records of all abortions performed, irrespective of the stage of pregnancy.
- requiring attending doctors to exercise a standard of care that strived to save the life of the fetus; physicians failing to follow such a standard would be subject to manslaughter charges.

The suit claimed these provisions intruded on a woman's fundamental right to choose an abortion and deprived doctors and their patients of assorted constitutional rights. Attorneys sought a declaratory judgment and asked for an injunction barring Missouri Attorney General John Danforth from enforcing the statute. The district court upheld all provisions except the one regarding a doctor's duty of care for the fetus. The U.S. Supreme Court then agreed to hear the family planning clinic's appeal of the lower federal court's judgment.

Legal Issues

Planned Parenthood challenged the Missouri law on a number of constitutional grounds. The statute, lawyers contended, alternately skirted the

Court's intent in **Roe** and out-and-out violated the holdings of the land-mark 1973 decision. They claimed the provision on viability, as worded, was unduly burdensome because it interfered with doctors' exercising their best medical judgment. On the issue of a woman's consent, counsel argued that the word "informed" was so vague and open to interpretation as to be unconstitutional. The written-consent requirement, moreover, represented impermissible state intrusion into the 1st trimester of preg-nancy—the period the Supreme Court had ruled in **Roe** was shielded from government interference.

Extending this same basic attack, Planned Parenthood claimed the consent regulations also conflicted with **Roe**. Requiring the husband's approval in the first three months of pregnancy abridged a woman's fun-damental privacy right. Counsel rejected suggestions that a father had an interest in the pregnancy equal to the mother's. Lawyers said the paren-tal consent requirement violated unmarried minors' rights to equal pro-tection under the law because it placed them under a restriction that married minors of the same age would not face. In addition, the rule on parental approval was said to invite the possibility mature minors would be totally excluded from a decision that might have an enormous impact on their lives.

The provision on mandatory record keeping was challenged as a threat to the confidentiality of the doctor-patient relationship. The attorneys characterized the rule as excessive and said it served no legitimate medi-cal purpose. The bar on the saline amniocentesis procedure was termed unconstitutional because it deprived women access to the safest and most commonly used method of abortion in the 2nd trimester. Finally, Planned Parenthood attacked the standard-of-care provision as overbroad and in violation of **Roe** because it did not exempt 1st-trimester abortions from its scope.

Attorney General Danforth, representing Missouri, defended the con-stitutionality of the contested law. He claimed the legislation's definition of viability conformed with **Roe** and was drafted in view of the state's compelling interest in protecting potential human life. Missouri con-tended the informed-written-consent rule supported the state's legitimate interest throughout a pregnancy to see that the abortion decision was made by the person "constitutionally empowered to do so." Danforth's primary justification for the spousal consent and parental approval re-quirements was that each served the state's long-standing and appro-priate interest in preserving family or marital relationships and in up-holding parental authority. He also argued the father had his own strong interest in the pregnancy that deserved to be weighed against the wom-an's right to choose to have an abortion. Moreover, Danforth claimed that allowing a child to make a decision to have an abortion without adult advice would be an "irresponsible abandonment of the state's duty to protect the welfare of minors."

Missouri defended the bar on saline amniocentesis as a measure taken in the interest of protecting maternal health as the pregnancy advances. Finally, the state argued the standard-of-care regulation had been misinterpreted by the Federal District Court and should be ruled constitutional.

Decision

On July 1, 1976, the Supreme Court issued a mixed ruling, upholding parts of the Missouri law and invalidating others. The Court ruled unanimously that the provision defining viability was not unconstitutional because it did not circumvent or go beyond the allowable limitations on state regulation of abortion described in **Roe**. It also held that states may validly require a woman to consent in writing prior to an abortion, so as to ensure that her consent is freely given and not "the product of coercion." The majority ruled that while the record-keeping provision might give rise to "questionable practices" by the state, it did not on its face abridge a woman's constitutional rights or infringe on the doctor-patient relationship. Such records were called an important source of information for disinterested medical research.

The parental consent requirement was found to infringe on the constitutional rights of minors. The Court said that a state may not impose "blanket" restrictions requiring all single women under 18 to obtain the consent of a parent to have an abortion. The majority ruled this provision impermissible, saying the state had no authority to give a third party, even a parent, absolute power to override the decision of a woman to have an abortion. Writing for the majority, Justice Blackmun remarked that "constitutional rights do not mature and come into being magically when one attains the state-defined age of maturity. Minors as well as adults are protected by the Constitution and possess constitutional rights."

By a vote of six to three, the Court ruled the spousal consent provision unconstitutional. States could not require a woman to get the husband's approval prior to an abortion. The majority said a state could not delegate a veto power that the state itself was absolutely prohibited from exercising during the 1st trimester of pregnancy. Blackmun took note of the father's interests and of the difficulties when husband and wife disagreed on an abortion decision. He explained the Court's stand in favor of the mother: "The obvious fact is that when the wife and husband disagree on this decision, the view of only one of the two marriage partners can prevail. Since it is the woman who physically bears the child

70

and who is the more directly and immediately affected by the pregnancy, as between the two, the balance weighs in her favor."

The provision barring saline amniocentesis was found unconstitutional because it failed as a reasonable regulation for the protection of maternal health, as defined by **Roe.** The Court ruled the prohibition an unwarranted regulation meant to inhibit most abortions after the 1st trimester. Finally, the majority struck down as too broad the standard-of-care provision requiring the attending doctor to preserve the life of the fetus. The Court held that because the provision did not exclude 1st-trimester abortions, it was in violation of **Roe's** bar on state interference in the initial 12 weeks of pregnancy.

Impact

As the first major abortion decision following **Roe v. Wade,** *Planned Parenthood v. Danforth* revealed how the Court intended to affect the balance between a woman's fundamental right and compelling public interests. The Missouri statute, emblematic of other state abortion laws passed in the aftermath of **Roe,** seemed designed to test the boundaries of the 1973 ruling. In dealing with sensitivities surrounding the issue of 3rd-party consent, the Court held firm to its stand in **Roe:** A woman's decision whether to have an abortion was secured under the Constitution by a fundamental right of privacy. States could not grant an absolute veto over such a decision to a husband, a parent, or a guardian.

Planned Parenthood v. Danforth was a prelude to two important cases on parental involvement in an unwed minor girl's abortion decision. In 1979 the Court suggested in **Bellotti v. Baird** that states might be able to require parental consent, but only so long as the law provided an alternative to the unmarried minor, such as letting her seek a judge's approval instead. In **H.L. v. Matheson** (1981), the Court said states could require doctors to notify parents of "immature," dependent minor girls prior to performing a requested abortion.

BEAL V. DOE AND MAHER V. ROE (1977)

On June 20, 1977, the U.S. Supreme Court ruled on two cases that dealt with the issue of whether states should have to make Medicaid monies available to indigent women to cover the cost of elective abortions. *Beal v. Doe* addressed the states' obligations under federal law. *Maher v. Roe* examined the broader constitutional question involved.

Some background on the Social Security Act is in order, as both cases largely hinged on this important federal statute. Medicaid is established under Title XIX of the Social Security Act. This program is a cooperative arrangement between the states and federal government to fund basic health care for indigent persons. Each level of government pays part of the cost of providing medical services to the poor. The program covers five general categories of treatment, one of which is pregnancy-related services. Under Title XIX, participating states set up their own mechanisms for reimbursing medical expenses within the guidelines of the Social Security Act. States are required to establish "reasonable standards" for determining the extent of medical assistance under the plan which are "consistent with the objectives of Title XIX."

BEAL V. DOE (1977)
Background

Pennsylvania's Medicaid plan excluded financial assistance for nontherapeutic abortions. The state provided funding only if the abortion was medically necessary to preserve the woman's life or health. Pregnant women applying for assistance were required to present a certificate of medical necessity from a licensed physician.

"Ann Doe" (a pseudonym), who was eligible for Medicaid under the Pennsylvania program, sought an elective abortion, but the state refused to pay for the procedure. She filed suit in Federal District Court against Pennsylvania and its secretary of public welfare, Frank S. Beal. Doe claimed the state's bar on payments for nontherapeutic abortions at the same time it funded childbirth costs contravened Title XIX and denied her equal protection of the laws under the 14th Amendment. The district court decided that neither the Constitution nor the language of the Social Security Act obligated states to pay for elective abortions.

Doe appealed this ruling to the U.S. Court of Appeals, which then departed from the lower court's reading of the Medicaid statute, declaring that indeed Title XIX did not allow a state to require a medical necessity certificate as a funding condition during the first two trimesters of pregnancy. Secretary Beal, on behalf of Pennsylvania, appealed the judgment to the Supreme Court.

Legal Issues

The core question before the Court was whether the Social Security Act required states to fund elective abortions. Its task was one of statutory interpretation: of discerning the meaning of the law's Medicaid provisions and Congress's intent in passing the legislation.

Doe claimed that by excluding all nontherapeutic abortions under its Medicaid plan, Pennsylvania was violating the "reasonable standards" test of Title XIX. Her counsel argued such blanket exclusion was unreasonable on both economic and health grounds. Noting that early abortion is generally less expensive than actual childbearing, her lawyers contended that a state electing to withhold funding of nontherapeutic abortions would eventually be faced with the greater costs incident to full-term pregnancy. They based the corresponding health argument on the view that an early abortion posed less risk to a woman's health than childbearing. Doe also argued that the Pennsylvania Medicaid plan denied her equal protection of the laws because it allowed funding for one pregnancy-related procedure, childbirth, but prohibited it for another, elective abortion.

Pennsylvania maintained that the Social Security Act's language in no way required the state to fund every medical procedure falling within the designated categories of medical care. Attorneys argued that Pennsylvania had broad discretion to define the extent of medical assistance "reasonable" under Title XIX. Moreover, the state contended that its choosing to pay for childbearing simply reflected Pennsylvania's traditional and valid interest in encouraging normal childbirth. This choice was said to be consistent with the aims of Title XIX.

Decision

The Supreme Court announced its decision on June 20, 1977. By a six-to-three margin, it held that states participating in the Medicaid program were not required by Title XIX to pay for elective abortions. At the same time, the ruling noted that a state was free to provide such funding if it so desired. The Court found that the language of the Social Security Act requiring states to establish "reasonable" standards for determining the extent of medical aid they would give in fact permitted states to ban financing for nontherapeutic abortions. It said in part that states had a valid and important interest in encouraging childbirth and that there was nothing in the words of the statute to show that it was "unreasonable" for a state to further such interest.

In a strong dissent to the ruling, Justice Harry Blackmun accused the majority of allowing the states to do indirectly—namely, interfere with a woman's decision in the 1st trimester whether to have a child—what it forbade them to do directly in its landmark 1973 ruling. Because the federal appeals court had not addressed the issue of equal protection, the Court did not touch on the constitutional question either.

Impact

This was the first Supreme Court decision on the issue of public funding of abortions, and it keyed on the principal government funding program: Medicaid. Importantly, Beal said Title XIX of the Social Security Act did not legally obligate states to pay for nontherapeutic abortions, though states remained free to do so if they chose. The ruling, in conjunction with the decision in *Maher v. Roe*, cleared the way after 1977 for states to refrain from paying for elective abortions, which is exactly what many states did.

Beal left unresolved the question of how far states could restrict Medicaid funding for medically necessary abortions. This issue was resolved in 1980 in **Harris v. McRae,** when the Supreme Court said neither the federal government nor the states were constitutionally required to pay for medically indicated abortions sought by women on welfare.

MAHER V. ROE (1977)

Background

A Connecticut law provided Medicaid funding only for those abortions judged by a physician to be medically necessary to preserve the woman's life or health. By regulation of its welfare department, the state refused to pay for elective abortions. Yet Connecticut's Medicaid plan fully subsidized childbirth costs for women on welfare. Two indigent women wanted abortions but neither claimed to seek them on grounds of medical necessity. Their requests for elective abortions were turned down by the Connecticut Department of Social Services. The women brought suit in Federal District Court against the state and Social Services Commissioner Edward Maher, the state official in charge of Medicaid. Challenging the Connecticut law as inconsistent with Title XIX, they also charged that state rules violated their constitutional guarantees to equal protection and due process.

The district court ruled funding of nontherapeutic abortions was required under Title XIX. On an appeal by the state of Connecticut, the U.S. Court of Appeals held that state funding of elective procedures was allowed under the Social Security Act, but not required. The appeals court sent the case back to the district court for a ruling on the constitutional issues raised by the women. The three-judge district panel at this point found that the equal protection clause of the 14th Amendment forbade the exclusion of nontherapeutic abortions from a state welfare program that generally paid for medical expenses incident to pregnancy and childbirth. Commissioner Maher, for Connecticut, appealed the district court's judgment on the constitutional challenge to the Supreme Court.

Court Cases

Legal Issues

Defending the constitutionality of the Medicaid regulations, Connecticut's counsel argued the ban on funding of nontherapeutic abortions did not curb a woman's fundamental right to choose to end her pregnancy. Nothing in the Connecticut regulations prevented indigent women from obtaining elective abortions with private resources. The state contended it had made a valid policy choice to favor normal childbirth over nonmedical abortion. The legislature had exercised its legitimate power in choosing among competing demands for limited public funds.

Counsel for Roe maintained that Connecticut's policy of selective subsidies was discriminatory and denied women who choose to have abortions equal protection of the laws. Women with ample private resources, the attorneys noted, were able without question to get nontherapeutic abortions while poor women dependent on public monies—meaning Medicaid—were refused abortions sought for the same reasons. In effect, an indigent woman's right to choose was abridged by her poverty. State encouragement of childbearing through allocation of public funds essentially pressured poor women into bringing their pregnancies to term. Counsel claimed this transgressed a woman's constitutionally protected, fundamental right to make the abortion decision without state intrusion.

Decision

On June 20, 1977, the Court decided, six to three, that the 14th Amendment's guarantee of equal protection of the laws did not require a state participating in the Medicaid program to finance elective abortions simply because it made a policy choice to pay expenses arising out of childbirth. The ruling found Connecticut's plan did not violate the fundamental privacy right that shielded a woman from unduly burdensome state interference with her liberty to choose whether or not to end her pregnancy. The majority held that the existence of this fundamental right did not prohibit a state from making a value judgment favoring childbirth. Public monies were limited and every state had the right and authority to choose how its revenues were to be spent.

Justice William Douglas, joined by Justices Marshall and Blackmun, wrote a powerful dissent, expressing the view that the Connecticut rule unjustifiably limited a pregnant woman's privacy right to decide about abortion because it forced the medically needy to bear children they would not otherwise have. In a separate dissent, Marshall said indigent women would find it increasingly hard to get legal abortions, and some might find it impossible. He noted the potential effects on women the ruling could have—unwanted children, unsafe but cheap clandestine abortions, and deaths from these illicit procedures. He also noted that nonwhite women would be most affected by the ruling, as they made up a disproportionate share of women dependent on Medicaid.

Impact

What *Beal* said about federal law, *Maher* extended to the Constitution. By dismissing equal protection and due process challenges to Medicaid programs that selectively omitted elective abortion costs, the Court essentially held that the only requirement on government was a "negative" one of not interfering with a woman's fundamental right of choice to an abortion. *Maher* declared that while a state could not forbid elective abortions, governments were under no obligation to provide the funding or facilities to perform them. The Court's reasoning here became the basis for its decision in **Harris v. McRae,** in which it held that the federal government did not have to fund even medically necessary abortions for poor women.

Maher galvanized opposition among women's and civil rights groups to more restrictive public financing policies by the states. Critics of the Court rulings in *Maher* and *Beal* contended these decisions condoned what effectively was the deliberate manipulation of a woman's economic condition to deny her a basic liberty, a fundamental right of choice to an abortion.

In a companion case decided the same day, *Poelker v. Doe,* the Court declared that cities with public hospitals were not required under the Constitution to provide or even permit elective abortions in those facilities. Repeating its reasoning in Maher, the Court said it found no constitutional violation by St. Louis in choosing to provide publicly financed hospital services for childbearing without offering corresponding funding for nontherapeutic abortions. The majority concluded the Constitution did not forbid cities from expressing, within the normal democratic process, their preference for normal childbirth. In a 1975 case, *Greco v. Orange Memorial Hospital Corporation*, the Supreme Court upheld a lower federal court's ruling that allowed a private hospital receiving public funds to forbid a doctor to perform abortions there.

COLAUTTI V. FRANKLIN (1979)

Background

The Pennsylvania Abortion Control Act was among a wave of restrictive state laws drafted after the 1973 Supreme Court ruling establishing a woman's fundamental abortion right. Passed in 1974 over Governor Milton Shapp's veto, the Pennsylvania statute regulated many phases of abortion. It imposed spousal and parental consent requirements, outlawed abortion after viability except to save the mother's life or health, prohibited public funding, and authorized state health officials to make rules governing performance standards.

An especially controversial provision of the new law, section 5(a), required a doctor performing an abortion to choose the procedure most likely to save the life of a fetus that "might be viable" or capable of surviving outside the womb. Under section 5(a), any doctor who did not attempt to save a potentially viable fetus could be subject to criminal charges.

Before the law was enacted, Dr. John Franklin, the medical director of a Pennsylvania Planned Parenthood chapter, filed suit in Federal District Court against state Secretary of Welfare Aldo Colautti, challenging most of the statute's provisions on constitutional grounds. When the district court overturned major portions of the law, Colautti appealed the ruling to the Supreme Court.

The case reached the Court in October 1976. By then most of the issues it raised had been considered in other key cases, notably **Planned Parenthood v. Danforth.** Thus the Court returned *Colautti* to the lower court for reconsideration; and in light of the recent rulings, the district court disposed of all the issues except those raised by section 5(a). The three-judge panel declared unconstitutional this part of the law regulating doctors' responsibilities for fetal survival. Once more Colautti appealed the ruling to the Supreme Court. The lone question remaining, then, was the permissibility of section 5(a).

Legal Issues

Counsel for Pennsylvania argued the statute was concerned only with abortions after viability and, by extension, with establishing a standard of care that safeguarded the state's interests in protecting potential human life. On both points, lawyers maintained, the law was consistent with **Roe v. Wade.** They rejected the claim that the phrasing "may be viable" was unconstitutionally vague and contended the meaning of section 5(a) would be adequately understood by attending physicians. Pennsylvania's lawyers said the standard-of-care provision simply meant that when faced with a choice of methods which could be applied with equal safety as concerned the mother, doctors would be required to select the method least likely to be fatal to the fetus.

In their brief, lawyers for Franklin argued the provision on determining fetal viability and standard of care was too ambiguous and interfered unduly with the exercise of a doctor's professional judgment. The law subjected physicians to possible criminal prosecution on the basis of a vague standard. The expression "may be viable" was so indefinite, counsel claimed, that attending doctors could not be entirely sure when their obligation to the fetus arose. The standard-of-care section was challenged as unconstitutionally restrictive because it denied the physician sufficient professional discretion in determining the appropriate abortion method.

Decision

On January 9, 1979, the Supreme Court voted six to three to invalidate the Pennsylvania law. The majority found the statute's requirements as to determination of fetal viability and standard of care for abortions unconstitutional. Writing for the Court, Justice Harry Blackmun declared the wording "may be viable" in section 5(a) was unconstitutionally vague. This provision of the law, dealing as it did with a clinical "gray area," was held to interfere with a doctor's discretionary judgment. Physicians faced the prospect of criminal liability for decisions rendered under the predictably difficult or even emergency circumstances surrounding late-term abortions. Blackmun concluded the Pennsylvania law did not give the doctor broad enough discretion; instead, it conditioned "possible criminal culpability on ambiguous and confusing criteria." The majority further described the law as a "trap for those who act in good faith" and suggested it would have a chilling effect on doctors' willingness to perform abortions anywhere near the point of viability.

Impact

Colautti was significant because it reaffirmed the Court's intention, first spelled out in **Roe**, to grant physicians broad discretion in determining just when a fetus was viable. The case was resolved at a time when many states were trying to make doctors subject to a nebulous, taxing standard at a very uncertain stage of pregnancy. *Colautti* supported the finding in **Roe** that states could legitimately seek to protect a fetus clearly able to survive outside the womb. However, when dealing with the inherently ambiguous area of potential viability, *Colautti* asserted that courts and legislatures should leave the hard decisions to the judgment of physicians. *Colautti* became the Court's precedent-setting ruling on the issue of what constitutes an acceptable standard-of-care requirement in late-term abortions.

BELLOTTI V. BAIRD (1979)

Background

In August 1974 the Massachusetts legislature passed an antiabortion statute over a gubernatorial veto. The measure required unmarried girls under age 18 to obtain parental approval before being able to have a legal abortion. If one of the parents refused consent, the law provided the minor girl could seek alternative consent from a state judge for "good cause shown." The judge's decision, according to the statute, was to be made in the "best interests of the minor." Any doctor performing an abortion who did not first obtain the required consent would be subject to criminal penalties.

William Baird, a long-standing advocate of abortion and director of an abortion clinic, brought suit in Federal District Court against Massachusetts and its attorney general, Francis X. Bellotti, challenging the new law as unconstitutional. Baird was joined in the action by "Mary Moe," an unmarried pregnant minor who was living at home with her parents and who wanted to have an abortion without telling them. Moe claimed she was capable of giving valid and informed consent to an abortion and therefore should not have to involve her mother or father in the decision.

When the three-judge panel held the statute unconstitutional and blocked its enforcement, Massachusetts appealed the ruling to the Supreme Court. After hearing arguments in 1976, the Court vacated the lower federal court's ruling, declaring the district panel should have refrained from deciding the case and sent it instead to the Supreme Judicial Court of Massachusetts for a determination of the precise meaning of the challenged law. On remand, the district court submitted questions to the Massachusetts high court about the statute. Following the Supreme Judicial Court's response, the federal court again declared the law unconstitutional and enjoined its enforcement. Once more the state appealed the ruling to the Supreme Court.

Legal Issues

In its advisory opinion to the district court, the Massachusetts high court made these key points: The statute in general did not permit unmarried minors, mature or immature, to obtain judicial consent to an abortion without first seeking both parents' consent; moreover, an available parent had to be notified of any judicial action brought by a daughter seeking court-ordered consent; and the law entitled a judge to withhold consent if he or she determined that the "best interests" of the minor would not be served by the abortion—even if that same judge had found the minor capable of making an informed and reasoned decision on her own.

The core issue in *Bellotti* concerned minors' legal rights. The Court was confronted first with the question of whether an unmarried girl under 18 enjoyed the same fundamental right of privacy to choose to have an abortion free of state interference as an adult woman. If such a fundamental right existed, could it be circumscribed by a state's traditional interest in ensuring that "vulnerable" minor children not make important decisions, the consequences of which they might not understand, without parental advice and emotional support?

Baird's counsel asked the Court to declare the law unconstitutional in violation of due process guarantees because it allowed no minor, no matter how mature and capable, to obtain an abortion without the permission of either a judge or both parents. This provision subjected a girl's fundamental abortion right to an absolute veto by others. The parental notification rule was challenged as too broad because it applied, without exception, to all situations and in every instance. Finally, lawyers argued the language in the statute directing state judges to decide in the "best interests" of the minor was too vague and allowed a judge to interject his or her personal values in reaching a decision on consent.

Decision

The Supreme Court announced its decision on July 2, 1979, with eight justices agreeing the Massachusetts law was unconstitutional. The Court first expressed its own theory of minors' rights, concluding that, because of differences in maturity and judgment, constitutional rights of children could not be equated with those of adults. But in striking down the statute, the majority reaffirmed the Court's **Planned Parenthood v. Danforth** judgment, saying it could not give a judge or parent an absolute and possibly arbitrary veto over a minor girl's decision to end her pregnancy, regardless of the reason for withholding permission. The law was found deficient because it required all minors to seek parental consent before going to a judge and because it created no exception for "mature" minors. Justice Lewis Powell summarized the Court's stand: "Every minor must have the opportunity—if she so desires—to go directly to a court without first consulting or notifying her parents. If she satisfies the court that she is mature and well-informed enough to decide on her own, the court must authorize her to act." Powell's words suggested that the state was left with some discretion and influence. He said that if a judge found a girl was not sufficiently mature, the judge could assess whether the abortion would be in the girl's best interest. If so, the court would be empowered to authorize the procedure. If not, the court could withhold approval.

Impact

Constitutional experts characterized *Bellotti* as a watershed decision in the Court's evolving position on minors' rights. A majority of Justices, standing strongly for due process protections for girls under 18, borrowed a dictum from the landmark case of *In Re Gault*: "Whatever may be their precise impact, neither the Fourteenth Amendment nor the Bill of Rights is for adults alone." The Court emphasized the key factor in the minors-and-abortion equation was not age but the capacity to make a competent decision on this very serious matter. *Bellotti* indicated the Court would not uphold a law that failed to differentiate mature from immature minors. While the Court recognized the importance of protecting adolescents' welfare and preserving family integrity, it made clear that under no circumstance should a minor's abortion decision be totally dependent on a parent's consent. In every case an alternative course of approval should be available, in all likelihood through the state courts. Justice Powell's opinion more than obliquely hinted that states might be able to pass laws giving judges complete discretion over an immature minor's decision so long as their ruling was made in the girl's best interests. To date, however, *Bellotti* has endured as the foundation case on the issue of minors and consent.

HARRIS V. MCRAE (1980)

Background

In September 1976 the U.S. Congress passed a controversial antiabortion rider to a major appropriations bill. The Hyde Amendment, named after sponsor Representative Henry J. Hyde (R-IL), barred the use of federal Medicaid funds for abortions except "where the life of the mother would be endangered if the fetus were carried to term." In 1977 the House reenacted the Hyde Amendment, but the Senate held out for language that would also allow funding of medically necessary abortions. A compromise between the chambers permitted Medicaid abortion in three situations: (1) to save the mother's life; (2) in the event of rape or incest; (3) when long-lasting health damage to the mother would result from continued pregnancy. The wording of the federal measure was important because most participating states keyed their own Medicaid funding rules to the federal government's criteria.

The debate in Congress over abortion funding and the Hyde Amendment would be repeated in each subsequent year, with the language becoming ever narrower. By 1979 Congress had once more limited Medicaid financing of abortions to life-threatening situations or when rape or incest had occurred.

The federal abortion rider was under legal attack from the start. Cora McRae and other low-income women ineligible under the narrow Hyde strictures, and thus unable to obtain Medicaid abortions, brought a class action in Federal District Court in New York in October 1976. They challenged the constitutionality of the embattled provision under the 1st and 5th amendments. Federal District Judge John F. Dooling, Jr., granted their request for an injunction blocking enforcement of the law. (The Hyde Amendment actually did not go into effect until August 1977.) The case reached the Supreme Court for the first time in July 1977. Meanwhile, the **Beal v. Doe** and **Maher v. Roe** decisions had been announced, declaring that nothing in either federal law or the Constitution required states to fund nontherapeutic abortions. The Court remanded the McRae case to Judge Dooling to reconsider in light of the rulings on state Medicaid financing.

Following a protracted trial in district court, Dooling ruled in January 1980 that the Hyde Amendment in fact violated liberty interests guaranteed to pregnant women by the 1st and 5th amendments. His decision invalidated the law. Secretary of Health and Human Services Patricia Harris, in charge of the federal Medicaid program, appealed the lower court ruling to the Supreme Court on behalf of the U.S. Government.

Legal Issues

The question before the Court was whether the federal government constitutionally could refuse to pay for medically necessary abortions under Medicaid when it funded virtually all other medically necessary pregnancy services. Was encouraging childbirth a legitimate government rationale for refusing to fund medically indicated abortions? Under the congressional ban, abortion funding was denied unless a woman was likely to die as a result of continuing pregnancy. The medical necessity standard, as defined under Title XIX, included non-life-threatening medical complications as well as emotional problems resulting from an unwanted pregnancy.

The U.S. government defended the constitutionality of the Hyde Amendment, arguing the Medicaid ban was "rationally related" to the state's valid interest in promoting childbirth. Endorsement of childbearing was a legitimate government reason to refuse to pay for non-life-threatening abortions. Government counsel, citing the Court's **Maher** ruling, claimed a basic difference existed between a law that abridged a fundamental right and one that simply promoted an alternative course of behavior. According to the government brief, the abortion right established by **Roe** was merely a right against state interference—not a right to government promotion or subsidization of the procedure.

McRae leveled a multifaceted challenge to the Medicaid rider. Attorneys argued the Hyde Amendment violated the 1st Amendment's ban on government establishment of religion because it effectively incorporated into federal law doctrines of the Roman Catholic Church concerning the sinfulness of abortion and the point at which life began. They also contended the Hyde measure unconstitutionally limited the religious liberty of women who believed their faiths required them, under some circumstances, to abort children they were unable to raise.

Citing the 5th Amendment's due process clause, counsel claimed the Hyde Amendment stripped indigent women of equal protection guarantees by excluding all medically necessary abortions from a Medicaid system that, at the same time, reimbursed all other medically necessary pregnancy services, including childbirth. The arguments evoked **Maher v. Roe**. Counsel claimed withholding public funding for abortions from women who had no other way to pay for them essentially denied such women their fundamental right of choice. The funding scheme was said to involve a discriminatory use of public monies that discouraged the exercise of a fundamental liberty.

Decision

On June 30, 1980, the Supreme Court voted five to four to uphold the Hyde Amendment, ruling the federal government and the states were under no constitutional obligation to pay for even medically necessary abortions. The Court held there was no significant difference constitutionally between elective and medically necessary abortions. Justice Potter Stewart said the key distinction for constitutional purposes was rather the difference between abortions and other medical procedures. Abortion was inherently different, he noted, because it alone involved the "purposeful termination of a potential human life."

The Court dismissed both 1st Amendment issues. It held that a law did not violate the establishment clause simply because it happened to coincide with the tenets of some religions. Second, the Court said McRae and her companion litigants had failed to establish religious standing under the law necessary to raise legitimately the claim of interference with free exercise of religion.

As it had in **Maher**, the Court declared the state had a proper interest in promoting childbirth by selective allocation of public monies if it so chose. The majority claimed the Hyde Amendment did not curb equal protection rights of poor women seeking abortions. Insofar as American constitutional law did not traditionally recognize poverty as a "suspect class" like race, a public policy that mainly burdened the indigent could be upheld as long as it related to a legitimate government aim. Encouraging childbirth, the Court reiterated, was such an objective.

The majority rejected the claim that the Hyde funding curbs violated due process by denying indigent women their fundamental right to choose to have an abortion. The Court held the law in no way stopped women from obtaining abortions through means other than public funding. Finally, it was held that individual states participating in the Title XIX Medicaid program were not obligated to fund their share of any service that Congress no longer financed, although the states were free to do so if they desired.

Justice Brennan, joined by Justices Marshall and Blackmun, wrote a sharp dissent to the majority ruling. He contended that the government's interest in protecting potential human life could not justify the exemption of financially needy women from the public health benefits to which they would otherwise be entitled solely because the medically necessary treatment involved an abortion.

Impact

With the enactment of the Hyde Amendment in 1977, the number of abortions funded by the federal government dropped precipitously, from about 300,000 to under 2,500 per year. The decision in *Harris v. McRae* signaled an end to court challenges seeking to reverse congressional policy on federal Medicaid financing. The Hyde Amendment has remained virtually unchanged to date.

Harris v. McRae focused on the intersection of poverty and abortion as no case before or since. Critics of the ruling claimed it victimized indigent women by denying them access to safe, legal abortions. There were predictions of a dramatic rise in illegal procedures and a concomitant decline in health standards. This did not materialize because most poor women were able to get abortions funded by their states or by local public agencies or private organizations. When confronted with concerns about the consequences of its decision, the majority reproved the Court's dissenters, emphasizing that the judiciary's job was not to rule on whether the Hyde Amendment was "wise social policy" but only if it violated constitutional rights.

The Court was asked to define the relevance of economic status to matters of personal liberty. Pro-choice advocates maintained that, with *Harris v. McRae*, the Court for the first time had condoned the manipulation of government benefits programs for the purpose of discouraging women's exercise of fundamental rights. The majority rejected the critics' premise that the Court had an obligation to remedy economic inequalities. For five Justices it did not follow that a woman's freedom of choice implied a constitutional entitlement to the financial resources needed to subsidize this right.

H. L. V. MATHESON (1981)

Background

An unmarried 15-year-old girl living with her parents in Utah and dependent on them for support became pregnant and was advised by her doctor that an abortion would be in her best interest. Because a state law required a physician to "notify, if possible" the parents of a minor before performing an abortion or face criminal penalties, the doctor refused to proceed without first contacting the mother or father. The girl sought to have the abortion without informing her parents. She filed suit in Utah district court, asking that the statute be declared unconstitutional and that an injunction against its enforcement be issued. The trial judge dismissed her complaint, saying the law did not unconstitutionally restrict the privacy right of a minor to get an abortion or to enter into a doctor-patient relationship. The Supreme Court of Utah upheld the district court ruling. H.L. appealed the judgment to the U.S. Supreme Court.

Legal Issues

H.L. argued the law violated her right to privacy because it unduly burdened her decision whether to end her pregnancy. Its failure to exempt "mature" or "emancipated" minors from the notice requirement, she claimed, made it unconstitutionally broad. Notably, the Utah statute did not explicitly require parental permission, and in this respect departed from other state laws mandating parental consent—laws that the Supreme Court had found unconstitutional in prior decisions in **Planned Parenthood v. Danforth** and **Bellotti v. Baird**.

The Court's ruling in **Roe v. Wade** held that a constitutionally protected right of privacy barred a state from interfering with a woman's decision to have an abortion. That ruling also said such a right was not absolute. A state could limit this right if the restriction served compelling state interests. In judging the legal legitimacy of the Utah measure requiring parental notification, the Court had to determine if this provision served an interest important enough to outweigh a minor's claim to constitutionally shielded privacy.

Decision

On March 23, 1981, the Supreme Court upheld the Utah law, ruling that states may require parents be notified before a minor daughter undergoes an abortion, at least when the girl is living at home and dependent on the parents. The majority, rejecting the violation of privacy claim of H.L., pointed out the Utah statute gave neither parents nor a judge an absolute veto over a minor girl's abortion decision. The decision emphasized the law served valid and compelling state interests. Writing for the Court, Chief Justice Warren E. Burger identified these interests as preserving family integrity and protecting adolescents from the possibly traumatic medical and psychological consequences of an abortion. Calling abortion a "grave decision," he declared that a "girl of tender years, under emotional stress, may be ill-equipped to make it without mature advice and emotional support."

The Court itself noted the decision was relatively narrow. The majority held that because H.L. was still living at home and did not claim to be either "emancipated" or "mature," she was not entitled to contest the law on behalf of all minors who might fit under these categories. Therefore the Court was limited to considering the constitutionality of the law only so far as it applied to an "immature and dependent" minor such as H.L.

Among the majority, Justices Powell and Stewart wrote a separate concurring opinion stressing that the Court's ruling did not apply either to mature minors or to minors able to demonstrate that parental notice would not be in their best interests. Such girls, they argued, have a constitutional right to an independent decision maker, like a judge, empowered to waive the notification requirement.

Impact

In *H.L. v. Matheson*, the Court refined its stand on the balance between minors' rights on the one hand and legitimate government interests on the other. The majority drew a distinction between notification and permission. While upholding its finding in **Bellotti** that states may not grant parents absolute power of consent, the Court said apprising a mother and father of a daughter's pending abortion was a valid requirement. It served a state's long-standing concerns for the welfare of adolescents and preservation of traditional lines of family authority. Importantly, the ruling limited itself to immature, dependent minors. Thus the Court avoided addressing whether a notification requirement applicable to mature minors would withstand constitutional review. This question is still being litigated in lower courts and has not yet appeared before the Supreme Court.

AKRON V. AKRON CENTER FOR REPRODUCTIVE HEALTH (1983)

Background

In February 1978 Akron, Ohio, enacted an ordinance regulating the performance of abortions within the municipality. The city council intended the measure to be a model code for towns nationwide. Akron made violation of the ordinance punishable as a misdemeanor. Key provisions of the code required: (1) all 2nd-trimester abortions be done in hospitals; (2) parental consent before doctors could perform abortions on unmarried minors under age 15; (3) an attending doctor to make any number of specified statements to a woman seeking an abortion to ensure her freely given consent (these included statements about the possibly dire emotional and physical consequences of abortion and about childbearing as an alternative option available to the woman); and (4) that doctors refrain from performing an abortion until 24 hours after the pregnant woman signed a consent form.

Three abortion clinics affiliated with the Akron Center for Reproductive Health brought suit in Federal District Court against the City of Akron, challenging its new abortion code. After mixed rulings in the district court and the U.S. Court of Appeals invalidating numbers of the ordinance's provisions, Akron petitioned the Supreme Court to review the lower court judgments.

Legal Issues

Before the Court was the question of whether the challenged rules conformed with the basic framework of **Roe v. Wade**, which described a shifting balance over the course of pregnancy between a woman's fundamental freedom to choose and state interests in protecting maternal health and potential human life. Did the Akron regulations serve valid public concerns, or were they intrusive and burdensome and thus unconstitutional?

The Justices were asked to determine if the hospital requirement reasonably related to a state's sole legitimate purpose in regulating abortion in the 2nd trimester: to safeguard the pregnant woman's health. The consent requirements reprised issues considered by the Court in such earlier cases as **Planned Parenthood v. Danforth** and **Bellotti v. Baird**. The informed-consent rule Akron defended as an appropriate way to make sure a woman's abortion decision was made freely and without coercion. The abortion clinics claimed, instead, that this rule was excessive and basically designed to pressure women to withhold consent. The

24-hour waiting period likewise was challenged as being arbitrary and burdensome, and unwarranted by any compelling government interest.

The provision on parents' approval once more brought before the Court the matter of minors' rights and the question of a state's responsibility to distinguish between mature minors who were competent to make their own decisions and immature minors who lacked the judgment and understanding to make a truly informed abortion choice.

The Justices faced an added element in this case. The Reagan administration had argued in a friend-of-the-court brief in support of the Akron ordinance. The Justice Department urged the Court to adopt a "deferential standard" in reviewing the city council's decision to restrict access to abortions. Generally, the White House sought the overturn of **Roe v. Wade** and the return of the whole issue to the states. The Reagan administration suggested the Court use the Akron case as an opportunity to reconsider and reverse its landmark 1973 ruling.

Decision

On June 15, 1983, the Supreme Court, by the vote of six to three, reaffirmed its ruling in **Roe v. Wade** establishing a woman's fundamental right to choose to have an abortion and struck down as unconstitutional a variety of local restrictions on access to abortion. The question of overturning **Roe** was not technically before the Court, but the Reagan Justice Department's participation in the Akron case led the majority to acknowledge the heightened sense of anticipation surrounding its decision.

In the opinion announcing the Court's ruling, Justice Powell emphasized that the Court intended to stand by the historic 1973 decision and had no plans to overrule it: "Arguments continue to be made that we erred in interpreting the Constitution. Nonetheless, the doctrine of stare decisis [bound by precedent], while perhaps never entirely persuasive on a constitutional question, is a doctrine that demands respect in a society governed by law. We respect it today and reaffirm **Roe v. Wade.**"

The Court found the Akron hospital requirement unreasonably infringed on a woman's constitutional right to have an abortion. Noting that new techniques had made 2nd-trimester abortions much safer than they were in 1973, the opinion held it was not necessary to have all such mid-pregnancy abortions done in a hospital. While Akron had a legitimate right to monitor maternal health, it could not simply pass a regulation mandating all abortions after the 12th week take place in a hospital without showing reasonable grounds for such a provision. The Court determined, at least in the early weeks of the 2nd trimester, that abortions could be done as safely in outpatient clinics as in full-service hospitals. The opinion also noted that the hospital rule typically doubled the cost of the procedure and so "imposed a heavy and unnecessary burden on women's access to a relatively inexpensive, otherwise safe and accessible procedure."

The highly detailed informed consent rule that required physicians to apprise women seeking abortions of a lengthy list of information and medical particulars was struck down as an infringement on the doctor-patient relationship and an impermissible curb on a woman's fundamental right to choose an abortion without state interference. Justice Powell suggested the requirement was designed "not to inform the woman's consent but rather to persuade her to withhold it altogether"—a motive, he added, forbidden by earlier abortion decisions by the Supreme Court.

Restating its decision in **Bellotti v. Baird** on a similar requirement in Massachusetts, the Court struck down the parental consent provision because it was a blanket rule covering all women 15 or younger. It did not distinguish between mature and immature minors and failed to adequately protect the right of competent and capable girls under this age to make their own abortion decisions. Finally, the Court invalidated the 24-hour waiting period, declaring Akron had not shown a legitimate state interest was furthered by this "arbitrary and inflexible interval." The majority concluded there was no compelling evidence suggesting that the abortion would be made safer by mandating a delay of one day from the time of the woman's consent.

In dissent, Justice Sandra Day O'Connor, quoting **Maher v. Roe**, held to the view that regulations placed on even lawful abortions are not unconstitutional unless they unduly burden the fundamental right to an abortion. She said she did not see where the Akron measure set up any requirements that placed an undue burden upon a woman seeking an abortion. Moreover, O'Connor stressed that the Court's trimester analysis, established in **Roe**, had become almost unworkable and should be abandoned since the Court was now extending the rules that applied in the 1st trimester well into the 2nd trimester. She argued improved medical technology was closing the gap between the threshold for safe abortions and the point of fetal viability—thus putting **Roe**'s trimester system on an inevitable "collision course with itself."

Impact

Akron had the immediate effect of invalidating regulations in 21 states that limited the performance of abortions to fully licensed hospitals. Because the ordinance had been promoted by antiabortion groups nationwide as a model of its kind, the Court's action sent a message to other municipalities to refrain from adopting measures patterned on the Akron model.

The ruling was called a major victory by many of the principal organizations in favor of free choice. Abortion-rights groups praised the Court for reaffirming **Roe** and holding the line against greater regulation of abortion by states or municipalities. The decision was also the first indication of Justice O'Connor's views on abortion since she joined the Court in 1981. Pro-choice forces characterized her dissent as a virtual call for a reversal of **Roe**.

Constitutional experts suggested that the split vote on Akron indicated an emerging division on the Court over the abortion issue, with Justices lining up on either side of the landmark 1973 decision. Evidence of such a gulf was made more apparent when, in 1986, in **Thornburgh** a sharply divided Court narrowly voted to strike down a restrictive Pennsylvania law and again reaffirm **Roe**.

THORNBURGH V. AMERICAN COLLEGE OF OBSTETRICIANS AND GYNECOLOGISTS (1986)

Background

After a previous Pennsylvania law regulating abortion was found unconstitutional by the U.S. Supreme Court in **Colautti v. Franklin** (1979), the state passed another measure in 1984 that contained strict limitations. The Abortion Control Act imposed detailed regulation of the procedure. It required: (1) doctors provide women seeking abortions with extensive information about the risks and alternatives to ensure their consent was informed and freely given; (2) doctors file detailed reports on all abortions to the state, open to public inspection; (3) women wait 24 hours between giving consent and actually having the abortion; (4) unemancipated minors obtain the consent of their parents or a state judge; (5) all 2nd-trimester abortions be done in a hospital; (6) two doctors be present at late-term abortions—moreover, that they use the method most likely to save the life of a possibly viable fetus, unless doing so would pose "significantly greater risk" to the woman's health.

Before the law was implemented, the American College of Obstetricians and Gynecologists filed a suit in Federal District Court against the state, alleging the law violated the Constitution and asking for an injunction to stop Governor Richard Thornburgh from enforcing its provisions. The district court blocked only the section requiring the 24-hour waiting period. Subsequently, the U.S. Court of Appeals struck down most of the rest of the legislation. Pennsylvania appealed the lower court judgments to the Supreme Court.

Legal Issues

Several previous major Supreme Court rulings had settled some of the issues raised by the Pennsylvania law. The state conceded that, based on **Akron v. Akron Center for Reproductive Health**, the 24-hour waiting period and the hospital requirement for all 2nd-trimester abortions were unconstitutional; and that, in light of **Bellotti v. Baird**, the parental consent regulation was impermissible. These provisions, then, were not presented to the Court.

Like **Akron**, the Thornburgh case drew increased attention because of the Reagan administration's intercession. The Justice Department had submitted a friend-of-the-court brief urging the Court to use Thornburgh as the chance to abandon **Roe v. Wade** and leave state legislatures free to allow, to regulate, or to bar abortion as they pleased. Once more the Court was under some pressure to clarify its position on the landmark 1973 ruling.

The Court was asked to judge whether the remaining parts of the law infringed on a woman's fundamental freedom to choose to end her pregnancy. The informed consent requirement obligated physicians to present their patients with specific information prior to performing an abortion: the possibly detrimental long-range physical and psychological effects; the specific risks associated with the particular abortion method to be used; the option of childbirth and availability of public funds for this alternative to abortion. The Justices were left to rule whether this provision was tailored to unconstitutionally deter women from having abortions, as those challenging the law contended. The reporting requirement, which mandated comprehensive abortion records and then made such records open to public scrutiny, raised the issue of confidentiality within the doctor-patient relationship and the extent to which this relationship was private and inviolable.

Probably the most complex matter presented by *Thornburgh* involved the requirement for a second doctor and the standard of care late in a pregnancy. Pennsylvania claimed these provisions were consistent with **Roe**'s holding that states may regulate abortion in the 2nd trimester to protect maternal health and in the final trimester to protect the state's "compelling" interest in keeping alive a fetus capable of living outside

---

the womb. American College countered that each of the rules unjustifiably required doctors to risk the health of the woman for the sake of the fetus.

Decision

On June 11, 1986, a divided Supreme Court reaffirmed **Roe v. Wade**, rejecting the Reagan administration's arguments for overturning the landmark 1973 decision that established a woman's fundamental right to an abortion. The five-to-four ruling struck down the Pennsylvania law on grounds several provisions of the statute unconstitutionally infringed on this right. Based on **Akron**, the majority concluded the Pennsylvania informed consent rule failed to withstand constitutional review because: (1) it was designed to "persuade a woman to withhold her consent altogether"; and (2) the requirement that a specific body of information be presented in all cases, regardless of the particular needs of the patient, intruded on the doctor's professional judgment.

The *Thornburgh* decision held that the reporting provision, which required a doctor to gather information on a patient's age, race, marital status, and number of prior abortions and then submit it to the state for possible public inspection, unjustifiably invaded a woman's privacy. The Court said the specter of public disclosure of this very personal information could dissuade many women from choosing an abortion and, therefore, the provision was impermissible. Finally, the decision declared the 2nd-doctor and standard-of-care guidelines for 3rd-trimester abortions were unacceptable because they might place the woman's welfare at peril in order to save the fetus.

Stressing what the majority saw as the fundamental issue at stake in *Thornburgh*, Justice Harry Blackmun concluded: "Our cases long have recognized that the Constitution embodies a promise that a certain private sphere of individual liberty will be kept largely beyond the reach of government. Few decisions are more personal, intimate, more properly private than a woman's decision—with the guidance of her doctor and within the limits specified in **Roe**—whether to end her pregnancy. A woman's right to make that choice freely is fundamental. Any other result, in our view, would protect inadequately a central part of the sphere of liberty that our law guarantees equally to all."

In a strong dissent, Justice White, joined by Justice Rehnquist, keyed on the benchmark case in the abortion issue. He said **Roe** departed from a proper understanding of the Constitution. It was "fundamentally misguided," had led the Court into "warped interpretations," and made the Court susceptible to charges of imposing its own choice of values on the people. For these reasons, White concluded, the 1973 decision should be overturned. Even accepting **Roe**, he continued, the majority's invalidation of the Pennsylvania law was not justified by prior Supreme Court rulings. Moreover, it limited the state's power to implement the legitimate policy of encouraging normal childbirth over abortion.

Impact

As it had in **Akron** (1983), the Court upheld abortion rights and reaffirmed its 1973 ruling making a choice to have an abortion a constitutionally protected privacy right. While the decision made no substantive change in abortion law, the five opinions by various Justices represented the most detailed Court debate yet on the complex moral and constitutional issue. Abortion-rights advocates, though pleased with the outcome, added a note of caution. To the pro-choice movement, the narrowing margin of support for **Roe**, the sharp dissenting opinions and the declaration for the first time by Chief Justice Burger that the Court should reexamine **Roe** signaled a troubling retreat and raised the possibility the 1973 decision might be undermined in the future.

WEBSTER V. REPRODUCTIVE HEALTH SERVICES (1989)

Background

Resuming its determination since **Roe v. Wade** to test the limits of state regulatory powers, the Missouri General Assembly in 1986 passed a restrictive abortion law. Twice before Missouri abortion statutes had been struck down as unconstitutional, either totally or in part, by the U.S. Supreme Court: in **Planned Parenthood v. Danforth** and in *Planned Parenthood v. Ashcroft*. Undeterred, the 1986 law laid out exacting rules on medical standards of care and virtually shut off public assistance or involvement in abortion. The statute opened with a declaration that "the life of each human being begins at conception." Its major provisions barred use of public hospitals for abortions not necessary to save a woman's life; prohibited public employees from performing or assisting an abortion; and required that doctors perform medical tests on any fetus thought to be at least 20 weeks old to determine its viability.

State pro-choice groups quickly mobilized against the measure. A number of doctors and a nonprofit abortion clinic filed a class action in Federal District Court, challenging the law and seeking to block its enforcement. In March 1987 the trial court declared most provisions of the law unconstitutional. In turn the U.S. Court of Appeals in January 1988 backed the district court's conclusions. Missouri Attorney General William Webster then appealed the lower court judgments to the U.S. Supreme Court, which agreed in January 1989 to review the case and decide on the constitutionality of the Missouri legislation.

The *Webster* case drew exceptional public attention and triggered widespread speculation because it raised the possibility the Court would reconsider its **Roe v. Wade** decision legalizing abortion. Such a possibility made *Webster* from the outset perhaps the most closely watched abortion case since 1973. While the reasoning of **Roe** had come under legal attack before, the decision basically had stood unchanged. Reflecting the tremendous concern on all sides with the case's outcome, the Court received 78 friend-of-the-court briefs, exceeding by 20 the greatest number ever before submitted for a single case.

Legal Issues

Attorney General Webster asked the Supreme Court both to reverse the federal appeals court ruling striking down most provisions of the Missouri law and to overrule **Roe v. Wade**. Missouri was joined by the U.S. Justice Department in a friend-of-the-court brief that called on the Court to use the Webster case as the vehicle to overturn the 1973 decision making abortion a fundamental right under the Constitution. The Justice Department contended **Roe** rested on two premises, neither of which was supported by the Constitution: first, that there was a fundamental right to have an abortion; second, that states had no compelling interest in protecting potential life throughout a pregnancy.

In its brief, Missouri further challenged as unworkable **Roe**'s trimester framework, which related allowable state regulation to three particular stages of pregnancy. State officials implored the Court to abandon the trimester analysis as inflexible and unable to adjust to changes in medical technology. Finally, Missouri contended that **Roe** let courts usurp the traditional function of the legislature to weigh competing social and scientific factors in setting the limits on appropriate state regulation of abortion.

Attorney General Webster argued that even if the Court chose not to reconsider **Roe**, it should declare the Missouri statute constitutional within the framework of the landmark 1973 ruling. He contended all the regulations at issue validly expressed the state's compelling interest in protecting unborn life. As to the controversial viability rule, Webster claimed Missouri chose the 20-week standard to allow for a 4-week margin of error by women and their doctors in estimating the start of a pregnancy. Missouri, Webster concluded, had simply chosen not to encourage abortion in any manner. Invalidating the law would be an unjustified judicial intrusion on the legislative arena. The Court should defer to the democratically expressed wishes of the people on this controversial issue of public policy.

Reproductive Health Services argued for full preservation of **Roe** and no limiting of abortion rights. Counsel claimed there was a strong historical basis for including abortion in the right to privacy and for deciding that a state's interest in protecting potential life was not compelling until the fetus becomes viable. Moreover, were the Court to scrap **Roe**, it would, for the first time in history, withdraw from constitutional protection a previously recognized fundamental personal freedom. Women denied control over their own childbearing were said to be subject to forced motherhood and for this reason could never enjoy a meaningful measure of ordered liberty. In addition, rescinding **Roe** would potentially lead to abrupt criminalization of a conduct undertaken daily by hundreds of citizens.

Counsel for Reproductive Health Services made several pointed constitutional challenges to the law. The provisions prohibiting any use of state workers, facilities, or monies for abortion were said to deny women 14th Amendment guarantees of equal protection and due process; also, that in practice they stripped poor women of their fundamental right to end an unwanted pregnancy. The lawyers claimed the law's preamble, defining as public policy the moment when human life begins, was a violation of **Roe:** The 1973 ruling declared a state could not adopt one theory of the start of human life if the intent was to justify the regulation of abortion.

Attorneys reserved their most ardent objections for the viability provision. Mandating tests to determine fetal viability at the 20th week was said to blatantly disregard **Roe,** which said states could not regulate abortion in the interest of protecting the fetus until the 24th week of pregnancy. Requiring doctors to measure fetal weight and lung capacity was an unjustified legislative interference with a matter of medical skill and judgment. They also pointed out these testing requirements added greatly to the cost and hence unfairly burdened a woman's access to abortion. Last, they rejected the state's claim that improved medical testing had pushed the point of viability back and in so doing had undercut **Roe**'s trimester framework. The earliest point of viability remained virtually unchanged at about 24 weeks, and no scientific evidence existed that a dramatic change was imminent. The reason viability had not been extended back was that critical internal organs almost never mature before the 23rd week. Medical advances, then, had not made the **Roe** trimester scheme obsolete.

Abortion

Decision

On July 3, 1989, a splintered U.S. Supreme Court gave states greater leeway to implement new restrictions on abortion. By five to four, the Court upheld the major provisions of the Missouri law but stopped short of abandoning **Roe v. Wade.** However, majority members expressed strong misgivings about **Roe** and indicated they were ready to overturn the decision in an appropriate case. No one opinion commanded a complete majority. Chief Justice Rehnquist wrote for the Court, joined by Justices White and Kennedy. Justices Scalia and O'Connor wrote separate concurring opinions.

By five-to-four margins, the Justices reversed the federal appeals court judgment. In upholding the provision requiring fetal testing at 20 weeks, the majority attacked **Roe**'s trimester analysis as an inflexible scheme that had made, in Rehnquist's words, "constitutional law in this area a virtual Procrustean bed." The Chief Justice concluded there was no valid reason why the state's interest in protecting potential human life should come into play only at the point of viability. He proposed an updated standard for reviewing abortion regulations, under which courts simply would gauge, case by case, whether the provision rationally furthered the state's interest in protecting the unborn. As the Missouri testing rules met this standard, they should be upheld. Significantly, the fact Missouri did not, in the majority's estimation, intend to curb abortion prior to viability meant there was no need in Webster to overturn **Roe v. Wade.**

Justice Scalia voted without qualification to overturn **Roe** and its trimester framework and return the issue to the state legislatures. He rebuked the rest of the majority for not doing so and suggested the Court was bowing to popular pressures to keep the landmark 1973 decision intact. O'Connor, a critic on previous decisions of the trimester approach, claimed the Court had no cause to rethink its previous abortion rulings because the Missouri viability testing rule conformed with these precedents.

In a bitter dissent, Justice Harry Blackmun, author of the historic **Roe** majority opinion, called the *Webster* ruling ominous and predicted the Court might abandon the 1973 decision and its holdings as early as the next term. He chided Rehnquist's opinion for repudiating every principle of accumulated abortion law. "I fear for the future," Blackmun wrote. "I fear for the liberty and equality of the millions of women who have come of age in the 16 years since Roe was decided."

The majority relied on Court rulings since 1973 in finding the Missouri restrictions on use of public funds, facilities, and workers legitimate. Adopting the reasoning employed in a line of earlier cases, the *Webster* opinion held that the Constitution did not forbid a state from expressing its preference for childbirth over abortion. The preamble was called a permissible "value judgment" and left untouched. The Court found no reason to rule on it because the preamble was legally nonbinding and no evidence existed it had ever been applied to limit abortion.

Impact

Webster guaranteed the abortion debate will continue to preoccupy American law and politics. The short-term, practical impact in one sense will be modest. The bar on public services, which the Court upheld, will not affect doctors' private offices and clinics, where most abortions are done and where women in Missouri and elsewhere can still obtain them. Viability testing will have marginal effect because only a negligible number of abortions are performed as late as the 20th week.

Within minutes of the release of the decision, leadership on each side of the abortion issue focused on the implications and suggested consequences beyond Webster's formal findings. **Roe** remains intact. Yet the majority certainly expressed mounting willingness to limit or possibly overturn the 1973 ruling. Five Justices indicated they are prepared to uphold state restrictions on abortion that for the past 16 years have been found unconstitutional. Importantly, the Court revealed it will hear three new cases in its next term. These concern rights of teenagers to obtain abortions without parental involvement in Ohio and Minnesota and an Illinois law that essentially requires private abortion clinics be equipped as full-scale hospitals. Any of these cases could offer the Court grounds for limiting or even overturning **Roe.**

Abortion-rights supporters portrayed *Webster* as a wrenching reversal, threatening women's rights to privacy and equality. Pro-choice groups, which in the past had relied on the courts to uphold their position, vowed they would now resort to political action to keep abortion legal and unrestricted. Abortion opponents predicted **Roe** soon would be overturned. They praised the Webster ruling, claiming it cleared the way for more restrictive state measures. Both sides concurred the decision will move the emotional issue to dead center of the nation's political debate. Partisans anticipate a 50-state showdown over further legislative bids to curb abortion. Already there are clear signs abortion will be made a litmus test issue for candidates in elections at the local, state, and national levels in 1990 and beyond.

Finally, *Webster* revealed something of the changing composition of the Court on this issue. Pro-choice forces said its fears had been confirmed; the balance had tipped and a clear majority of Justices was in place to cast aside precedents and return the whole matter to the states. Observers on all fronts basically agree that Justice O'Connor will emerge as the swing vote in future abortion cases. Past opinions suggested she was ready to vote to overrule **Roe.** But in *Webster*, a reluctant O'Connor declined to criticize the 1973 decision and called on her colleagues to let it stand.

CHAPTER 4

BIOGRAPHICAL LISTING

This chapter contains brief biographical sketches of a cross-section of significant figures in the recent history of abortion in the United States. Each entry identifies the relationship of the individual to the issue of abortion and summarizes the person's involvement and impact. Court cases appearing in bold print are addressed separately in Chapter 3.

Arlin M. Adams   A retired federal appeals court judge from Philadelphia, he served as chairman of the advisory panel to the National Institutes of Health that in 1988 studied the controversial practice of using human fetal remains for medical science. His committee concluded in September 1988 that the designation of fetal tissue from legal abortions for medical research and therapy is morally acceptable.

William R. Baird   He established the nation's first abortion clinic in 1965 in Hempstead, New York. The facility was the target of a bombing by antiabortion activists in 1986. Baird continues to run a series of clinics between New York and Boston and is an outspoken advocate of full abortion rights for all women. He was a litigant in two major Supreme Court cases: *Eisenstadt v. Baird*, which extended the fundamental right of privacy to single persons, and **Bellotti v. Baird,** which declared states could not give judges absolute veto over a minor girl's abortion decision.

Etienne Baulieu   A French medical researcher, he developed the controversial new drug RU 486 for the company Groupe Roussel Uclaf. First marketed in October 1988, the abortion-inducing pill prevents the fertilized egg from implanting itself in the uterine wall. In September 1989 Dr. Baulieu received the prestigious Lasker Award for his pathbreaking work.

Joseph L. Bernardin   Appointed Roman Catholic archbishop of Chicago in 1982, he was elevated to the Sacred College of Cardinals in 1983. As president of the National Conference of Catholic Bishops since 1974, Bernardin has led efforts in the American church to link its battle against abortion to renewed commitment on such related social issues as poverty and equal rights for women.

Harry A. Blackmun   An Associate Justice of the U.S. Supreme Court since 1970, he wrote the majority opinion for the landmark **Roe v. Wade** decision in 1973. That ruling established a woman's constitutional right to have an abortion. Blackmun devised the trimester analysis of a pregnancy that became the basis for balancing a woman's right of privacy with the state's interest in safeguarding maternal health and protecting potential life. A steadfast supporter of abortion rights, Blackmun has consistently rebuked all efforts on the Court to have **Roe** overturned.

Robert H. Bork   A former U.S. Circuit Judge, his nomination to the U.S. Supreme Court by President Ronald Reagan was rejected by the U.S. Senate in October 1988 by a greater margin than any previous failed nominee. The abortion issue figured prominently in Bork's confirmation hearings before the Senate. His criticism of the judicial analysis behind the high court's **Roe v. Wade** (1973) decision legalizing abortion led to bipartisan mobilization against confirmation.

James L. Buckley   A member of the U.S. Senate (R-NY) from 1971 to 1977, he led the unsuccessful initial efforts in Congress to overturn the U.S. Supreme Court's 1973 **Roe v. Wade** decision establishing abortion as a constitutionally protected right. In each of the three years following **Roe,** Buckley sponsored constitutional amendments to ban all abortions except those necessary to save the life of the mother.

George H. Bush   A moderate Republican through most of his political career, Bush moved toward more conservative positions on social issues during his two terms as Ronald Reagan's vice president. While in favor of abortion in cases of rape, incest, or to save the mother's life, President Bush endorses a proposed constitutional amendment that would in effect overturn **Roe v. Wade** and return the issue to the states. During the 1988 campaign candidate Bush drew attention to the divergence in views between himself and Democratic candidate Governor Michael Dukakis, an ardent supporter of broad abortion rights. In his first year in office, Bush resisted a developing pro-choice tide in Congress by vetoing four bills that would have eased long-standing curbs on federal funding of abortion.

Joseph A. Califano   As Secretary of the Department of Health, Education and Welfare (1977–81) under President Jimmy Carter, he endorsed congressional efforts to limit federal Medicaid payments for elective abortions. Califano spearheaded the Carter administration efforts to promote adoption as an alternative to abortion.

James E. Carter/President Carter (1977–81), while personally opposed to abortion, guided a policy respectful of evolving rights as defined by the courts and Congress through the mid and late 1970s. His administration acquiesced on the point of a woman's constitutional right to an abortion. Carter nonetheless supported legislative steps to bar public funding of abortions and advocated federal efforts to encourage adoption as an alternative.

Mario M. Cuomo   Democratic governor of New York since 1983, he has garnered national attention with his outspoken views on the need for moral tolerance regarding the complex issue of abortion. A Roman Catholic, Cuomo has faced criticism from church officials for refusing to interject his personal religious opposition to abortion into the debate over public policy. In a set of speeches in 1984, he insisted that public officials in a pluralist society who personally believe abortion is immoral should nonetheless refrain from trying to outlaw the practice if it is approved of by a majority of citizens.

Charles E. Curran   A Roman Catholic priest and leading liberal theologian, his well-publicized dispute with the church hierarchy over sexual issues was a major news story in the United States. In 1986 the Vatican revoked Curran's authority to teach theology at Catholic University of America after he argued that the church's opposition to abortion should not be absolute. The episode marked the first time censure had been used to discipline an American Roman Catholic theologian.

John F. Dooling, Jr.   U.S. District Judge for Brooklyn, he blocked implementation in all 50 states of the controversial 1976 Hyde Amendment prohibiting federal Medicaid funding of abortions. The congressional measure went into effect in August 1977 when Dooling lifted his injunction. He continued to hear challenges to the law through the late 1970s and in 1980 declared the legislation unconstitutional. The U.S. Supreme Court, in **Harris v. McRae,** overruled Dooling and upheld the Hyde Amendment, thus finally resolving the Medicaid financing issue.

Kenneth C. Edelin   Chief resident in obstetrics at Boston City Hospital, Edelin was convicted in 1975 of manslaughter in the death of a fetus he legally aborted. The verdict capped a controversial and much-publicized trial that attracted nationwide attention. Edelin's indictment followed revelation that hospital physicians were using aborted fetuses for medical research. Edelin's conviction was overturned in 1976

101

by the Massachusetts Superior Judicial Court on grounds that the state had not clearly proved the fetus was ever actually alive outside the mother's womb.

Geraldine Ferraro   A former congresswoman from New York, she was Democratic presidential candidate Walter Mondale's nominee for vice president in 1984. A Roman Catholic and the first woman selected to run on a major party ticket, Ferraro drew attention to the abortion issue in the campaign. While personally opposed, she contended that the decision to end a pregnancy should remain the woman's alone. This stance involved her in a public dispute with Archbishop John J. O'Connor of New York, who accused Ferraro of misrepresenting the traditional Roman Catholic position.

Sherri Finkbine   A television hostess and mother of four, her well-publicized story in 1962 attracted national attention to the issue of eugenic abortion. Finkbine had taken the drug thalidomide while she was pregnant with a fifth child. When she discovered that thalidomide was reported to cause severe birth defects, she sought an abortion in her home state of Arizona. A Phoenix Hospital denied her request and she finally elected to travel to Sweden in order to obtain a legal abortion.

Nellie J. Gray   Founder and president of March for Life, Gray has organized the yearly January protests in Washington, D.C., on the anniversary of the Supreme Court's **Roe v. Wade** decision legalizing abortion. Gray has established this annual march as a key political forum for the pro-life movement to galvanize congressional and White House support for anti-abortion policies.

Alan F. Guttmacher   An obstetrician with Mt. Sinai Hospital in New York, he served as the president of the Planned Parenthood Federation of America from 1962 until his death in 1974. In books and lectures Guttmacher advocated unlimited access to contraceptive information and liberal abortion regulations. Planned Parenthood's research institute is named in his honor.

Orrin G. Hatch   An attorney, he has served in the U.S. Senate (R-UT) since 1977. He remains one of the key spokespersons in Congress for the positions of the national pro-life movement. Twice in the early 1980s Hatch introduced constitutional amendments tailored to overturn the Supreme Court's 1973 **Roe v. Wade** decision. The proposed Hatch "Human Life Federalism" amendments declared that the Constitution does not secure a right to abortion. They empowered both Congress and the states to regulate or prohibit the practice. Neither of the measures survived Senate deliberations.

Jesse A. Helms   Elected to the U.S. Senate (R-NC) in 1972, he has been a leading antiabortion voice and consistent supporter since 1974 of legislative efforts to curb abortion rights. While in the Congress Helms has backed strict prohibitions on federal funding of abortion, proposed constitutional amendments guaranteeing a "right to life" to the unborn, sponsored "human life" bills declaring that life begins at conception, and resisted appointment of persons to the federal judiciary or executive agencies who favor pro-choice positions.

Henry J. Hyde   Republican congressman from Illinois since 1975, he gained national notice his freshman term for sponsoring the controversial Hyde Amendment. Withstanding a number of legal challenges, the amendment has prohibited federal funding of abortions except under strictly limited circumstances every year since 1977.

C. Everett Koop   A renowned pediatrician and outspoken political conservative, his avowed personal opposition to abortion almost prevented his confirmation by the Senate in 1981 as U.S. Surgeon General. Koop served in the post throughout the Reagan administration. In January 1989 he issued the findings of a major study that showed no conclusive scientific evidence of any adverse psychological effect on women from abortion.

Ellen McCormack   A cofounder of the Right to Life Party, she ran for President in 1980 on a single-issue, antiabortion platform. McCormack mounted the candidacy out of dissatisfaction with Republican nominee Ronald Reagan's refusal to oppose abortion under all circumstances.

Norma McCorvey   She was the plaintiff in the landmark 1973 case of **Roe v. Wade,** in which the U.S. Supreme Court first recognized a woman's right to an abortion and legalized the practice nationwide. McCorvey had challenged a 100-year-old Texas law forbidding abortion except to save the life of the mother. In 1987 she revealed that she had lied when she declared upon bringing the historic suit that it was rape that had caused her pregnancy. In April 1989 she announced she was moving to Washington, D.C., to work full time on political activities for the organized pro-choice movement.

Kate Michelman   Executive director of the National Abortion Rights Action League (NARAL) and one of the most visible spokespersons in the pro-choice movement, she was the principal organizer of the massive demonstration in April 1989 that drew 300,000 abortion rights advocates to the nation's capital. Following the Supreme Court's decision in **Webster v. Reproductive Health Services,** in which the majority suggested it might narrow or overturn **Roe v. Wade** and return the whole issue of abortion regulation to the states, Michelman moved to organize NARAL politically and mobilize it nationwide to target antiabortion candidates for defeat in 1989 and 1990 elections.

Richard M. Nixon   An opponent of unrestricted abortions, President Nixon (1969–74) in 1972 rejected the key recommendations of his own Commission on Population Growth and the American Future. That panel had urged liberal state abortion laws and government funding of abortion services for poor women. Also in 1972 he endorsed a campaign by the Roman Catholic Church to seek the repeal of New York State's 1970 statute legalizing abortion.

John J. O'Connor   Appointed Roman Catholic archbishop of New York in 1984, he was elevated to the Sacred College of Cardinals in 1985. O'Connor's outspoken denunciations of abortion often have commanded national headlines. His insistence on the church's absolute and doctrinal prohibition has frequently put him at odds with Catholic politicians obliged to uphold the laws and policies of legal abortion.

Sandra Day O'Connor   The first woman to serve on the U.S. Supreme Court, she was sworn in as an associate Justice in September 1981. O'Connor was reproved by the national pro-life movement when she refused during confirmation hearings to critique the Court's reasoning in **Roe v. Wade.** In her time on the Court, O'Connor has criticized colleagues in the majority for too liberally invoking the "unduly burdensome" standard in order to strike down state laws regulating abortion. She created a stir in 1983 in **Akron v. Akron Center for Reproductive Health** when, in dissent, she said **Roe** was becoming increasingly unworkable and that its very framework placed the landmark decision on a "collision course with itself." She has stopped short of saying it should be reversed.

Ronald W. Reagan   Governor Reagan in June 1967 signed the law eliminating most curbs on abortion in California. Thereafter, opposition to abortion became a cornerstone of Reagan's politics. As President (1981–89) he articulated strong, steady support for the aims of the national pro-life movement. Regulating and restricting abortion were key objectives of administration social policy. The Justice Department consistently urged the Supreme Court to reconsider and overturn its 1973 ruling legalizing abortion. Reagan backed congressional curbs on federal funding of abortion services and initiated the withholding of U.S. foreign aid from international family planning agencies that promoted abortion. Prior to leaving office, Reagan vowed continued personal involvement in the antiabortion movement.

William H. Rehnquist   Appointed to the U.S. Supreme Court in 1973, he became Chief Justice in 1986 following the resignation of Warren

Burger. Rehnquist wrote the dissent to the 1973 **Roe v. Wade** decision, challenging the majority's establishment of abortion as a privacy right protected under the Constitution. He has favored returning the issue to the states. As Chief Justice, Rehnquist has indicated a willingness to narrow or even overturn the Court's **Roe v. Wade** ruling.

Nelson A. Rockefeller   As governor of New York (1959–73), he provided the leadership essential to the passage in 1970 of a state law legalizing abortion up to the 24th week of pregnancy. The statute was the most liberal of its kind, permitting virtual abortion on demand through the end of the second trimester. In 1972 Rockefeller vetoed a bill sponsored by his own Republican party that would have repealed the 1970 law and recriminalized abortion.

Antonin Scalia   An associate justice of the U.S. Supreme Court since 1986, he has characterized abortion as an issue for the state legislatures rather than the courts. In a sharp dissent to the 1989 **Webster v. Reproductive Health Services** decision, Scalia held that the Constitution does not guarantee a fundamental right to an abortion. He criticized the judicial reasoning behind the 1973 **Roe v. Wade** decision and called on the current court to overturn the ruling outright.

Louis Sullivan   Secretary of the Department of Health and Human Services since February 1989, his selection to the Bush cabinet nearly foundered on the abortion issue. Prior to confirmation hearings, rumors that Sullivan supported a woman's right to abortion led some antiabortion senators to call for President Bush's withdrawal of the nomination. Sullivan assured pro-life skeptics that his views on the issue conformed with those of the President. He weathered the controversy and was confirmed.

Randall Terry   He is the founder and current leader of the antiabortion organization Operation Rescue. Terry's group has gained national headlines by staging highly organized demonstrations outside of abortion clinics. Operation Rescue has employed the tactics of nonviolent civil disobedience in its campaign against legal abortion in the United States. Protests planned and carried out by Terry at the site of the Democratic National Convention in Atlanta in July 1988 resulted in hundreds of arrests, commanded nationwide headlines, and made the Operation Rescue director a national figure.

Richard Thornburgh   As governor of Pennsylvania (1983–87), he signed into law a highly contested 1982 bill imposing detailed regulation of abortions. The statute was later struck down as unconstitutional by the U.S. Supreme Court in **Thornburgh v. American College of Obstetricians and Gynecologists** (1986). Thornburgh has been U.S. Attorney General since August 1988. He ordered the Justice Department brief that was filed with the Supreme Court in the case of **Webster v. Reproductive Health Services** (1989). That brief urged the Court to overturn its 1973 **Roe v. Wade** ruling.

Faye Wattleton   President of the Planned Parenthood Federation of America since 1978, she has guided the transformation of the organization into an aggressive advocate for the preservation of abortion rights. Following the Supreme Court decision in **Webster** upholding a restrictive Missouri abortion law, she initiated a program to mobilize Planned Parenthood politically in all 50 states to fight to uphold women's abortion rights.

William L. Webster   Attorney General of Missouri since 1984, he appeared before the U.S. Supreme Court to defend the constitutionality of a state statute regulating abortions. The Court's subsequent ruling in **Webster v. Reproductive Health Services** (1989) upheld the key provisions of the Missiouri law barring state funding of abortion services and mandating tests for fetal viability after the 20th week of pregnancy.

John C. Wilkie   A physician and outspoken leader in the national prolife movement, he is coauthor with his wife of *The Abortion Handbook*, an early antiabortion manifesto. Wilkie is president of the National Right to Life Committee.

Molly Yard   Leader of the National Organization of Women, Yard has ardently advocated women's complete reproductive freedom and abortion on demand. She has called on women nationwide to make abortion a litmus test issue in evaluating candidates for elective public office at all levels of government.

PART II

GUIDE TO FURTHER RESEARCH

CHAPTER 5

INFORMATION ON ABORTION

Information sources on abortion include an expansive literature, a range of nonprint and audiovisual (AV) materials, and organizations. This chapter is a brief primer on basic abortion research. It describes the principal reference tools used in finding information on abortion and then profiles some of the primary works on the subject. Chapter 6 provides an extensive annotated bibliography on abortion and Chapter 7 identifies organizations that can be contacted for further information.

Much of the abortion information that students and beginning researchers normally seek is available at a standard, medium-size municipal or school library. Several basic library reference resources are indispensable aids to identifying and locating abortion materials.

CARD CATALOGS

The card catalog remains a key reference tool. It is a central inventory of a library's holdings, from books and periodicals, to AV materials and microforms. The catalog contains individual bibliographic citations on all items in the library. Rather than consolidate all holdings in a single catalog, some libraries maintain separate ones for AV materials, noncirculating reference works, government documents, and special collections.

Libraries continue to utilize manual card catalogs. Increasingly, though, facilities are converting to automated systems. The advent of automated catalogs has marked a parallel trend toward interlibrary networks. Computers allow libraries to cross-reference holdings more readily. With this capability, public and school facilities are joining in cooperative lending systems. A library that is part of such a network now has access to vastly enlarged resources.

AUTOMATED SYSTEMS

Automated, or computer-based, information systems and services have emerged as major research tools. Online and CD ROM systems offer quick access to numerous databases encompassing a broad range of subjects. "Online" means the library, as a subscriber, is tapped into a regional, national, or international database network over a phone line. CD ROM is a system of information storage on laser disks for use with microcomputers.

Most of these databases furnish bibliographic citations and abstracts of articles, documents, books, and reports. Some provide the full text of articles. Political developments, legal actions, and statistical shifts continually supplement or change the store of information on abortion. Computer-based systems are particularly helpful because they are updated frequently and therefore capture the most current resources.

Several automated databases and information systems are valuable guides to the extensive book and periodical literature on abortion. *InfoTrac*, which indexes mainstream and generally accessible periodical sources, is easy to use and widely available. It provides bibliographic records from more than 900 business, technical, and general-interest magazines and newspapers. *InfoTrac* covers the current year plus the three preceding years. *WILSONLINE* provides the full range of printed H. W. Wilson Co. indexes. Users have access to *Reader's Guide to Periodical Literature*, *Book Review Digest*, *General Science Index*, *Social Science Index*, and the *Humanities Index*. These and the other indexes available on *WILSONLINE* provide access to some of the most recent abortion sources.

MEDLINE, an online service of the National Library of Medicine, provides post-1980 bibliographic citations to technically oriented articles on abortion research, clinical aspects, demographics, and health policy issues. The *Health Information Network* (HIN) is a full-text database network that provides health care professionals access to up-to-date abortion information from journalism, agencies of the federal government, and the courts.

INDEXES

Indexes are an integral part of a library's reference complement. These guides compile citations on books, magazine literature, newspaper articles, scholarly tracts, government publications, filmstrips, audio recordings, and historical materials. There is significant overlap of the book-

and pamphlet-form indexes and the automated information systems. Some guides appear both in the traditional printed form and in automation. Other indexes are converting from print to computer-based systems.

Book Review Index is a guide to book reviews published in over 300 magazines and newspapers. This bimonthly publication furnishes just the citation to reviews. The monthly *Book Review Digest* provides citations to reviews of current English-language fiction and nonfiction. In addition, the *Digest* prints excerpts from the reviews, which are drawn from some 900 selected periodicals and journals. A good source for annotated citations to abortion reference books is Sheehy's *Guide to Reference Books*.

Major city daily newspapers can be excellent sources on many aspects of abortion. *The New York Times* gives full coverage to major legal, political, medical, social, and cultural developments. *The New York Times Index* is an invaluable research tool for anyone interested in contemporary abortion issues. It concisely summarizes all articles and gives citations to the dates, pages, and columns on which they appeared. Back issues of *The New York Times* and some other major dailies are recorded on microfilm. The *Newspaper Index* is a monthly publication that indexes major newspapers such as the *Chicago Tribune, Los Angeles Times, Denver Post, Detroit News,* and *San Francisco Chronicle*.

The periodical literature on abortion is massive. Two sources stand out as useful citators to articles in mainstream publications. *Reader's Guide to Periodical Literature* indexes more than 200 general-interest periodicals published in the United States; *Magazine Index* compiles citations to the approximately 370 popular magazines and professional journals. Other indexes track the periodical literature on subject areas in the hard sciences and liberal arts. *General Science Index, Social Science Index, Humanities Index,* and *Education Index* cite abortion articles from publications devoted to these disciplines.

The *Encyclopedia of Associations* is standard to any basic library reference collection. A guide to national and international organizations, it provides short explanatory abstracts on each entry. *The Encyclopedia of Associations: Regional, State and Local Organizations* is a seven-volume, geographically organized guide to more than 50,000 nonprofit organizations on the state, city, or local level. Both of these indexes also are available online.

GOVERNMENT DOCUMENTS

When the federal and state governments issue information on abortion, they make these materials publicly available through their respective depository library systems. A depository member library—it could be a college facility or a municipal library—receives government publications and maintains a government documents collection. The *Monthly Catalog of United States Government Publications* has bibliographic entries for virtually all documents published by federal agencies, including books, reports, studies, and serials. The *Monthly Catalog* also is on CD ROM. This automated version is called *GPO Silverplatter.*

The *Index to U.S. Government Periodicals* covers periodicals of the federal government. *Congressional Information Service Index* (CIS), a directory to the publications of the U.S. Congress, is an excellent source. It is the primary tool for locating documents issued by the various committees of both houses of Congress: hearings, committee prints, reports, treaties, and public laws. This source is issued in two parts: One volume is the index; the other volume contains abstracts on the cited publications.

The methods for cataloging public documents vary. Generally, libraries will maintain a separate catalog for federal and state government sources. Certain government documents may also be housed in the reference or general book collections, in which event they most likely are listed in the main card catalog.

LEGAL RESEARCH

The law and the courts have figured hugely in the abortion issue in the past quarter century. Facility with a few basic legal research tools will benefit anyone who is interested in following legal developments. Morris L. Cohen's *How to Find the Law* is a helpful guide for newcomers to legal research. It discusses key techniques and describes the main references encountered in researching court decisions and legislative history. *The Guide to American Law: Everyone's Legal Encyclopedia,* a comprehensive source written for the layperson, covers all aspects of the American legal system and includes helpful articles on landmark court cases.

Decisions of the United States Supreme Court, published since 1965 by the Lawyer's Cooperative Publishing Company, is an excellent guide for the legal novice. Cases ruled on by the nation's high court are reviewed and summarized in this handy, readable series. Yearly volumes coincide with completed terms of the court. *The New York Times* also is quite good on major Supreme Court rulings. Normally, the *Times* has extensive background coverage and analysis, along with excerpts from the majority decision.

Computerized research can accelerate dramatically the process of locating legal resources. But these online services are expensive, and legal nonprofessionals invariably have problems gaining access to them. The two leading services are *LEXIS* (Meade Data) and *WESTLAW* (West Publishing Company). Both are full-text databases containing federal and state case law, statutes, and administrative regulations.

In the literature on abortion, a number of basic sources cover the main aspects and major issues. Following is a discussion of a sampling of the primary works on abortion.

General texts on the subject abound. These titles are a fitting place to begin. Two brief and very readable overviews are tailored to young adult readers: *The Abortion Controversy*, by Carol A. Emmens, examines moral, legal, social, and medical aspects and includes a history of the practice through the centuries; Susan N. Terkel's *Abortion: Facing the Issues* combines statistics and the personal testimony of women who have undergone abortions to illustrate the complexities of the issue. Still useful is *Abortion*, by Malcolm Potts, Peter Diggary and John Peel, a comprehensive and objective discussion of historical, ethical, clinical, and demographic aspects of abortion. A trio of books outlines the different views on abortion issues: *A Matter of Choice: An Essential Guide to Every Aspect of Abortion*, by Myron K. Denney, presents pro- and antiabortion arguments and perspectives; *Abortion Opposing Viewpoints*, edited by Bonnie Szumski, uses primary documents—articles, essays, addresses, book excerpts, court opinions, and so on—to illustrate the differing vantage points on the major abortion issues; in a similar vein, *Abortion: An Eternal Social and Moral Issue*, the Information Series on Current Topics, compiles excerpts from major Supreme Court rulings, congressional legislation, statistical studies, and public leaders' statements on social and moral aspects of the issue.

Many general overviews and much of the social literature examine the history of abortion, at least briefly. The pre-20th-century American experience is profiled in *Abortion in America: The Origins and Evolution of National Policy, 1800–1900* by James C. Mohr. This standard work traces social, legal, and political developments in the 19th century. Lawrence Lader's *Abortion II: Making the Revolution* chronicles the 20th-century development of the pro-choice movement, with particular attention on political and legal events from the end of World War II through *Roe v. Wade*. *The Right-To-Lifers: Who They Are, How They Operate, Where They Get Their Money*, by Connie Paige, is a social history of the right-to-life movement since the Supreme Court's landmark 1973 legalization ruling.

Familiarity with the medical aspects of abortion will help readers to better grasp the interconnected political, ethical, and legal debates. A solid starting source is *Abortion Practice*, by Warren Hern, a textbook that discusses medical techniques, patient screening, counseling, and long-term health prospects. Arthur F. Ide's *Abortion Handbook: History, Clinical Practice and Psychology of Abortion* is a primer on the medical procedures and psychological impact. *Abortion and the Private Practice of Medicine*, by Jonathan B. Imber, examines the clinical realities of abortion by describing the experiences of 26 obstetricians/gynecologists in one town.

The social literature on abortion is abundant and wide-ranging. Numerous works examine the ethical and moral dimensions. Two, in particular, weigh evenly the competing views and vantage points: *The Ethics of Abortion: Pro-life v. Pro-choice*, edited by Robert M. Baird and Stuart E. Rosenbaum, part of the Contemporary Issues in Philosophy Series, is a collection of essays on how Western moral, religious, social, and intellectual traditions have shaped abortion attitudes; *Abortion: A Case Study in Law and Morals*, by Fred M. Frohock, outlines pro-life and pro-choice arguments. Daniel Callahan's *Abortion: Law, Choice, and Morality*, an exhaustive study of moral, legal, sociological, and psychological aspects of the issue, is considered a classic. A scholarly evaluation of theological and philosophical views of abortion, from a feminist perspective, is *Our Right to Choose: Toward a New Ethic of Abortion*, by Beverly Wildung Harrison.

Any number of personalized accounts describe the human toll of abortion. *The Ambivalence of Abortion*, by Linda Bird Francke, uses case histories of women who underwent abortion as a backdrop against which to examine personal, political, and sociological views of the practice. In *Back Rooms: Voices From the Illegal Abortion Era*, authors Ellen Messer and Kathryn E. May use oral history techniques to recount women's experiences with illegal abortion in the era before *Roe v. Wade*. Bernard N. Nathanson's *Aborting America* is the memoir of a gynecologist and former abortionist who revoked his long-standing advocacy of legal abortion. Nathan explains why he came to support abortion only when the mother's life is endangered.

For a discussion of politics and an analysis of public policy responses since the early 1970s, consult *Abortion Politics: Private Morality and Public Policy*, by Frederick S. Jaffe, Barbara L. Lindheim and Philip R. Lee. Nanette J. Davis's *From Crime to Choice: Transformation of Abortion in America*, part of the Women's Studies Series, is a political history of abortion from a feminist perspective.

For those interested in abortion worldwide, two helpful works are *Induced Abortion: A World Review*, by Christopher Tietze, which supplies an international overview of public policy and demographic patterns; and the *International Handbook on Abortion*, edited by Paul Sachdev, which provides extensive data from 33 nations on legal status of abortion, policy development, abortion rates, and availability of services.

Information on Abortion

Numerous pro-life and pro-choice sources spell out the movements' ideas, positions, and criticisms of one another. *Rachel Weeping and Other Essays on Abortion*, by James Tunstead Burtchael, and *Abortion: The Silent Holocaust*, by John Powell, each makes the case against abortion. *The Handbook of Abortion* by Dr. and Mrs. John C. Wilkie is a manifesto of the pro-life cause authored by the leader of the National Right to Life Committee. On the pro-choice side, *The Right to Choose*, by Gisele Halimi, argues for a woman's control over her reproductive choices. In *A Woman's Guide to Safe Abortion* authors Maria Corsaro and Carole Korzeniowsky outline basic pro-choice premises and follow with an explanation of clinical procedures, costs, and insurance.

Legal issues predominate in the abortion debate. A fine overview text on abortion and the law is *A Lawyer Looks at Abortion*, by Lynn D. Wardle and Mary Ann Wood. It gives a balanced analysis of the full range of abortion-related legal issues and has an excellent chapter on the history of legal restriction of abortion in the United States. *Abortion, Politics and the Court*, by Eva R. Rubin, describes the evolution of American abortion law through the late 1970s, summarizing the key court cases and legal precedents. Barbara Milbauer and Bert N. Obrentz's *The Law Giveth: Legal Aspects of the Abortion Controversy* examines how decisions of the state and federal courts have shaped abortion law. The *ACLU Reproductive Freedom Project Legal Docket*, edited by Diana Traub and updated periodically, provides case-by-case summaries of current abortion litigation and can be obtained by contacting the Freedom Project in New York (see Chapter 7 for address).

Probably the finest easily accessible source on the federal government's activities is the *Congressional Quarterly Almanac*. Published annually, it provides a comprehensive overview of political developments, legislative initiatives, and activities of Congress, the White House, and the Supreme Court. For brief summaries of Senate and House bills and information on the status of legislation before Congress, readers should check Commerce Clearing House's *Congressional Index*.

Several major national advocacy organizations serve as information outlets. Planned Parenthood Federation of America, (212) 541-7800, which seeks to make abortion accessible and available to all women, operates more than 800 centers nationwide that provide family planning services and educational programs. The National Abortion Rights Action League (NARAL), (202) 371-0779, spearheads the political efforts of the organized pro-choice movement to keep abortion legal. Its 41 state chapters furnish up-to-date information on abortion-related developments and keep track of legislation pertaining to abortion. The National Right to Life Committee (NRLC), (202) 626-8800, is an antiabortion organization that provides ongoing public education programs, conducts research, and compiles statistics. Its biweekly *NRTL News* covers the activities of the prolife cause.

Current national and global statistics on numbers of abortions, rates, and demographic distribution are available from the Alan Guttmacher Institute, (212) 254-5656, which also publishes *Family Planning Perspectives*, an ongoing series of research reports. Similar statistics are available from the NRLC. The Centers for Disease Control's annual publication, *Abortion Surveillance*, offers a statistical profile of abortion in the United States.

CHAPTER 6

ANNOTATED BIBLIOGRAPHY

This chapter is an annotated bibliography of abortion sources. It includes materials drawn from a broad spectrum of print and other media. Separate listings are provided for bibliographies, books, encyclopedias, periodicals, articles, government documents, brochures and pamphlets, and audiovisual materials. Each item is identified by a standard library citation. A brief annotation then describes the resource's contents and scope.

There is a vast amount of information on abortion. Two basic rules have guided the inclusion of materials in this bibliography. First, emphasis is on sources that are available in a medium-size public or school library. Second, items have been selected for their usefulness to students and others doing general research on abortion. Highly technical works on the subject have not been included. Readers desiring further specialized information should consult either the listing of bibliographies in this chapter or the discussion of reference sources in Chapter 5.

BIBLIOGRAPHIES

Abortion Bibliography For . . . Troy, NY: Whitston Publishing Co., 1970–.

Annual international listing of all materials published on abortion within a given year. Includes journals searched, subject headings, and author index.

Bibliography of Bioethics. Washington, DC: Kennedy Institute of Ethics, Georgetown University, 1975–.

Annual bibliography covering a wide range of bioethical issues, including abortion. Emphasizes medical, scientific, and philosophical journals; includes major news media, such as *Time* and *The New York Times.*

Current Literature in Family Planning. New York: Planned Parenthood Federation of America (monthly).

Annotated subject list of articles and books in the family planning field received by Planned Parenthood's library.

Hughes, Marija Matich. *The Sexual Barrier: Legal, Medical, Economic and Social Aspects of Sex Discrimination.* Washington, DC: Hughes Press, 1977.

A bibliography covering a number of legal issues related to women. Includes approximately 620 entries on abortion, surveying the literature circa 1962 to 1975. Subheadings cover areas such as abortion's legal status pre- and post-1973; medical complications; rights of the fetus and the father; and statistics.

Loeb, Catherine R., et al. *Women's Studies: A Recommended Core Bibliography, 1980–1985.* Littleton, CO: Libraries Unlimited, 1987.

A continuation of Stineman and Loeb's 1979 work (q.v.). Both volumes include annotations of feminist periodicals.

Stineman, Esther, with Catherine Loeb. *Women's Studies: A Recommended Core Bibliography.* Littleton, CO: Libraries Unlimited, 1979.

An extensive annotated bibliography, ranging from literature to medicine and sexuality. Emphasizes works from the 1970s.

Winter, Eugenia B. *Psychological and Medical Aspects of Induced Abortion: A Selective, Annotated Bibliography, 1970–1986.* Westport, CT: Greenwood Press, 1988.

A 500-entry annotated bibliography of articles, books, and audiovisual materials covering the psychological and medical aspects of abortion, including such areas as abortion clinics, techniques, counseling, and effects on subsequent pregnancy. Many of the articles are from health and science periodicals.

BOOKS

GENERAL

Abortion: An Eternal Social and Moral Issue. The Information Series on Current Topics. Wylie, TX: Information Aids, 1988.

A biennial compilation that includes excerpts from Supreme Court rulings since 1973, congressional legislation, United States and world statistics, and public leaders' statements supporting both sides of the social and moral aspects of the issue.

Benderly, Beryl Lieff. *Thinking About Abortion*. New York: Dial Press, 1984.

A thoughtful, readable account of the experiences a woman may undergo while making a decision about abortion. Describes both hostile and helpful medical situations and various psychological reactions to abortion.

Bluford, Robert, and Robert E. Petres. *Unwanted Pregnancy: The Medical and Ethical Implications*. New York: Harper & Row, 1973.

A theologian and a physician explore a woman's alternative responses to unwanted pregnancy.

The Boston Women's Health Collective. *The New Our Bodies, Ourselves*, rev. ed. New York: Simon and Schuster, 1984.

Chapter 16 covers the physical and emotional aspects of abortion. Discusses medical techniques, abortion facilities, what occurs during an abortion, and the risks and complications.

Callahan, Daniel. *Abortion: Law, Choice, and Morality*. New York: Macmillan, 1971.

An exhaustive study that considers the moral, medical, legal, sociological, philosophical, demographic, and psychological angles of the issue.

Chandrasekhar, S. *Abortion in a Crowded World: The Problem of Abortion with Special Reference to India*. Seattle: University of Washington Press, 1974.

An in-depth discussion of abortion in India, focusing on that country's particular historical, religious, and political contexts.

Collins, Anne. *The Big Evasion: Abortion, the Issue That Won't Go Away*. Toronto: Lester & O. Dennys, 1985.

An account of the abortion issue in Canada since the 1960s. Draws on interviews with women active in pro-life and pro-choice organizations.

Corsaro, Maria, and Carole Korzeniowsky. *A Woman's Guide to Safe Abortion*. New York: Holt, 1983.

A clear overview, describing pregnancy tests, choice of an abortion facility, costs and insurance, procedures, and precautions following abortion.

Davis, Nanette J. *From Crime to Choice: The Transformation of Abortion in America*. Women's Studies Series. Westport, CT: Greenwood Press, 1985.

A social and political history of abortion, from a feminist vantage point.

Denes, Magda. *In Necessity and Sorrow: Life and Death in an Abortion Hospital*. New York: Basic Books, 1976.

Mostly interviews with doctors, nurses, patients, and lovers. While pro-abortion, conveys the negative realities of the actual process.

Denney, Myron K. *A Matter of Choice: An Essential Guide to Every Aspect of Abortion*. New York: Simon and Schuster, 1983.

An overview of the subject. Presents both pro- and antiabortion viewpoints as well as medical and psychological aspects, the roles of partners and doctors, and alternatives to abortion.

The Diagram Group. *Woman's Body: An Owner's Manual*. New York: Paddington Press, 1977.

Section on abortion methods presents information in clear diagrams. Gives concise descriptions of techniques.

Dolan, Edward F., Jr. *Matters of Life and Death*. New York: Franklin Watts, 1982.

An introduction to abortion, euthanasia, and in vitro fertilization, discussing the legal, medical, moral, and religious factors of each.

Dornblaser, Carole, and Uta Landy. *The Abortion Guide: A Handbook for Women and Men*. New York: Playboy Press, 1982.

General coverage. Topics range from history and methods to contraception and psychological reactions.

Ebon, Martin. *Every Woman's Guide to Abortion*. New York: Universe Books, 1971.

Where to go for help and guidance. Reviews case histories. Includes public statements on abortion by medical groups.

Emmens, Carol A. *The Abortion Controversy*. New York: Julian Messner, 1987.

Basic overview of the moral, legal, social, and medical aspects of abortion. Includes the history of abortion through the centuries. Uses statistics to illustrate the reactions of different populations to the various aspects.

Francke, Linda Bird. *The Ambivalence of Abortion.* New York: Random House, 1978.

A feminist exploration of personal, political, and sociological views of abortion, presented through case histories and interviews with women who underwent abortion, and with friends and relatives. Emphasizes the complexities and anguish of the decision to abort.

Francome, Colin. *Abortion Freedom: A Worldwide Movement.* London: George Allen and Unwin, 1984.

Reviews debates on contraception since the late 19th century and the status of abortion rights worldwide. Focuses on abortion movements in Great Britain and the United States.

Gardner, Joy. *A Difficult Decision: A Compassionate Book About Abortion.* Freedom, CA: Crossing Press, 1986.

Suggests options to those facing an unplanned pregnancy, with equal advocacy for bearing the child or aborting. Discusses the emotions that may stem from having had a previous abortion.

Greer, Germaine. *Sex and Destiny: The Politics of Human Fertility.* New York: Harper & Row, 1984.

Explores in international terms topics such as attitude toward children, sexuality, birth control, abortion and infanticide, and the family. Pays particular attention to the varied views held by industrialized and developing nations.

Halimi, Gisele. *The Right to Choose.* St. Lucia, Queensland, Australia: University of Queensland Press, 1977.

Translation of *La Cause des Femmes* (1973), first published in France. An autobiography by one of the organizers of the "Manifesto of 343," a public admission by 343 Frenchwomen (among them Simone de Beauvoir) that they had had illegal abortions. The effect of the manifesto on the signers' lives encouraged the founding of an organization promoting legalized abortion.

Howe, Louise Kapp. *Moments on Maple Avenue: The Reality of Abortion.* New York: Macmillan, 1984.

Observations of one day in an abortion clinic, showing the spectrum of women who decide to abort and their varied reasons for that decision.

McDonnell, Kathleen. *Not an Easy Choice: A Feminist Re-examines Abortion.* Toronto: Women's Press, 1984.

Examines psychological, philosophical, and moral questions. Discusses men's roles as fathers and doctors and comments on the effect new technologies, such as gender engineering and prenatal sex determination, may have on the issue of abortion.

Messer, Ellen, and Kathryn E. May. *Back Rooms: Voices From the Illegal Abortion Era.* New York: St. Martin's Press, 1988.

An oral history of illegal abortions, unwanted marriages, and adoptions in the era before *Roe v. Wade.*

Morgentaler, Henry. *Abortion and Contraception.* Toronto: General Publishing, 1982.

General discussion, including the complexities of the decision, methods of abortion, physical and psychological aftereffects, and legal issues.

Nathanson, Bernard N. *Aborting America.* New York: Doubleday, 1979.

A memoir by an obstetrician/gynecologist, once an activist for abortion legalization, who now advocates abortion only if the mother's life is endangered.

Petchesky, Rosaline Pollack. *Abortion and Woman's Choice: The State, Sexuality, and Reproductive Freedom.* Boston: Northeastern University Press, 1984.

Charts abortion practice and regulation in social and historical terms. Surveys abortion practice during the 1970s in the United States. Explores abortion as a political issue in the 1980s. Discusses ethics and "personhood."

Potts, Malcolm, Peter Diggary, and John Peel. *Abortion.* Cambridge: Cambridge University Press, 1977.

A comprehensive, objective discussion of the issue, reviewing historical, sociological, ethical, clinical, and demographic factors.

Rodman, Hyman, et al. *The Abortion Question.* Irvington, NY: Columbia University Press, 1987.

An academic presentation of the moral positions on each side of the controversy, the recent legal history of abortion in the United States, and information on the medical and psychosocial context of the ongoing debate. An update of Sarvis and Rodman's *The Abortion Controversy* (1973).

Sachdev, Paul, ed. *International Handbook on Abortion*. Westport, CT: Greenwood Press, 1988.

An extensive collection of data from 33 nations, covering the legal status of abortion, policy development, abortion rates, and service availability. Covers few Latin American and African countries.

Sarvis, Betty, and Hyman Rodman. *The Abortion Controversy*. New York: Columbia University Press, 1973.

Discusses legal, psychological, ideological, and medical factors. Uses a wealth of statistical data and recent studies, pointing out the possible manipulation of such data to support opposing views.

Sass, Lauren R., ed. *Abortion: Freedom of Choice and the Right to Life*. New York: Facts On File, 1978.

A collection of editorials from U.S. newspapers, 1973 to 1978, covering the constitutional aspects of the issue, the political and legislative processes, pregnancy and population control, and science and morality.

Schulder, Diane, and Florynce Kennedy. *Abortion Rap*. New York: McGraw-Hill, 1971.

An important early compilation of legal papers, public statements, and essays collected by the plaintiffs' lawyers in the case that tested New York State's abortion law, before the law's revision in 1970.

Shostak, Arthur B., and Gary McLouth, with Lynn Seng. *Men and Abortion: Losses, Lessons, and Love*. Westport, CT: Praeger, 1984.

Analyzes the attitudes and demographics of those who accompany their partners to American abortion clinics.

Skowronski, Marjory. *Abortion and Alternatives*. Millbrae, CA: Les Femmes, 1977.

Written simply, this work is intended for women, men, parents, and friends who participate in a decision about abortion. Discusses the law, the ethical debate, medical questions, alternatives, fears, and consequences.

Sloane, R. Bruce, ed. *Abortion: Changing Views and Practice*. Seminars in Psychiatry. New York: Grune and Stratton, 1971.

A collection of articles presenting a range of viewpoints. Describes the "transition period" before the Supreme Court's 1973 decision.

Sloane, R. Bruce, and Diane F. Horvitz. *A General Guide to Abortion.* Chicago: Nelson-Hall, 1973.

A general overview. Includes information on socioeconomic trends and international patterns.

Smetana, Judith G. *Concepts of Self and Morality: Women's Reasoning about Abortion.* New York: Praeger, 1982.

Explores how decision making about abortion is affected by how a woman views and relates to the social world. Discusses social and cognitive development and psychological perspectives.

Szumski, Bonnie, ed. *Abortion Opposing Viewpoints.* San Diego: Greenhaven Press, 1986.

Presents differing perspectives on major abortion issues through the use of primary documents—articles, essays, book excerpts, court opinions, and so on.

Terkel, Susan Neiburg. *Abortion: Facing the Issues.* New York: Franklin Watts, 1988.

A general overview that illustrates the complexities of the issue with both statistics and quotes from women with firsthand experience.

Tietze, Christopher. *Induced Abortion: A World Review*, 5th ed. A Population Control Fact Book. New York: The Population Council, 1983.

Overview of international abortion data.

Wilkie, John C., Dr. and Mrs. *The Handbook of Abortion.* Cincinnati: Hayes Publishing, 1985.

A general primer on abortion authored by the leader of the National Right to Life Committee and a principal spokesperson for the pro-life movement in America.

Zimmerman, Mary K. *Passages Through Abortion: The Personal and Moral Reality of Women's Experiences.* New York: Praeger, 1977.

An analysis of the abortion process. Includes statistics and interview findings for each stage, from pregnancy through postabortion emotions.

ETHICAL

Baird, Robert M., and Stuart E. Rosenbaum, eds. *The Ethics of Abortion: Pro-life v. Pro-choice.* Contemporary Issues in Philosophy Series. Buffalo, NY: Prometheus Books, 1989.

Essays examine ideological and pragmatic considerations in the context of Western moral, religious, social, and intellectual traditions. Includes extensive excerpts from the *Roe v. Wade* (1973) and *Webster v. Reproductive Health Services* (1989) decisions.

Batchelor, Edward, Jr., ed. *Abortion: The Moral Issues.* New York: Pilgrim, 1982.

Explores the moral issues framed by abortion.

Brody, Baruch. *Abortion and the Sanctity of Human Life: A Philosophical View.* Cambridge, MA: MIT Press, 1975.

A philosophical analysis of the morality of abortion.

Brown, Harold O. J. *Death Before Birth.* New York: Thomas Nelson, 1977.

Antiabortion positions, both secular and religious, examined through a conservative Christian perspective.

Burtchaell, James Tunstead. *Rachel Weeping and Other Essays on Abortion.* Fairway, KS: Andrews and McMeel, 1982.

A collection of logical, reflective analyses from a pro-life stance.

Connery, John. *Abortion: The Development of the Roman Catholic Perspective.* Chicago: Loyola University Press, 1977.

A scholarly historical survey of the development of the Roman Catholic perspective on abortion from early Christianity to the first half of the 20th century.

Cornelio, David A. *A Descriptive Study of the Attitudes of Males Involved in Abortion.* New York: Columbia University Teachers College, 1981.

Interviews with 60 males involved in abortion decisions show that they want and need to take part in such decisions. Most men felt they should be equally responsible both for the pregnancy and the decision about abortion.

Dedek, John F. *Human Life: Some Moral Issues.* New York: Sheed and Ward, 1972.

A theological analysis of the evolution of Catholic teaching on abortion, euthanasia, war, and genetic manipulation.

Falwell, Jerry. *If I Should Die Before I Wake —.* Nashville, TN: Thomas Nelson, 1986.

Falwell describes the program he instituted when challenged to address the complexities of renouncing abortion. His chapters alternate with those of "Jennifer," who took part in the program. The program includes a network of homes for pregnant young women.

Ganz, Richard L., ed. *Thou Shalt Not Kill: The Christian Case Against Abortion.* New Rochelle, NY: Arlington House, 1978.

A collection of articles criticizing justifications for abortion from various perspectives, including the medical, psychological, biblical, historical, legal, moral, and feminist.

Gardner, R. F. R., and J. A. Stallworthy. *Abortion: The Personal Dilemma.* Grand Rapids, MI: Wm. B. Eerdmans, 1972.

Essays about the medical, social, and spiritual issues, by two British physicians. Topics include pregnancy out of wedlock, the pregnant student, and the consequences of being refused an abortion.

Garfield, Jay L., and Patricia Hennessey, eds. *Abortion: Moral and Legal Perspectives.* Amherst: University of Massachusetts Press, 1985.

A compilation of articles addressing moral and legal dimensions of abortion.

Gorman, Michael J. *Abortion and the Early Church: Christian, Jewish and Pagan Attitudes in the Greco-Roman World.* Downers Grove, IL: Inter-Varsity Press, 1983.

A survey of the Greco-Roman, Jewish, and early Christian philosophical and moral opinions regarding abortion. Also attempts to link abortion to pacifism.

Hardin, Garrett J. *Mandatory Motherhood: The True Meaning of "Right to Life."* Boston: Beacon Press, 1974.

The author feels that the Right-to-Life movement "is dedicated to forcing motherhood onto women who don't want to be mothers."

Harrison, Beverly Wildung. *Our Right to Choose: Toward a New Ethic of Abortion.* Boston: Beacon Press, 1983.

A scholarly, thoughtful evaluation of theological and philosophical views of abortion, from a feminist perspective.

Hurst, Jane. *History of Abortion in the Catholic Church.* Washington, DC: Catholics for Free Choice, 1987.

Historical account of Catholic teaching and doctrine on abortion prepared by a Catholic organization that advocates a woman's right of choice.

Hursthouse, Rosalind. *Beginning Lives.* New York: Basil Blackwell, 1987.

A philosophical discussion of the multiple factors to be considered in abortion cases.

Kluge, Eike-Henner W. *The Practice of Death.* New Haven, CT: Yale University Press, 1975.

A philosophical analysis of the taking of life through abortion, suicide, euthanasia, infanticide, and senicide. Intended as an introduction to contemporary ethical issues.

Kohl, Marvin. *The Morality of Killing: Sanctity of Life, Abortion and Euthanasia.* Atlantic Highlands, NJ: Humanities Press, 1974.

Essays concerning the sanctity of life, abortion and euthanasia, examined from theological and linguistic standpoints.

Merton, Andrew H. *Enemies of Choice: The Right-to-Life Movement and Its Threat to Abortion.* Boston: Beacon Press, 1982.

An account of the right-to-life movement, with a strong pro-choice bias.

Noonan, John T., ed. *The Morality of Abortion: Legal and Historical Perspectives.* Cambridge, MA: Harvard University Press, 1971.

A collection of essays examining the medical, legal, and moral foundations for abortion in the Western Christian tradition.

Paige, Connie. *The Right-to-Lifers: Who They Are, How They Operate, Where They Get Their Money.* New York: Summit Books, 1983.

A social history of the right-to-life movement, since the 1973 Supreme Court decision.

Powell, John. *Abortion: The Silent Holocaust.* Allen, TX: Argus Communications, 1981.

An apologia for the antiabortion movement.

Ramsey, Paul. *Ethics at the Edges of Life: Medical and Legal Intersections.* Bampton Lectures. New Haven, CT: Yale University Press, 1978.

A moral theologian's exploration of the legal aspects of abortion, euthanasia, and other life-and-death issues.

Rice, Charles E. *Beyond Abortion: The Theory and Practice of the Secular State.* Chicago: Franciscan Herald Press, 1979.

An erudite search for the philosophical roots of societal support for legalized abortion and similar issues.

Satenberger, Ann. *Every Woman Has a Right to Know the Dangers of Legal Abortion*, 3rd ed. Glassboro, NJ: Air-Plus Enterprises, 1985.

Summarizes abortion's medical hazards, from a strong antiabortion stance. Cites both objective research and antiabortion position papers.

Sumner, L. W. *Abortion and Moral Theory*. Princeton, NJ: Princeton University Press, 1981.

Defends 2nd trimester sentient activity as a "criterion for moral standing" and grounds for not permitting abortion.

Vetterling-Braggin, Mary, et al., eds. *Feminism and Philosophy*. Totowa, NJ: Littlefield, Adams, 1977.

A collection of articles on feminism, sex roles and gender, sexism in language, marriage, rape, and abortion.

LEGAL

Briscoe, Clarence B. *Abortion: The Emotional Issue*. San Francisco: Dorrence, 1984.

Examines the contentious nature of abortion in American politics and society.

Burtchaell, James Tunstead, ed. *Abortion Parley*. Papers delivered at the National Conference on Abortion at the University of Notre Dame, October 1979. Fairway, KS: Andrews and McMeel, 1980.

Essays, many based on social science research, examine policy issues from pro-choice and pro-life viewpoints.

Butler, J. Douglas, and David F. Walbert. *Abortion, Medicine and the Law*. New York: Facts On File, 1986.

A lengthy and fairly technical examination of the legal and medical dimensions of abortion.

Decisions of the United States Supreme Court. Rochester, NY: The Lawyer's Co-operative, 1970–.

This handy series reviews and summarizes cases ruled on by the Supreme Court. Annual volumes coincide with a completed court term.

Faux, Marian. *Roe v. Wade: The Untold Story of the Landmark Supreme Court Decision That Made Abortion Legal*. New York: Macmillan, 1988.

Describes the events leading to the Supreme Court decision in 1973. Focuses on the two women attorneys who challenged a Texas abortion law.

Frankfort, Ellen, with Frances Kissling. *Rosie: The Investigation of a Wrongful Death*. New York: Dial Press, 1979.

An investigation into the death of a young Mexican-American mother following an illegal abortion, after federal funds for abortion were cut off in August 1977. Focuses on the attitudes of the government, middle class, and medical establishments toward such a case.

Frohock, Fred M. *Abortion: A Case Study in Law and Morals*. Contributions in Political Science. Westport, CT: Greenwood Press, 1983.

Presents arguments for both the pro-choice and pro-life positions. Discusses historical background, ethical issues, and the relationship between abortion law and morality.

Glendon, Mary Ann. *Abortion and Divorce in Western Law*. Rosenthal Lectures, 1986. Cambridge, MA: Harvard University Press, 1987.

Discusses differing European and American attitudes toward law and the impact of such attitudes on abortion and divorce laws.

Goldstein, Robert L. *Mother-love and Abortion: A Legal Interpretation*. Berkeley: University of California Press, 1988.

Discusses the "dyadic" relationship of mother and fetus, arguing that mother-love cannot be decreed by the legal system. Analyzes conflicting standpoints and proposes a redefinition of the mother-fetus relationship in terms of the rights and duties of each member.

Hilgers, Thomas W., and Dennis J. Horan, eds. *Abortion and Social Justice*. New York: Sheed and Ward, 1972.

Essays opposing the reform of abortion law, from medical, legal, and sociological viewpoints. All center on the concept that a fetus is a being from the moment of conception.

Hindell, Keith, and Madeleine Simms. *Abortion Law Reformed*. New York: Humanities Press, 1971.

An account of events leading to the passage of Great Britain's Abortion Act of 1967.

Jaffe, Frederick S., et al. *Abortion Politics: Private Morality and Public Policy*. New York: McGraw-Hill, 1981.

An analysis of public policy development since 1973.

Krason, Stephen. *Abortion: Politics, Morality, and the Constitution, A Critical Study of Roe v. Wade and Doe v. Bolton*. Lanham, Maryland: University Press of America, 1984.

Exhaustively examines political and moral contexts of two landmark U.S. Supreme Court decisions.

Lader, Lawrence. *Abortion II: Making the Revolution.* Boston: Beacon Press, 1973.

Continuing from an earlier book (*Abortion*, 1966), Lader presents a history of the U.S. abortion movement from 1966 to 1973, focusing on the author's own political work.

Luker, Kristin. *Abortion and the Politics of Motherhood.* California Series on Social Choice and Political Economy. Berkeley: University of California Press, 1984.

A study of the sociological factors leading to pro-life and pro-choice partisanship.

Milbauer, Barbara, in collaboration with Bert N. Obrentz. *The Law Giveth: Legal Aspects of the Abortion Controversy.* New York: Atheneum, 1983.

A discussion of the legal background and current status of abortion law, for the layperson.

Mohr, James C. *Abortion in America: The Origins and Evolution of National Policy, 1800–1900.* New York: Oxford University Press, 1978.

A history of the development of United States abortion law in the 19th century.

Nolen, William A. *The Baby in the Bottle: An Investigative Review of the Edelin Case and Its Larger Meanings for the Controversy Over Abortion Reform.* New York: Coward, McCann and Geoghegan, 1978.

An account of the case of Dr. Kenneth Edelin, a Massachusetts surgeon who was convicted, then later acquitted, of manslaughter after he performed a legal abortion. Within this context, describes abortion itself, the judicial process, and the implications of the practice.

Noonan, John T. *A Private Choice: Abortion in America in the Seventies.* New York: Free Press, 1979.

Recommends a constitutional amendment overturning *Roe v. Wade.* Explores the legal, social, and political elements that led to the legalization of abortion.

Rubin, Eva R. *Abortion, Politics and the Courts.* Westport, CT: Greenwood Press, 1982.

Recounts the evolution of American abortion law through the late 1970s. Summarizes the key court cases and the legal precedents they yielded.

Sloan, Irving J. *The Law Governing Abortion, Contraception and Sterilization.* Legal Almanac Series. London: Oceana Publications, 1988.

Covers both historical and contemporary legislation that relate to abortion, contraception and sterilization, and the rights of minors to these services. Appendixes include selected state statutes and federal laws.

Traub, Diana, ed. *ACLU Reproductive Freedom Project Legal Docket.* New York: American Civil Liberties Union Foundation, 1988.

Issued by the pro-choice ACLU, this compendium provides case-by-case summaries of current abortion litigation. Background, legal issues, and plaintiff and defense positions are outlined for each case.

Wardle, Lynn D., and Mary Ann Wood. *A Lawyer Looks at Abortion.* Salt Lake City, UT: BYU Press, 1982.

A balanced analysis of the full range of abortion-related legal issues. The work opens with an excellent chapter summarizing the history of legal restriction of abortion in the United States.

MEDICAL

Arditti, Rita, et al., eds. *Test-Tube Women: What Future for Motherhood?* Boston: Pandora Press, 1984.

A largely feminist anthology covering ethical, legal, and political implications of reproductive technologies—including genetic engineering, in vitro fertilization, surrogate motherhood, abortion, and sex selection.

Berger, G. S., et al., eds. *Second Trimester Abortion.* Boston: John Wright/PSG Inc., 1981.

This comprehensive report on 2nd-trimester abortion discusses methods, socioeconomic aspects, morbidity and mortality, and future reproduction. Evaluates the future of 2nd-trimester abortion in the United States and internationally, and suggests ways to make 2nd-trimester abortion unnecessary.

Chilman, Catherine S. *Adolescent Sexuality in a Changing American Society: Social and Psychological Perspectives.* Bethesda, MD: National Institutes of Health, 1979.

Chapter 8, "Abortion Alternatives," includes statistics on abortion risks among adolescents. Discusses studies on the psychological effects of abortions and the sociological characteristics of those choosing abortion.

Corea, Gena. *The Hidden Malpractice: How American Medicine Treats Women as Patients and Professionals.* New York: Morrow, 1977.

A feminist exploration of women's health care and its shaping by a patriarchal medical profession. Includes a critique of health care practices relating to birth control, sexually transmitted diseases, abortion, sterilization, and childbirth.

Crabtree, Paula Hinckley. *Personality Correlates of the Delayed Abortion Decision.* Garden City, NY: Adelphi University, 1980.

Results of a study of 80 women, half in their 1st trimester, half in their 2nd. A substantial difference is revealed in their psychological reactions to pregnancy and abortion. Women having later abortions reported more external influence on the decision.

Driefus, Claudia., ed. *Seizing Our Bodies: The Politics of Women's Health.* New York: Vintage Books, 1977.

A collection of articles on women's health, from a range of periodicals such as *Health/PAC Bulletin, Mother Jones,* and *The New York Times Magazine.* Organized into five sections: history; reproductive means and control (including abortion); institutionalized medical practice; men workers in medicine; and the women's health movement.

Federation of Feminist Women's Health Centers. *A New View of a Woman's Body.* New York: Simon and Schuster, 1981.

Sections describe various abortion techniques, including performing menstrual extraction at home or in a self-help group.

Francome, Colin. *Abortion Practice in Britain and the United States.* London: George Allen and Unwin, 1986.

Drawing from his own research, the author recommends several social improvements that would lower the number of abortions in the United States from a rate of more than twice that of Great Britain.

Frankfort, Ellen. *Vaginal Politics.* New York: Quadrangle Books, 1972.

An exposé of the patriarchal American medical establishment. Urges women to be knowledgeable about themselves and to seek nonsexist, high-quality care. Discusses legal and economic aspects of the abortion issue.

Group for the Advancement of Psychiatry. Committee on Psychiatry and the Law. *The Right to Abortion: A Psychiatric View.* New York: Scribner's, 1970.

The GAP Committee on Psychiatry and the Law recommends that abortion be wholly separated from the realm of criminal law. The psychiatrists recommend that physicians explore the motivation of a pregnant woman wishing to abort, in case it is based on impulse or self-destructive tendencies.

Hern, Warren. *Abortion Practice*. Philadelphia: Lippincott, 1984.

A general textbook. Discusses medical techniques, patient screening, counseling, long-term risks, and program evaluation. Lengthy bibliographies.

Himes, Norman Edwin. *Medical History of Contraception*. New York: Schocken Books, 1970.

Originally published in 1936, this study remains a solid background source, providing an exhaustive look at 3,000 years of the theory and practice of contraception. Includes a 1,500-entry bibliography surveying the literature to the mid-1930s.

Hodgson, Jane E., ed. *Abortion and Sterilization: Medical and Social Aspects*. London: Academic Press, 1981.

Textbook on the medical and social aspects of abortion and sterilization. Topics include epidemiology of induced abortion; morbidity and mortality statistics; abortion and sterilization techniques; abortion services in the United States; and abortion and mental health.

Ide, Arthur F. *Abortion Handbook: History, Clinical Practice and Psychology of Abortion*. Las Colinas, TX: Liberal Press, 1985.

Essays on medical, psychological, legal, and historical issues. Analyzes the film *The Silent Scream* from a pro-abortion standpoint.

Imber, Jonathan B. *Abortion and the Private Practice of Medicine*. New Haven: Yale University Press, 1986.

Focusing on the private practices of 26 obstetrician/gynecologists in a single town, the author describes the factors influencing a physician's response to a request for abortion.

Institute of Medicine of the National Academy of Sciences. *Legalized Abortion and the Public Health*. Washington, DC: National Academy of Sciences, May 1975.

Reviews data on the correlation between legalized abortion and the public health. Includes medical and demographic data on legal abortion, the risk of death or complications, selective abortion and birth defects. Also contains a summary of Supreme Court decisions and a glossary of pertinent terms.

Joffe, Carole E. *The Regulation of Sexuality: Experiences of Family Planning Workers.* Philadelphia: Temple University Press, 1986.

Observing a private, nonprofit family planning clinic, the author explores the role played by birth control and abortion counselors as they interweave conflicting ideologies with clients' complex lives.

Keith, Louis G., et al., eds. *The Safety of Fertility Regulation.* New York: Springer, 1980.

"Pregnancy Termination" (Chapter 5) discusses midtrimester abortion, reproduction after 1st trimester induced abortion, and abortion mortality.

Legge, Jerome S., Jr. *Abortion Policy: An Evaluation of the Consequences for Maternal and Infant Health.* Albany: State University of New York Press, 1985.

An effort to trace the relationship between abortion policy and infant and maternal health, using data from the 1950s to 1981. Analyzes the impact of policy changes in the United States, Britain, and Romania.

Luker, Kristin. *Taking Chances: Abortion and the Decision Not to Contracept.* Berkeley: University of California Press, 1975.

A study of 50 women who had abortions at a California clinic. Examines their perceptions about pregnancy and contraception.

Mace, David R. *Abortion: the Agonizing Decision.* Nashville, TN: Abingdon Press, 1972.

A medical school professor's discussion of unbiased abortion counseling. Includes a physiological explanation of fetal development and termination; counsels that abortion should be an "informed decision," to lessen psychological aftereffects.

Pritchard, Jack A., et al. "Abortion" in *Williams Obstetrics,* 17th ed. Norwalk, CT: Appleton-Century-Crofts, 1985.

Classic textbook on obstetrics includes an outline and definitions for various abortion methods. Also includes information on managing complications.

Sciarra, John J., et al., eds. *Gynecology and Obstetrics,* vol. 6. Philadelphia: Harper & Row, 1986.

This loose-leaf textbook discusses demographics, mother and child health, contraception, sterilization, and abortion.

Shapiro, Howard I. *The Birth Control Book.* New York: Avon Books, 1977.

Chapters on postcoital contraception and abortion describe abortion techniques, possible complications, and psychological aftereffects.

Tooley, Michael. *Abortion and Infanticide.* Oxford: Oxford University Press, 1984.

An extensive dissertation on abortion and infanticide, arguing that if abortion is justified, so is infanticide during the first few months of life.

ENCYCLOPEDIAS

Abernethy, Virginia. "Abortion" in *The World Book Encyclopedia*, vol. 1. Chicago: World Book, 1990, 15–16.

Concise overview of arguments for and against abortion, historical background, relevant laws, and methods of abortion.

"Abortion" in *Academic American Encyclopedia*, vol. 1. Danbury, CT: Grolier, 1988, 60.

A brief overview of the subject, focusing on medical, ethical, and legal aspects and the impact of legalization in the United States.

"Abortion" in *The Encyclopedia Americana International Edition*, vol. 1. Danbury, CT: Grolier, 1986, 44–45.

Provides a concise definition of abortion. Reviews the legal history of the issue, moral questions, and medical aspects.

"Abortion" in *The Encyclopedia of Judaism.* New York: Macmillan, 1989, 19.

A concise explanation of the considerations of Jewish law involved in induced abortion.

"Abortion" in *The Guide to American Law*, vol. 1. St. Louis, MO: West Publishing, 1983, 13–17.

Overview of *Roe v. Wade* (1973), *Doe v. Bolton* (1973), and subsequent landmark cases. Discusses the issue of federal financing of abortions and the constitutionality of certain restrictions.

Abortion

"Abortion" in *Illustrated Encyclopedia of Family Health*, vol. 1. New York: Marshall Cavendish, 1983, 7–9.

Basic information on reasons for having an abortion, how abortions are carried out, and aftereffects of the procedure. Includes frequently asked questions.

"Abortion" in *The New Encyclopaedia Britannica Micropaedia Ready Reference*, vol. 1. Chicago: Encyclopaedia Britannica, 1987, 35–36.

Medically defines abortion, describes clinical aspects, and briefly covers the historical highlights, legal issues, and moral questions.

"Abortion" in *The New Good Housekeeping Family Health and Medical Guide*. New York: Hearst, 1989, 548–551.

Clear explanation of reasons, medical and nonmedical, for induced abortions and of the procedures for early and late abortions. Includes information on safety, counseling, and aftereffects.

"Abortion" in *Reader's Digest Family Legal Guide*. Pleasantville, NY: Reader's Digest Association, 1981, 3–5.

Provides statutory definition of abortion in layman's terms; furnishes summations of *Roe v. Wade, Doe v. Bolton,* and more recent Supreme Court rulings; discusses such issues as consent, standards of care, and qualifications of abortionists.

Appleton, Susan Frelich. "Abortion" in *Encyclopedia of Crime and Justice*, vol. 1. New York: Free Press, 1983, 1–9.

Overview of abortion law: its historical development, more recent reforms, and the problem of legislating the beginning of life.

Burch, T. K. "Abortion, I" in *New Catholic Encyclopedia*, vol. 1. Washington, DC: Catholic University of America, 1981, 27–28.

Societal sources of knowledge about abortion: its extent, motivation, and incidence.

Connery, John R. "Abortion: Roman Catholic Perspectives" in *Encyclopedia of Bioethics*, vol. 1. New York: Free Press, 1978, 9–13.

Roman Catholic perspectives on abortion, beginning with the Hebrew and early Christian traditions. Discusses the status of the fetus and the question of intentionality through the centuries. Concludes with theological controversies in the mid-twentieth century.

Curran, Charles E. "Abortion: Contemporary Debate in Philosophical and Religious Ethics" in *Encyclopedia of Bioethics*, vol. 1. New York: Free Press, 1978, 17–26.

Discusses the status of religious and ethical debates in the 3rd quarter of the 20th century on issues such as the beginning of human life and the value and rights of the fetus.

Ducat, Craig R. "Abortion" in *The Guide to American Law*, vol. 1. St. Louis, MO: West Publishing, 1983, 18–20.

An essay quoting extensively from the *Roe v. Wade* opinions and summarizing subsequent rulings.

Feldman, David M. "Abortion: Jewish Perspectives" in *Encyclopedia of Bioethics*, vol. 1. New York: Free Press, 1978, 5–9.

Jewish perspectives on abortion, from Talmudic law and Maimonides' Code through mid-20th century rabbinic teachings.

Finnis, J. M. "Abortion: Legal Aspects" in *Encyclopedia of Bioethics*, vol. 1. New York: Free Press, 1978, 26–32.

Outlines basic models for the legal regulation of abortion: restriction for the child's sake or for uniform medical practice; availability for the sake of women's freedom.

Fletcher, David B. "Abortion" in *Dictionary of Christianity in America*. Downers Grove, IL: InterVarsity Press, 1990, 24–26.

Overview of American Protestant stances on abortion.

Ginsburg, Ruth Bader. "Reproductive Autonomy" in *Encyclopedia of the American Constitution*, vol. 3. New York: Macmillan, 1986, 1552–1558.

The history of U.S. governmental policy on reproductive choice, from *Skinner v. Oklahoma* (1942) to a battery of Supreme Court decisions in 1983.

Hellegers, Andre E. "Abortion: Medical Aspects" in *Encyclopedia of Bioethics*, vol. 1. New York: Free Press, 1978, 1–5.

Medical context of abortion covering clinical procedures and ethical considerations.

Huser, R. J. "Abortion, III (Canon Law)" in *New Catholic Encyclopedia*, vol. 1. Washington, DC: Catholic University of America, 1981, 29–30.

Describes the nature of canonical law regarding abortion; discusses the penalty for "perpetrators" of abortion.

Karst, Kenneth L. "Roe v. Wade, Doe v. Bolton" in *Encyclopedia of the American Constitution*, vol. 3. New York: Macmillan, 1986, 1602–1604.

Discusses these two 1973 Supreme Court decisions and the constitutional issues they addressed.

Nelson, James B. "Abortion: Protestant Perspectives" in *Encyclopedia of Bioethics*, vol. 1. New York: Free Press, 1978, 13–17.

Begins with Lutheran and Calvinist perspectives. Focuses on American Protestant views from the 18th century on.

"Obstetrics" in *Collier's Encyclopedia*, vol. 18. New York: Macmillan Educational Corporation, 1976, 53.

An explanation of abortion appears under the heading for obstetrics.

O'Donnell, T. J. "Abortion, II (Moral Aspect)" in *New Catholic Encyclopedia*, vol. 1. Washington, DC: Catholic University of America, 1981, 28–29.

Discusses the notion and morality of induced abortion.

Perry, Michael J. "Abortion and the Constitution" in *Encyclopedia of the American Constitution*, vol. 1. New York: Macmillan, 1986, 4–6.

An overview of the constitutional dimensions of the abortion issue.

Quay, E. "Abortion, IV (U.S. Law of)" in *New Catholic Encyclopedia*, vol. 1. Washington, DC: Catholic University of America, 1981, 30–31.

Overview of U.S. abortion law to the mid-1960s.

Tietze, Christopher. "Fertility Control" in *International Encyclopedia of the Social Sciences*, vol. 5. New York: Macmillan and Free Press, 1968, 382–388.

Discusses contraceptive methods, practice, and sociological importance. Includes a brief overview of abortion in this context.

PERIODICALS

Abortion Research Notes. Bethesda, MD: Transnational Family Research (3 per year).

International abortion services and research.

Abortion Surveillance. Atlanta, GA: Center for Disease Control (annual).

Reports incidence and rate of abortion in the United States.

Action Line. Falls Church, VA: Christian Action Council (monthly).

Reports on the pro-life movement.

Annotated Bibliography

All About Issues. Stafford, VA: American Life League (9 per year). Reports on the pro-life movement.

All News. Stafford, VA: American Life Lobby (biweekly). Pro-life newsletter on abortion legislation and related issues.

Conscience: A Newsjournal of Prochoice Catholic Opinion. Washington, DC: Catholics for a Free Choice (bimonthly).
Forum for discussion of the ethical questions raised by human reproduction issues.

Contraception. Stoneham, MA: Butterworth Legal Publishers (monthly).
Addresses international experimental and clinical research.

Family News Digest. Manassas, VA: Pro-Family Press Association (monthly).
Covers developments in legislative, health, education, and the law related to family issues.

Family Planning Perspectives. New York: Alan Guttmacher Institute (bimonthly).
Reports on pro-life developments and initiatives.

Heartbeat Magazine. Orlando, FL: Alternatives to Abortion International (quarterly).
Reports on pro-life developments and initiatives.

Hotline. Tulsa, OK: Christian Americans for Life (monthly).
Reports on religiously affiliated elements of the pro-life movement.

Human Life Issues. Steubenville, OH: University of Steubenville, Human Life Center (quarterly).
Articles on the social, ethical, and moral aspects of abortion from an editorial perspective that supports the teachings of the Catholic church.

Human Life Review. New York: Human Life Foundation (quarterly).
Articles on abortion, bioethics, and family issues.

International Family Planning Perspectives. New York: Alan Guttmacher Institute (quarterly).
Articles on international reproductive health care and population issues.

International Review of Natural Family Planning. Collegeville, MN; St. John's University, Human Life Center (quarterly).

International developments and research in natural family planning.

Lex Vitae: A Reporter on Life and Death Issues in the Law. Chicago: Americans United for Life (quarterly).

Newsletter covering legal issues and current court cases involving abortion.

Life Date. St. Paul, MN: Lutherans for Life (monthly).

Newsletter on abortion, adoption, and related issues. Covers church policies and includes book reviews and legislative updates.

Life Docket. Chicago: Americans United for Life Legal Defense Fund (quarterly).

Information on abortion-related legal issues and developments.

The Life-Guardian. Woodbury, NJ: Birthright (bimonthly).

Newsletter on actions and initiatives to encourage pregnant women to find alternatives to abortion.

Lifeletter. Washington, DC: AD HOC Committee in Defense of Life (18 per year).

Newsletter on pro-life lobbying efforts.

Living World. Los Angeles: International Life Service (quarterly).

Journal directed toward those engaged in pro-life endeavors, specifically those who work with and minister to others.

NARAL News. Washington, DC: National Abortion Rights Action League, (quarterly).

Tracks legislation related to abortion.

National Right to Life News. Washington, DC: National Right to Life Committee (weekly).

Reports on abortion issues and the pro-life movement.

The NOEL News, Fairfax, VA: National Organization of Episcopalians for Life (quarterly).

Newsletter of the Christian-oriented pro-life organization.

Options. Washington, DC: Center for Population Options (quarterly).

Information on family planning services and adolescent reproductive health issues. Includes legislative updates.

Planned Parenthood-World Population Washington Memo. Washington, DC: Alan Guttmacher Institute (20 per year).

Newsletter reporting on legislative and other developments pertaining to abortion and pregnancy-related services. Covers federal appropriations, congressional actions, Supreme Court decisions, and international programs.

Pro-Life Action News. Chicago: Pro-Life Action League (quarterly).

Reports on the pro-life movement.

Pro-Life Reporter. Export, PA: U.S. Coalition for Life (quarterly).

Monitors legislative and other developments in abortion and family planning areas.

Religious Coalition for Abortion Rights-Options. Washington, DC: Religious Coalition for Abortion Rights (quarterly).

Pro-choice newsletter that monitors legislative, regulatory, and religious efforts to halt government funding of abortion.

Sisterlife. Kansas City, MO: Feminists for Life of America (quarterly).

Information and research on abortion and feminism.

Sorrow's Reward. Gaithersburg, MD: Human Life International (quarterly).

Newsletter on international developments in the study and treatment of Post Abortion Syndrome.

Studies in Family Planning. New York: Population Council (bimonthly).

Addresses all aspects of family planning with emphasis on policies and programs affecting fertility. Provides international scope with focus on developing countries.

Update, Washington, DC: National Abortion Federation (quarterly).

Newsletter that reports on the pro-choice movement.

ARTICLES

GENERAL

"Abort/Adopt." *Time,* November 2, 1987, 60.

An abortion clinic offering adoption as an alternative.

"Abortion: The Democrats Shift to the Right." *Newsweek*, May 25, 1987, 21.

Discusses the potential impact of various voting blocs on the abortion stances taken by the candidates for the Democratic presidential nomination.

"Abortion: The Gathering Storm." *Ms.* 17 (April 1989): 87–95.

A special section on the attempt to reverse *Roe*. Analyzes congressional opinion, the issues involved and pro-choice support, and reports on the antiabortion group Operation Rescue.

"Abortion: What Does 'Webster' Mean?" *Commonweal*, August 11, 1989, 425–428.

A symposium on the moral, social, medical, and political impact of the *Webster* ruling.

Adessa, M. "Where We Stand Now on Abortion." *Psychology Today* 23 (October 1989): 10.

In the wake of *Webster*, several major American pollsters show support for *Roe* to be at a record high.

Akers, J. N. "Abolition Revisited." *Christianity Today*, March 3, 1989, 13.

Compares the contemporary antiabortion movement with the antislavery movement 150 years ago.

Allen, Glen. "A Crusader's Challenge." *Maclean's*, November 6, 1989, 14–15.

Despite a Nova Scotia law banning abortions outside hospitals, Dr. Henry Morgenthaler challenges the ban in his Halifax clinic.

Arena, John, and Patrick Buchanan. "Civil Disobedience Against Abortion Is Heroic." *Opposing Viewpoints SOURCES: Human Sexuality, 1989 Annual*. San Diego, CA: Greenhaven Press, 1989, 71–74.

A diverse group of citizens uses tactics of civil disobedience and nonviolence to protest legalized abortion. The authors applaud these efforts.

Bader, Eleanor. "The Pro-Life Movement Works to Deny Women's Rights." *Opposing Viewpoints SOURCES: Death/Dying, 1986 Annual*. St. Paul, MN: Greenhaven Press, 1986, 137–139.

Pro-choice activists must work to defend the right to choose in the face of antiabortion attacks.

Annotated Bibliography

———. "March on Washington." *The Humanist* 49 (July/August 1989): 26–28 ff.

An account of the largest pro-choice rally ever held.

Baer, Donald. "The Abortion Decision: Readers Respond." *U.S. News & World Report*, August 7, 1989, 23–24.

An analysis of readers' opinions on the issue.

Baker, James N. "Blacks Agonize over Abortion." *Newsweek*, December 4, 1989, 63.

Many black leaders have opposed abortion in the past, but the leadership's attitude is changing as the general stance in the black community has changed.

Ball, Judy. "Real Prolifers Defend Women, Too." *U.S. Catholic* 52 (August 1987): 16–21.

A "prolife feminist" advocates increased cooperation between right-to-life activists and feminists and a broadening of the pro-life focus to encompass more than the abortion issue alone.

Barnes, Fred. "Bringing Up Baby." *The New Republic*, August 24, 1987, 10–12.

The Reagan administration's antiabortion strategy, including the cutoff of funds to clinics providing abortion counseling, was the result of political maneuvering by White House aides.

———. "Tar Baby." *The New Republic*, February 13, 1989, 12–13.

Discusses President Bush's difficulties in dealing with antiabortion groups, because he lacks an unequivocal stance on the issue.

———. "Abortive Issue." *The New Republic*, December 4, 1989, 10–11.

Discusses the possible positions of the two major political parties on the abortion issue since the resurgence of the pro-choice movement.

———. "Republicans Miscarry Abortion." *The American Spectator* 23 (January 1990): 14–15.

Suggests means by which pro-life Republicans can continue to carry their stance effectively in a pro-choice political environment.

"Black Women's Plight Cited at Pro-choice Rally in D.C." *Jet*, April 24, 1989, 13.

The mammoth pro-choice rally in Washington had special meaning for black and poor women: 75% of abortion-related mortalities were women of color before the 1973 *Roe* decision legalized abortion.

Bole, W. "Liberals Join Abortion Battle." *Christianity Today*, October 7, 1988, 32–33.

Announces the formation of a coalition of religious right-to-life groups whose members are affiliated with traditionally liberal Protestant churches.

Bond, Leslie. "Men Should Participate in the Abortion Decision." *Opposing Viewpoints Sources: Human Sexuality 1989 Annual*. San Diego, CA: Greenhaven Press, 1989, 85–86.

Fathers should have input in the abortion decision as part of their responsibility for the pregnancy.

Breslau, K. "Overplanned Parenthood." *Newsweek*, January 22, 1990, 35.

The Romanian dictator Nicolae Ceausescu, in an attempt to increase the country's population and so strengthen socialism, outlawed sex education, birth control, and abortion. Women who did not produce children were taxed. The policy was reversed when Ceausescu was overthrown.

Brode, Marjorie. "The Consequences of Abortion Legislation." *Women and Therapy* 2 (Summer–Fall 1983): 81–90.

Summarizes gains made possible by abortion legalization and the effect on maternal and infant health. Emphasizes that education and improvements in contraception, not force, will decrease abortions.

Carlin, David R., Jr. "It's My Party." *Commonweal*, October 7, 1988, 521–522.

An antiabortionist who belongs to the (pro-choice) Democratic party discusses the impact the abortion issue is having on the political party's membership among certain demographic groups.

———. "A Tragedy Without Villains." *Commonweal*, October 6, 1989, 517–518.

The political battle over abortion, viewed as a struggle between two goods.

Carlson, Margaret B. "The Battle over Abortion." *Time*, July 17, 1989, 62–63.

The *Webster* ruling may precede a "corrosive" political fight akin to that over Vietnam.

———. "Can Pro-Choicers Prevail? Feminists Squabble over Strategy for Protecting Rights." *Time*, August 14, 1989, 28.

In the midst of the resurgence of pro-choice activism, opinions differ as to strategy, which may endanger the cohesion of the movement.

Carr, Pamela, and Faye Wattleton. "Which Way Black America: Anti-Abortion or Pro-Choice?" *Ebony* 44 (October 1989): 134–138.

Black leaders present opposing viewpoints on the impact of abortion on black women.

Christiano, Donna. "Abortion: Just the Facts, Not the Hype." *Glamour* 87 (November 1989): 228–231.

A compilation of current statistics.

Church, G. J. "Five Political Hot Spots." *Time*, July 17, 1989, 64.

Spotlights the pro- and antiabortion stances of the 50 states.

Clift, E. "Taking Issue with NOW." *Newsweek*, August 14, 1989, 21–22.

The National Organization for Women's suggestion of a political party devoted to women's rights and issues has met opposition among feminists.

Colen, B. D. "Trouble in the Streets." *Health* 20 (August 1988): 78–79.

Discusses Operation Rescue's antiabortion demonstrations at New York abortion clinics. The author argues that abortion is inevitable, and that women who cannot afford safe abortions will attempt self-abortion or risk their lives at the hands of ill-qualified abortionists.

Cryderman, L. "They'd Rather Switch than Fight." *Christianity Today*, February 5, 1990, 12.

The issue of pro-life politicians changing their stance on the abortion issue is viewed from a Christian perspective.

Distelheim, Rochelle. "A Day in the Life of an Abortion Clinic." *Glamour* 85 (February 1987): 238–239 ff.

A day at Planned Parenthood's Midwest Center clinic in Chicago. Illustrates the difficulty of the decision to abort.

Doerr, E. "Abortion: Right or Wrong?" *USA Today* (periodical), 117 (January 1989): 51–53.

An overview of abortion rights in America.

———. "Abortion Rights Imperiled." *The Humanist* 49 (July/August 1989): 39.

Underlying motives for the antichoice movement.

Ehrlich, Elizabeth. "If Pro-Choice Is Mainstream, Now's the Time to Prove It." *Business Week*, July 17, 1989, 64.

Polls show majority support for abortion in some circumstances. The *Webster* ruling now puts the issue in the political arena.

Eisenstein, Z.R. "Fetal Position." *The Nation*, November 20, 1989, 588–589.

Discusses President Bush's inconsistency on the abortion issue.

Engle, Margaret. "Abortion: The Battle Heats Up Again." *Glamour* 85 (October 1987): 192–194.

The confirmation of pro-life Judge Robert Bork would tip the pro-choice balance on the Supreme Court.

Erens, P. "Anti-abortion, pro-feminism?" *Mother Jones* 14 (May 1989): 31 ff.

Profiles a group, Feminists for Life of America, that supports both fetal rights and women's equal rights.

Fineman, Howard. "Pro-choice Politicking." *Newsweek*, October 9, 1989, 34–36.

Pro-choice politicians are taking advantage of the resurgence of support following *Webster*.

"The First March." *National Review*, May 5, 1989, 9–10.

Discusses the status of the abortion issue 16 years after the *Roe* decision, in the context of a pro-choice rally in Washington and the anticipated Supreme Court ruling in the *Webster* case.

Fly, Richard. "The Surging Armies of Abortion." *Business Week*, October 16, 1989, 130–135.

Pro-choice activists include "nonpolitical" women.

"The Future of Abortion." *Newsweek*, July 17, 1989, 14–21 ff.

A special section. Examines the *Webster* decision's impact on political candidates, the medical profession's views on abortion, the dangers of performing one's own abortion, and the Supreme Court's present conservatism.

Glazer, Sarah. "Abortion Policy." *Editorial Research Reports*, 2:14 (1987) 15

If *Roe v. Wade* were changed or reversed, states would have more say in abortion rights. Also discusses morality and women's rights.

Goodman, Eric. "Men and Abortion." *Glamour* 87 (July 1989): 178–179 ff.

Men's emotional experiences of abortion.

Grant, Charity. "Sarabeth Eason." *Ms.* 15 (January 1987): 60–61 ff.

Interview with 11-year-old expelled from a Catholic school for actively supporting women's right to have abortions. Eason was selected as one of *Ms.*'s "Women of the Year."

Gustafson, K. "The New Politics of Abortion." *Utne Reader* (March/April 1989); 19 ff.

A compendium of recent opinions on antiabortion activism.

Harbrecht, Douglas. "Will the GOP Trip Itself as It Backpedals on Abortion?" *Business Week*, December 4, 1989, 47.

Following the *Webster* decision and campaign losses, the Republicans position themselves on both sides of the issue.

Harper's. "Abortion: An Overview." *Opposing Viewpoints SOURCES: Death/Dying, 1986 Annual*. St. Paul, MN: Greenhaven Press, 1986, 113–118.

Debates political and moral issues: pro-life advocates hold for fetal rights, pro-choice for maternal rights.

Henry, Horah F., and Milton E. Harvey. "Social, Spatial and Political Determinants of U.S. Abortion Rates." *Social Science and Medicine* 16 (1982): 987–996.

Examines geographic and sociopolitical patterns of growth in abortion rates in the five years following *Roe v. Wade*. Regional patterns appeared. Urbanization and number of abortion facilities had a positive correlation.

Henshaw, Stanley K., et al. "Abortion Services in the United States, 1979 and 1980." *Family Planning Perspectives* 14 (1982): 5–15.

Analyzes data from the Alan Guttmacher Institute's 7th national survey on known providers of abortion services in the United States: In 1980 about 25% of pregnancies were terminated by abortion.

Hern, W. M. "Abortion as Insurrection." *The Humanist* 49 March/April (1989): 18–20 ff.

Suggests that abortion rights change the power balance in Western society and that the most aggressive antiabortionists are men who do not wish to view women as equals.

Hertzberg, H. "People's Choice." *The New Republic*, May 1, 1989, 4 ff.

Discusses the complex message of a recent pro-choice march in Washington.

Hitchens, C. "Minority Report." *The Nation*, April 24, 1989, 546.

Urges compromise between pro-choice and pro-life factions. Suggests a national health service providing free counseling and care, free contraception, and free abortions in specific circumstances.

"Instant Philosopher." *The New Republic*, October 17, 1988, 4.

The Bush-Dukakis debates show Bush to have illogical views on the abortion issue. He therefore cannot be labeled a secret extremist. Dukakis evidences a definite viewpoint, which hurts him politically.

Jenish, D. "Support for Women's Rights." *Maclean's*, January 1, 1990, 44–45.

Part of a cover story on the status of the abortion issue in Canada.

Kantrowitz, Barbara. "Defying Simple Slogans: Why 'Adoption, Not Abortion' Won't Work." *Newsweek*, May 1, 1989, 36.

Part of a special section: emphasizes that adoption is not a realistic substitute for abortion.

Kasindorf, Jeannie. "Abortion in New York." *New York*, September 18, 1989, 32–41.

An extensive report on pro-life, pro-choice, and abortion activists in New York.

Kinsley, M. "The New Politics of Abortion." *Time*, July 17, 1989, 96.

Discusses the divergent views on abortion held by American voters. Suggests that extremism may be traceable to *Roe*'s all-or-nothing view of abortion, which *Webster* has tempered somewhat.

Klein, Joe. "Short Honeymoon?" *New York*, February 6, 1989, 16–19.

On his first day in office, President Bush spoke out for the reversal of *Roe v. Wade* and called for a pro-life constitutional amendment.

Lacayo, Richard. "The Shifting Politics of Abortion." *Time*, October 23, 1989, 35–36.

Abortion-rights groups report growing membership. Pro-life politicians are trying to realign their positions in the wake of the *Webster* decision.

————. "Pro-choice? Get Lost: Antiabortion Views Are a Must at Health and Human Services." *Time*, December 4, 1989, 43–44.

HHS Secretary Louis Sullivan is finding pro-life opposition in the Bush administration toward several of his pro-choice candidates for positions in the department.

Lawton, K. A. "Promises to Keep." *Christianity Today*, February 3, 1989, 44–45.

Discusses the status of governmental action on abortion in the early days of the Bush administration.

Leepson, Marc. "Abortion: Decade of Debate." *Editorial Research Reports* 1 (1983): 25–43.

Discusses the legal debates since *Roe v. Wade* and the impact of legalized abortion in public arenas.

Lerner, R., et al. "Abortion and Social Change in America." *Society* 27 (January/February 1990): 8–15.

Reviews the impact on American thinking of pro-choice leaders in a variety of high-impact fields, such as the media, the law, and business.

McLoughlin, Merrill. "America's New Civil War." *U.S. News & World Report*, October 3, 1988, 22–25 ff.

Cover story assessing the civil rights questions inherent in both sides of the abortion question, 15 years after *Roe v. Wade*. Sidebar interviews give viewpoints of activists, former spouses, and women who chose to abort.

————. "The Abortion Debate: An Overview," *Opposing Viewpoints 1989 annual*. San Diego, CA: Greenhaven Press, 1989, 67–70.

Debate on the abortion issue focuses on its morality, the beginning of life, and the appropriateness of governmental regulation.

Mertus, Julie A. "Pro-life Clinics Are Deceptive." *Opposing Viewpoints SOURCES: Human Sexuality, 1989 Annual*. San Diego, CA: Greenhaven Press, 1989, 79–80.

Right-to-life advocates have set up clinics that in the guise of providing abortion alternatives, pressure women with antiabortion information.

Mills, Sarah. "Abortion Under Siege." *Ms.* 18 (July/August 1989): 48–51.

A woman about to have an abortion faces antiabortion demonstrators outside a clinic.

"The Missionary Doctor." *Time*, June 8, 1987, 22.

Portrait of C. Everett Koop, conservative pro-life Surgeon General with liberal views on AIDS prevention.

Mithers, Carol Lynn. "Abortion and His Responsibility." *Glamour* 85 (July 1987): 180.

Discusses men's responsibility to provide support, both emotional and financial, to a partner making the abortion decision. Stresses the need for open communication between the partners.

Monmaney, T. "When Abortion Is Denied." *Newsweek*, August 22, 1988, 64.

Excerpts a study of 440 Czechoslovakian children, focusing on 220 whose mothers were denied abortions between 1961 and 1963. Matching these with 220 from similar backgrounds but whose parents definitely wanted them, the researchers found that the "unwanted" children were more likely to suffer psychological and social problems.

Morain, Lloyd R. [Untitled.] *The Humanist* 49 (September/October 1989): 2.

Abortion and flag-burning controversies are obscuring other issues.

Mosher, Stephen W. "A Mother's Ordeal." *Reader's Digest* 130 (February 1987): 49–55.

An account of mandated abortion in China as a population control measure.

———. "Their Baby Is Illegal." *Reader's Digest* 133 (August 1988): 33–36.

A Chinese couple living in the United States have had a second child, despite China's one-child policy. The Chinese government has threatened them with reprisals; the U.S. government, at press time, had refused their request for permission to stay in the country.

Neff, D. "Life After *Webster*." *Christianity Today*, August 18, 1989, 14.

A possible effect of the *Webster* decision is the rise of single-issue politics. Encourages the support of pro-life candidates who also hold firm, responsible views on other equally important issues.

Neuhaus, R. J. "After *Roe*." *National Review*, April 7, 1989, 38–40.

Discusses the possible moral and cultural effects were *Roe* overturned.

"New Abortion Fights." *U.S. News & World Report*, April 24, 1989, 22–23 ff.

Report on the April pro-choice rally in Washington, D.C.

Orenstein, P. "Does Father Know Best?" *Vogue* 179 (April 1989): 314 ff.

Explores the growing impact of the fathers' rights movement.

———. "The Politics of Abortion." *Vogue* 179 (June 1989): 250–251.

Right-to-life groups are expanding their activism to encompass issues besides abortion, such as sex education and contraception.

"Our Bodies, Our Business." *Ms.* 18 (July/August 1989): 6, 38–44 ff.

A special section provides an overview of the issue just before the Supreme Court's ruling in the *Webster* case.

Perkins, S. "The Prolife Credibility Gap." *Christianity Today* April 21, 1989, 21–22.

Discusses conflicts among pro-life supporters who clash on other issues, such as racial equality.

Pierard, R. V. "Wanted: Consensus on Abortion." *Christianity Today*, October 6, 1989, 8.

Compares the pro-life movement to the Prohibition movement, particularly in terms of mistakes that were made.

"Politicians Reconsider Their Prolife Positions." *Christianity Today*, January 15, 1990, 46.

Following several gubernatorial losses by pro-life candidates, many pro-life politicians are tempering their stances to placate pro-choice electorates.

"The Politics of Evasion." *Commonweal*, November 3, 1989, 579–580.

Argues that legal and moral issues are being avoided by poorly focused legislators and activists.

Pollitt, Katha. "Babies, Anyone?" *The Nation*, October 17, 1988, 332.

George Bush's "adoption not abortion" advocacy is not a solution—the number of couples seeking to adopt is far less than the number of abortions performed each year.

———. "Children of Choice." *The New York Times Magazine*, November 20, 1988, 28 ff.

The focus of the abortion debate has shifted from a matter of personal control or family planning to a matter of convenience. Both pro-choice and pro-life advocates fuel the debate with emotional imagery.

Rees, Grover. "The True Confession of One One-Issue Voter." *National Review*, May 25, 1979, 669–672 ff.

A discussion of "what makes a one-issue voter tick," focusing on the issue of abortion. With commentary by James J. Kilpatrick.

"Regain the Body Politic." *The Nation*, February 13, 1989, 181.

Sixteen years after *Roe*, a look at the alliance of pro-life groups and political conservatives.

Rosenbaum, Ron. "Movies: Abortion in Film—A One-sided Story." *Mademoiselle* 95 (November 1989): 104 ff.

Movies routinely view abortion as a tragedy.

Sadler, Martha L. "The Social Determinants of Attitudes Toward Abortion." *Sociological Viewpoints* 1 (1985): 23–40.

Discusses the results of a 1983 survey that explored demographic and attitudinal characteristics that may influence acceptance of legalized abortion.

Salholz, E. "Pro-choice: 'A Sleeping Giant' Awakes." *Newsweek*, April 24, 1989, 39–40.

A recent, enormous pro-choice rally illustrated the resurgence of pro-choice activist support. Leaders are revitalizing the issue, fearing a reversal of the 1973 *Roe* decision.

Scott, Jacqueline, and Howard Schuman. "Attitude Strength and Social Action in the Abortion Dispute." *American Sociological Review* 53 (October 1988): 785–793.

Explores the strength of attitude held by pro-choice and pro-life supporters. Found the two sides equally strong when individuals with mixed feelings were excluded from the study. Focuses on several psychosocial characteristics affecting the outcome.

Simmons, Judy. "A Matter of Choice." *Essence* 18 (October 1987): 55 ff.

Discusses her own abortion experience, advocating women's right to control their reproductive choices and thus their destinies.

Annotated Bibliography

Simpson, Peggy. "The War Has Just Begun." *Ms.* 18 (September 1989): 88.

The post-*Webster* growth of pro-choice activism.

Sobran, J. "The Non-Debate of 1988 Is on Abortion." *Conservative Digest* 14 (October 1988): 95–100.

The author finds the argument that a woman has a "right to control her own body" to be specious. If a fetus is part of its mother, then abortion is self-mutilation. Republicans must fight abortion as part of the liberalistic indifference to family bonds.

Stafford, T. "The Abortion Wars." *Christianity Today*, October 6, 1989, 16–20.

Discusses abortion in a historical perspective.

Starr, Mark. "Playing Single-Issue Politics: Abortion and the Massachusetts Governor's Race." *Newsweek*, August 14, 1989, 22.

An example of the impact of single-issue politics: Most of the commonwealth's voters are pro-choice, but the current legislature is more conservative.

Stengel, Richard. "Nothing Less than Perfect." *Time*, December 11, 1989, 82–84.

Profiles Faye Wattleton, president of the Planned Parenthood Federation of America.

Strothers, E. "Our Big Choice." *Essence* 20 (July 1989): 116.

Pro-choice supporters often have not been as vocal as antiabortion proponents. Suggests that it is time for black women to combat sexism in tandem with racism, rather than setting it aside as less important to them.

Suh, Mary. "Pols Feel the Heat: Candidates Scramble for Pro-Choice Votes." *Ms.* 18 (November 1989): 72–73.

A rundown on political candidates who clarified their stances as pro-abortion support increased.

Szegedy-Maszak, Marianne. "Calm, Cool and Beleagured." *The New York Times Magazine*, August 6, 1989, 16–19 ff.

Cover portrait of Faye Wattleton, president of Planned Parenthood. Discusses Planned Parenthood's response to the *Webster* decision.

Tax, M. "March to a Crossroads on Abortion." *The Nation*, May 8, 1989, 613 ff.

Discusses protection of abortion rights in the context of broader issues of women's rights.

Thomas-Bailey, Jane. "How to Keep the Pro-Life Movement Small." *Commonweal*, May 22, 1987, 308–309.

A pro-life political liberal finds pro-life rhetoric unpersuasive.

Tierney, B. "Planned Parenthood Didn't Plan This: Abortion Foes Are Attacking the Agency's Corporate Sponsors." *Business Week*, July 3, 1989, 34.

Pro-life groups are targeting Planned Parenthood's corporate donors. The organization says its corporate grants have been halved since the mid-1970s.

"Too Many Abortions." *Commonweal*, August 11, 1989, 419–420.

The *Roe* decision cannot be blamed for the attitude that allows 1.5 million abortions annually in the United States, nor can the *Webster* decision be expected to alter that attitude. Urges rational thought about abortion policy.

"Turning Back Webster." *The Nation*, October 30, 1989, 477.

Since the Supreme Court handed down its *Webster* decision, the Republican pro-life bloc has been challenged by renewed feminist activism.

Waldman, S. "Attacking the Real 'Jane Roe.' " *Newsweek*, April 17, 1989, 22.

The woman called "Jane Roe" in the 1973 Supreme Court case is now speaking out in favor of abortion. The FBI is investigating attacks against her property.

Webb, M. "The Great Debate." *Harper's Bazaar* 112 (July 1989): 64–65 ff.

An overview of the issue in the wake of *Webster*.

Weiss, Michael J. "Equal Rights: Not for Women Only." *Glamour* 87 (March 1989): 276–277 ff.

Fathers' rights in the abortion decision.

Whitman, David. "A Fall from Grace on the Right." *U.S. News & World Report*, May 25, 1987, 27–28.

Surgeon General Koop, strongly antiabortion, who advocates candid sex education, clashes with conservative supporters.

"Whose Life Is It?" *Time*, May 1, 1989, 20–24.

Cover story discusses abortion as Supreme Court reviews *Roe v. Wade.*

"Why I Decided to March for Abortion Rights." *Glamour* 87 (July 1989): 96.

An interview with actress Cybill Shepherd, spokesperson for Voters for Choice, a nonpartisan political action committee.

Wilcox, Clyde. "Political Action Committees and Abortion: A Longitudinal Analysis." *Women & Politics* 9 (1989): 1–19.

Discusses the formation and activities of both pro-choice and pro-life groups as well as the strategies of political action committees supporting each side of the issue, from 1977–1984.

Witt, K. "Abortion in the Soviet Union." *World Press Review* 36 (August 1989): 55.

Excerpted from a Viennese newsmagazine. Abortion is the Soviets' most common method of birth control, given the unavailability of contraceptives and attitudes toward sex. Abortions are free at public clinics. Soviet women average three to four abortions each.

Woodward, Kenneth L. "Abortion and the Churches." *Newsweek*, July 24, 1989, 45–46.

Traditionally pro-choice Protestant organizations find pro-life support growing in their ranks.

ETHICAL

"Abortion: Common at Christian Colleges?" *Christianity Today*, July 14, 1989, 42–43.

Several prominent leaders raise concern over the problem of unwanted pregnancy among students at Christian colleges.

"Abortion: The Life You Destroy May Be Your Own." *U.S. Catholic* 52 (July 1987): 20–27.

An interview with Father James T. Burtchaell in which he discusses his participation in the abortion controversy and the ethics of abortion in personal and societal contexts.

Baker, James N. "The Church Strikes Back." *Newsweek*, December 18, 1989, 28.

Growing pro-choice support has triggered a stronger Roman Catholic antiabortion movement. There is concern that the church's pressure on Catholic politicians and colleges could in turn cause a political backlash.

Bassen, Paul. "Present Stakes and Future Prospects: The Status of Early Abortion." *Philosophy and Public Affairs* 11 (Fall 1982): 314–337.

A philosophical examination of the fetus's moral status at several stages of its development.

Bernardin, J. L., Cardinal. "Abortion: Catholics Must Change Hearts as Well as Laws." *U.S. Catholic* 54 (December 1989): 31–33.

Encourages Catholics not to let the legal debate obscure the need for understanding and assistance for those whose circumstances may lead them to view abortion as the necessary option.

Brandl, John E. "Dear Constituent: Here's Where I Stand." *Commonweal*, December 1, 1989, 661–662.

A Minnesota state senator's views on abortion and political responsibility.

Buckley, William F. "Can a Church Take Sides?" *National Review*, September 16, 1988, 64–65.

An attempt to deny tax exemptions to religious organizations has been a vehicle for attacks on the Roman Catholic Church because of its stand on abortion. A question raised is whether or not a tax-protected institution should have the right to advocate the legal codification of a moral belief.

———. "On Criminalizing Abortion." *National Review*, November 7, 1988, 76–77.

Discusses the nature of "crime" as opposed to branding someone a "criminal," in context of remarks on abortion by Massachusetts Governor Dukakis and Vice-President Bush.

———. "Give Them That Credit." *National Review*, December 30, 1988, 62.

Discusses the social idealism of the right-to-life movement in the face of the real social benefits of legalized abortion.

———. "Abortion and the Rapee." *National Review*. December 8, 1989, 53–54.

An ethical perspective on a presidential veto of funding for abortions.

Buckley, William F., et al. "Abortion: The Debate, the Politics, the Morality." *National Review*, December 22, 1989, 25–31.

A debate on the extent to which morality and politics can, or should, be divorced.

Burtchaell, James T. "In a Family Way." *Christianity Today*, June 12, 1987, 24–27.

Advocates ending legal abortion; advocates compassion for, and discouragement of, the attitudes and conditions that lead to the decision to abort.

———. "Abortion Is Not Justified." *Opposing Viewpoints SOURCES: Human Sexuality*, vol 1. St. Paul, MN: Greenhaven Press, 1985, 109–110.

Views abortion as unjustifiable in any circumstances.

Byrne, Harry J. "Abortion Should Not Be Considered a Contraceptive Option." *Opposing Viewpoints SOURCES: Human Sexuality*, vol. 1. St. Paul, MN: Greenhaven Press, 1985, 101–103.

Views abortion as separate from, and more serious than, contraception.

Cavanaugh-O'Keefe, John. "New Questions—Same Old Debate." *America*, April 25, 1987, 334–335.

Examines the theological debate, formulated 20 years before, that does not allow for ethical situations arising in the present society.

Chervenak, Frank A., et al. "When Is Termination of Pregnancy During the Third Trimester Morally Justifiable?" *New England Journal of Medicine*, February 23, 1984, 501–504.

Argues that 3rd-trimester abortion is justified if (1) the fetus is not likely to survive birth for more than a few weeks, or has little or no cognitive function, and (2) the prenatal diagnosis of the condition is highly reliable. If one of these factors does not exist, 3rd trimester abortion is not justified.

Church, F. Forrester. "A Just-War Theory for Abortion." *Christian Century*, August 26–September 2, 1987, 733–734.

Both pro-choice and pro-life stances on abortion are based on individualism: for pro-choice, maternal rights take precedence; for pro-life, fetal rights. The author argues that a "just-war" theory would recognize both the option of abortion and the destruction of a prospective life, thereby providing a less individualistic context for abortion decisions.

Colen, B. D. "Quiet, Please." *Health* 19 (November 1987): 6 ff.

Rational abortion debate will take place only when both sides recognize that the main issue is whether a woman's right to control reproduction is important enough to justify legal sanction for the killing of fetuses.

Colson, Charles W. "The Fear of Doing Nothing." *Christianity Today*, May 15, 1987, 72.

Discusses antiabortion activism and the conflict between religious and secular obedience.

———. "How Prolife Protest Has Backfired." *Christianity Today*, December 15, 1989, 72.

Advises the pro-life movement to establish the immorality of abortion through appeals to human dignity rather than through legislative means.

Dahlquist, Anna Marie. "Aborting a Handicapped Fetus Should Not Be Allowed." *Opposing Viewpoints SOURCES: Death/Dying*, vol. 1. St. Paul, MN: Greenhaven Press, 1984, 57–58.

Maintains that abortion under these circumstances is immoral.

Davis, Nancy. "Abortion and Self-Defense." *Philosophy and Public Affairs* 13 (Summer 1984): 175–207.

Examines the view that the right of self-defense justifies abortion when the mother's life is endangered.

DeCelles, Charles. "Abortion Is a Legal Issue." *Opposing Viewpoints SOURCES: Death/Dying*, vol. 1. St. Paul, MN: Greenhaven Press, 1984, 19–24.

Argues for laws to defend the sanctity of life.

DeParle, J. "Beyond the Legal Right: Why Liberals and Feminists Don't Like to Talk About the Morality of Abortion." *The Washington Monthly* 21 (April 1989): 28–29.

Urges the left to recognize obligations to the life of the fetus and the increasing importance of such obligations as the fetus matures.

Dornblaser, Carole, and Uta Landy. "Abortion Is Justified." *Opposing Viewpoints SOURCES: Human Sexuality*, vol. 1. St. Paul, MN: Greenhaven Press, 1985, 105–108.

Argues that the life and well-being of the woman should prevail over that of the fetus.

Dreifus, C. "Out of Order." *Ms.* 17 (December 1988): 64–67.

Chronicles the case of two members of a Catholic religious order who refused to rescind their pro-abortion stance and eventually resigned from their order.

Drummey, James J. "The Right to Abortion Must Be Revoked." *Opposing Viewpoints SOURCES: Death/Dying, 1986 Annual*. St. Paul, MN: Greenhaven Press, 1986, 127–132.

Asserts that pro-life forces must prevail against society's trend toward a loss of respect for life.

"Ecumenical War Over Abortion." *Time*, January 29, 1979, 62–63.

Two January marches related to the abortion issue—one pro-life, the other pro-choice—signify the deepening differences between largely Roman Catholic conservative forces and more liberal mainstream Protestants and Jews.

Ellingsen, M. "The Church and Abortion: Signs of Consensus." *The Christian Century*, January 3–10, 1990, 12–15.

Emphasizes the influence humans' interactions have on each other. Discusses the human status of a fetus in light of this concept.

Erde, Edmund L. "Studies in the Explanation of Issues in Biomedical Ethics: The Example of Abortion." *Journal of Medicine and Philosophy* 13 (November 1988): 329–347.

In-depth discussion of the ethics of abortion.

Fager, Charles. "Abortion Should Not Be a Legal Issue." *Opposing Viewpoints SOURCES: Human Sexuality, 1988 Annual*. San Diego, CA: Greenhaven Press, 1988, 103–104.

Abortion, like smoking and alcohol, is both legal and destroys human life. Outlawing abortion would no more stop it than Prohibition stopped alcohol consumption.

Farrell, W. L. "A Note on the Abortion Debate." *America*, January 27, 1990, 52–53.

Emphasizes the importance of distinguishing between the moral and legal elements of the issue.

Frame, R. "Presbyterians Consider Four Views on Abortion." *Christianity Today*, December 15, 1989, 52–53.

The Presbyterian Church in the United States, evaluating the abortion issue, outlines four possible justifications for abortion.

Gardner, C. A. "Is an Embryo a Person?" *The Nation*, November 13, 1989, 557–559.

The abortion-rights debate appears to be influenced by acceptance in some quarters of the view that human life begins at conception.

"Good News on Abortion." *The New Republic*, July 31, 1989, 5–6.

Issues such as abortion should not be settled in the courts.

Gramick, J. "Catholic Nuns and the Need for Responsible Dissent." *The Christian Century*, December 7, 1988, 1122–1125.

Discusses the case of two Catholic nuns who publicly supported the freedom of choice. Explores ways the case might have produced a more fruitful dialogue between the dissenters and church leadership.

Hentoff, Nat. "You Don't Have to Believe in God to Be Prolife." *U.S. Catholic* 54 (March 1989): 28–30.

If the pro-life movement were to draw in nonreligious people who nevertheless are against abortion, the movement would be viewed as less parochial and therefore stronger.

Higdon, John F. "The Right to Abortion Must Be Protected." *Opposing Viewpoints SOURCES: Death/Dying, 1986 Annual.* St. Paul, MN: Greenhaven Press, 1986, 119–125.

An atheistic discussion of antiabortion "propaganda."

Himes, Kenneth R. "Single-Issue Politics and the Church." *America*, May 9, 1987, 377–381.

Discusses political polarization caused by single-issue advocacy groups and the impact of Catholic focus on the abortion issue in a political context.

Holden, Constance. "U.S. Antiabortion Policy May Increase Abortions." *Science*, November 27, 1987, 1222.

Family planning groups project that the long-term impact of the Reagan administration's 1984 antiabortion policy may be to increase the rate of unwanted pregnancies, abortions, and maternal mortality in Third World countries.

Ivey, Julie K. "Aborting a Handicapped Fetus Is a Private Decision." *Opposing Viewpoints*. St. Paul, MN: Greenhaven Press, 1984, 53–56.

Argues that the parent, not the state, should make the abortion decision.

Annotated Bibliography

Johnsen, Dawn, and Lynn Paltrow. "Men Should Not Participate in the Abortion Decision." *Opposing Viewpoints SOURCES: Human Sexuality, 1989 Annual.* San Diego, CA: Greenhaven Press, 1989, 87–88.

As the woman carries the fetus, she alone should retain the right to decide whether or not to bear the child.

Johnson, Stephen B., and Joseph B. Tamney. "Factors Related to Inconsistent Life-views." *Review of Religious Research* 30 (September 1988): 40–46.

Discusses the inconsistency of some U.S. antiabortionists who favor, for example, capital punishment.

Kantzer, K.S. "A Winning Prolife Strategy." *Christianity Today*, December 15, 1989, 19.

Encourages a shift in evangelical pro-life thinking away from women's right to freedom and toward ideas of justice.

Kelly, James R. "Residual or Prophetic? The Cultural Fate of Roman Catholic Sexual Ethics of Abortion and Contraception." *Social Thought* (Spring 1986): 3–18.

Explores the differences and similarities of Catholic and general attitudes and practices regarding abortion and contraception.

———. "Ecumenism and Abortion: A Case Study of Pluralism, Privatization and the Public Conscience." *Review of Religious Research* 30 (March 1989): 225–235.

Examines the responses of religious denominations to the abortion issue in terms of such historic ideologies as objective moral truth and subjective conscience.

———. "Catholic Abortion Rates and the Abortion Controversy." *America*, February 4, 1989, 82–85.

A Guttmacher Institute study on abortion rates found that Catholic women were as likely to have abortions as most of the population, but that Jewish and Protestant women had an abortion rate lower than the national average.

Kelly, James R. "Residual or Prophetic? The Cultural Fate of Roman Catholic Sexual Ethics of Abortion and Contraception." *Social Thought* (Spring 1986): 3–18.

Explores the differences and similarities of Catholic and general attitudes and practices regarding abortion and contraception.

Kett, Joseph F. "The Search for a Science of Infancy." *Hastings Center Report* 14 (April 1984): 34–39.

Surveys the history of attitude changes regarding childbirth, child care and welfare, handicapped infants, and unwanted pregnancies, from the early decades of the 20th century.

Kocol, Cleo. "Let's Take the Guilt Away." *The Humanist* 48 (May/June 1988): 33.

Abortion is still stigmatized 15 years after it became legal. The author argues that in fact women choosing abortion have saved themselves, relatives, and society the consequences of an unwanted birth. Pro-choice activists should focus on defusing the stigma.

———. "Poor Women: The Sacrificial Lambs." *The Humanist* 49 (July/August 1989): 37 ff.

Expresses concern over the blurring of lines between church and state in the abortion issue.

LeGuin, Ursula K. "So Much for Prince Charming." *Ms.* 17 (January/February 1989): 101–102 ff.

Suggests that the pro-life goal of the preservation of life is perhaps more a slogan than a goal and that women in the antiabortion movement really want to control women, as men do.

Leo, John. "Baby Boys, to Order." *U.S. News & World Report.* January 9, 1989, 59.

Discusses sex-selective abortions in the context of medical geneticism and an international tradition of female infanticide.

———. "On Abortion: The Moral Complexity of Choice." *U.S. News & World Report*, December 11, 1989, 64.

The sensitivity of the moral issue, in light of other moral choices in today's society.

McManus, Robert J. "Bishops, Politicians and Abortion." *America*, November 4, 1989, 294–296 ff.

In the wake of the *Webster* decision, how should U.S. bishops and Catholic politicians approach the formation of "morally appropriate" abortion legislation?

Maguire, Daniel C., and James T. Burtchaell. "The Catholic Legacy and Abortion: A Debate." *Commonweal*, November 20, 1987, 657–663 ff.

Transcript of a debate on reconsideration of the church's disapproval of abortion.

"A Mistake in San Diego." *America*, December 9, 1989, 416.

A California politician is barred from communion for her pro-choice stance.

Mithers, Carol Lynn. "Sexual Ethics: Abortion and Responsibility." *Glamour* 85 (July 1987): 180.

Asserts that the responsibility for abortion, like conception, should be shared by women and men.

Mott, G. "A Blow Against Blind Obedience.' " *Newsweek*, June 20, 1988, 8.

A Roman Catholic religious order refused to dismiss two nuns who signed a newspaper ad stating that abortion can be "a moral choice." The decision is hailed as a victory for the right of clergy to contradict a Vatican order.

Nathanson, Bernard N., with Richard N. Ostling. "The Case Against Abortion." *Opposing Viewpoints SOURCES: Death/Dying*, vol. 1. St. Paul, MN: Greenhaven Press, 1984, 5–8.

Rational arguments negating pro-choice reasoning.

The New Republic. "Abortion Should Not Be a Legal Issue." *Opposing Viewpoints SOURCES: Death/Dying*, vol. 1. St. Paul, MN: Greenhaven Press, 1984, 25–27.

Abortion should be a private, moral decision. Laws should not be formulated to deal with something for which no moral consensus exists.

Pollitt, Katha. "The Mind of an Anti-Abortionist." *The Nation*, January 24, 1987, 65 ff.

Relates encounters with an ill-informed antiabortion protestor. Weighs the methods and reasoning of antiabortion activists.

"Pro-Con Debate: Ban All Abortions?" *U.S. News & World Report*, September 27, 1976, 27–28.

Interviews with Archbishop Joseph L. Bernardin, who advocates banning all abortions, and Rabbi Richard S. Sternberger, who advocates a woman's right to choose as her conscience and religious beliefs may dictate.

" 'Prolife': What Does It Really Mean?" *Christianity Today*, July 14, 1989, 27–38.

A special section provides a variety of Christian interpretations of the term "prolife."

Quinn, J. R. "Abortion: The Axe at the Root of Human Rights." *America*, April, 1989, 284–285.

Sees the widespread practice of abortion as indicative of a growing lack of sensitivity to the inviolability of human life.

Quinn, Warren. "Abortion: Identity and Loss." *Philosophy and Public Affairs* 13 (Winter 1984): 24–54.

The author argues that as the fetus becomes more human, the range of rights increases and abortion is more like infanticide.

Rosenberg, Leon. "Point of View: On the 'Human Life' Bill." *Science*, May 22, 1981, 907.

Excerpts from testimony in Senate hearings on S.158, the "human life" bill. Yale University geneticist Rosenberg says no scientific evidence exists as to the moment when human life begins.

Rosenthal, Peggy, et al. "Challenges Facing U.S. Catholics: The Next Ten Years." *Commonweal*, November 17, 1989, 617–623.

Examines changes in Catholic attitudes on a number of issues, including abortion.

Ross, Steven L. "Abortion and the Death of the Fetus." *Philosophy and Public Affairs* 11 (Summer 1982): 232–245.

Discusses abortion as both the end of the fetus's physical dependency on the mother and as the termination of the fetus's life. Concludes that there is logical justification for the act of abortion and the woman's decision to seek the death of the fetus.

Scheidler, Joseph M. "The Pro-Life Movement Works to Prevent Murder." *Opposing Viewpoints SOURCES: Death/Dying, 1986 Annual*. St. Paul, MN: Greenhaven Press, 1986, 133–135.

Pro-life activists view abortion as murder and must work to stop it.

Spring, Beth. "Prolife and Prochoice Activists Renew the Battle." *Christianity Today*, February 20, 1987, 48–50.

Assesses the status of abortion activism and the claims by both advocates and opponents to significant progress.

Sher, George. "Subsidized Abortion: Moral Rights and Moral Compromise." *Philosophy and Public Affairs* 10 (Fall 1981): 361–372.

Discusses the morality of subsidized abortions in light of the welfare rights and freedom of indigent women.

Stanton, Joseph R. "A Fetus' Right to Life Must Be Protected." *Opposing Viewpoints SOURCES: Death/Dying,* vol. 1. St. Paul, MN: Greenhaven Press, 1984, 9–13.

Defends the view that life begins at conception and sees all abortion as murder.

Steinem, Gloria. "Our Bodies, Our Business: A Basic Human Right." *Ms.* 18 (July/August 1989): 38–41.

A consideration of the control of one's own body as a basic right, akin to freedom of speech.

"Strategy Time II." *Commonweal,* February 9, 1990, 68–69.

Discusses the impact of "private" beliefs, such as the right to choose abortion, in the public arena.

Walker, Alice. "What Can the White Man . . . Say to the Black Woman?" *The Nation,* May 22, 1989, 691–692.

An address by the author of *The Color Purple,* on the relationship between white male leadership and black women and their unborn children.

Wallis, Claudia. "Abortion, Ethics and the Law." *Time,* July 6, 1987, 82–83.

In the context of the Constitution's bicentennial, focuses on the clouding of legal definitions of viability by advances in medical technology.

Willis, G. "Evangels of Abortion." *The New York Review of Books,* June 15, 1989, 15 ff.

A discussion of the theology of the late evangelical author Francis Schaeffer and those antiabortion activists who base their arguments on his writings.

Wreen, Michael. "Abortion: The Extreme Liberal Position." *Journal of Medicine and Philosophy* 12 (August 1987): 241–265.

Critiques philosophical views leading to the opinion that neither the fetus nor the infant has a right to life. Examines the impact of this notion on the abortion issue.

LEGAL

"The Abortion Furor." *U.S. News & World Report,* July 17, 1989, 8–9, 18–23 ff, 68.

A special section on *Webster v. Reproductive Health Services.* Discusses fetal viability, the Supreme Court's struggle over the ruling, and the case's impact on state politics.

"Abortion, Gay Rights Hit by Loss of Funds." *Christianity Today*, November 4, 1988, 45.

The District of Columbia Appropriations Bill, signed by President Reagan, prohibits the use of government funds for abortions unless the mother's life is in danger. The District's congressional representative argued that the bill attacks the District's ability to govern itself.

"Abortion Law Complications." *Christianity Today*, December 11, 1987, 47 ff.

The U.S. Supreme Court is hearing an Illinois case, *Hartigan v. Zbaraz*, regarding parental notification. About 30 states have comparable statutes.

"Abortion on Trial." *Maclean's*, July 31, 1989, 14–21.

A cover section explores the state of the issue in Canada, focusing on two much-publicized cases.

"Abortion Still a Constitutional Issue." *Lancet*, April 16, 1983, 866–867.

Brief report on continuing attempts in the United States to regulate abortion. Notes the status of efforts in the Supreme Court, the Congress, and the Reagan administration.

"Abortion: The International Agenda." *Feminist Review* 29 (Spring 1988): 23–132.

An international symposium on abortion rights considers the effect in the United Kingdom and elsewhere of a proposed bill that would restrict the permitted time limit for abortions as set forth in the 1967 British Abortion Act.

"After the Webster Decision." *America*, July 29–August 5, 1989, 51.

The Supreme Court's *Webster* ruling may moderate the "disastrous" *Roe* policy. Encourages temperate legislative debate with the emphasis on a pro-life attitude while respecting citizens' right to the freedom of choice.

"After 'Webster': An Uphill Struggle." *America*, October 14, 1989, 227.

Abortion restrictions in the months following the *Webster* decision will not be rapid. But one poll shows a slight majority of the American public favors stringent restrictions on circumstances in which abortion would remain legal.

Ammas, George J. "Roe v. Wade Reaffirmed." *Hastings Center Report* 13 (August 1983): 21–22.

Discusses the U.S. Supreme Court decision in *City of Akron v. Akron Center for Reproductive Health* (1983).

"And Now, a Feminist Full Court Press." *U.S. News & World Report*, November 28, 1988, 12–13.

Drive by feminist lobbyists to prevent the reversal of *Roe v. Wade*, as sensitive cases head for the Supreme Court.

Anderson, Carl A. "Abortion Is Unconstitutional." *Opposing Viewpoints SOURCES: Death/Dying*, 1987 Annual. St. Paul, MN: Greenhaven Press, 1987, 241–244.

A summary of the evolution of abortion law concludes that the distinction between fetus and infant in *Roe v. Wade* will be changed as medical technology progresses.

Annas, George J. "Roe v. Wade Reaffirmed, Again." *Hastings Center Report* 16 (October 1986): 26–27.

A review of the Supreme Court decision in *Thornburgh v. American College of Obstetricians and Gynecologists*, which reversed six provisions of Pennsylvania's 1982 Abortion Control Act. The Court reaffirmed earlier principles such as the right to privacy and the weight of precedent in the American legal system.

"Another Storm Brewing Over Abortion." *U.S. News & World Report*, July 24, 1978, 63.

Discusses the annual review of Congress' health budget and increased action on abortion funding at the state level.

Arkes, Hadley. "How to Roll Back Roe." *National Review*, October 28, 1988, 30–31ff.

A "modest proposal" that full public understanding of the "radical" contents of *Roe v. Wade* would undermine the pro-choice position.

Asnes, Marian. "Mary Ann Glendon: 'We Have Let Our Love of Individual Liberty Trump Everything Else, Such as Our Sense of Community.'" *Vogue* 177 (November 1987): 238–240.

Interview with the author of *Abortion and Divorce in Western Law*.

Baer, Donald. "The Politics of Abortion Takes an Unexpected Turn." *U.S. News & World Report*, July 31, 1989, 26.

The ramifications of the Supreme Court's *Webster* ruling.

"The Battle Over Abortion." *Newsweek*, May 1, 1989, 28–32ff.

A special section considers the possibility that *Roe v. Wade* may be revised by the *Webster* decision. Articles report on pro-life protesters; Justice O'Connor, who may be the Court's "swing vote"; and adoption as a nonviable alternative to abortion.

"The Battle Over Abortion." *Time*, July 17, 1989, 62–63.

The Supreme Court's *Webster* decision has brought a resurgent political fight that may impel the combatants to move toward more central positions.

Blum, Robert W., et al. "The Impact of a Parental Notification Law on Adolescent Abortion Decision-making." *American Journal of Public Health* 77 (May 1987): 619–620.

Results of a 1984 investigation of Minnesota's parental notification statutes. Interviews at Minnesota and Wisconsin clinics determined that notification rates were similar in the two states, although Wisconsin has no parental notification statute.

Brahams, Diana. "Charge of Attempted Murder of an Infant by a Gynecologist Dismissed." *Lancet*, October 1, 1983, 804–805.

Describes the case of a British gynecologist charged with attempted murder for performing an abortion that resulted in the birth of an infant in the 33rd week of pregnancy. The gynecologist had believed the pregnancy to be in the 23rd week. Charges were dismissed.

———. "An Action by Putative Father and Unborn Fetus to Prevent Termination." *Lancet*, March 7, 1987, 576–577.

An unwed father sought an injunction to prevent his former girlfriend from terminating her pregnancy of about 18 to 21 weeks. He asked the court to recognize the fetus's legal rights on the grounds that it was alive. The action was rejected by the High Court, the Court of Appeal, and the House of Lords.

———. "Consent to Abortion on Behalf of a Mentally Handicapped Adult." *Lancet*, June 13, 1987, 1386–1397.

A British judge declared abortion to be in the best interests of a mentally handicapped woman whose mental age was four to seven years, declaring it could not be considered illegal solely on the grounds that the woman could not give her informed consent.

———. "Mentally Incapable Adults: Consent to Treatment." *Lancet*, July 25, 1987, 228.

Changes in Britain's Mental Health Act in 1983 have made the law unclear about who can give informed consent for a mentally handicapped person to have an abortion.

"Bush's No-no on Abortion." *Time*, November 6, 1989, 30.

Several presidential vetoes represent setbacks for the pro-choice movement.

Callahan, Daniel. "How Technology Is Reframing the Abortion Debate." *Hastings Center Report* 16 (February 1986): 33–42.

Discusses technological developments since *Roe v. Wade* that, by changing attitudes toward fetal status, could challenge legalized abortion.
Developments such as the lowered age of fetal viability may make earlier decisions more difficult and lead to conflicts between the rights of the fetus and of the woman.

"Can States Restrict a Minor's Access to Abortion?" *Christianity Today*, April 3, 1987, 44 ff.

Discusses parental notification laws. Focuses on three U.S. Supreme Court rulings in cases challenging the constitutionality of such statutes.

Carlin, David R., Jr. "As American as Freeways: Abortion's Roots in Our Culture." *Commonweal*, July 14, 1989, 392–393.

Argues the constitutional reasoning in the *Roe v. Wade* and *Plessy v. Ferguson* decisions was similarly flawed.

Cartoof, Virginia G., and Lorraine V. Klerman. "Parental Consent for Abortion: Impact of the Massachusetts Law." *American Journal of Public Health* 76 (April 1986): 397–400.

A study of the impact of Massachusetts's parental consent law revealed that conception, abortion, and birth rate among Massachusetts minors were roughly equivalent before and after the law took effect.

Chopko, Mark E., et al. "Abortion Should Be Illegal." *Opposing Viewpoints SOURCES: Death/Dying, 1989 Annual.* San Diego: Greenhaven Press, 1989, 5–12.

Roe v. Wade should be overturned. Abortion has negative impact, psychologically and morally, on women and those around them.

Clary, Freddie. "Minor Women Obtaining Abortions: A Study of Parental Notification in a Metropolitan Area." *American Journal of Public Health* 72 (March 1982): 283–285.

A study exploring the reasons 141 minors chose not to notify parents of planned abortions. Fear of negative reactions and concern for parents' feelings were the most often-cited reasons for not informing parents. Discusses implications for legislation requiring parental notification.

Colt, G. H. "Save My Law." *Life* 12 (May 1989): 111–112 ff.

The woman known as "Jane Roe" in the 1973 case *Roe v. Wade* speaks out in favor of the continued legalization of abortion.

Cook, Rebecca J., and Bernard M. Dickens. "International Developments in Abortion Laws: 1977–88." *American Journal of Public Health* 78 (October 1988): 1305–1311.

Between 1977 and March 1988, 35 countries relaxed their abortion laws and four countries passed more restrictive laws. A number of indicators, such as AIDS/HIV infection, and the extremes of maternal age, have been added to the more traditional reasons for abortion eligibility.

Copelon, Rhonda, and Kathryn Kolbert. "Imperfect Justice." *Ms.* 18 (July/August 1989): 42–44.

An account of the opening arguments in the Supreme Court's *Webster* hearing.

Corelli, Rae. "An inflamed debate." *Maclean's*, July 17, 1989, 36–37.

The U.S. Supreme Court's *Webster* ruling inspires new protests in Canada.

Cryderman, L. "A Movement Divided." *Christianity Today*, August 12, 1988, 48–49.

Pro-life activists are divided over the efficacy of civil disobedience strategies for achieving change.

Culliton, Barbara J. "Abortion: Liberal Laws Do Make Abortion Safe for Women." *Science*, June 13, 1975, 1091.

A study by the Institute of Medicine on legalized abortion and public health found that a competent, legal abortion is safer than an illegal one and that a 1st-trimester legal abortion will have the least adverse physical or psychological effect on the woman.

"Day in Court." *The New Republic*, May 8, 1989, 11–12.

Essay observing that the expected result of the Webster case would make abortions less accessible to the less well-off.

"The Defenders of Abortion Win One." *U.S. News & World Report*, October 16, 1989, 24 ff.

A Florida supreme court upholds a state constitution privacy clause that gives women the option to abort during the 1st trimester.

Degnan, D. A. "When (If) 'Roe' Falls." *Commonweal*, May 5, 1989, 267–269.

Cover story. If *Roe* were reversed, it is unlikely that every state would prohibit all abortions.

Dellinger, W. "Day in Court." *The New Republic*, May 8, 1989, 11–12.

Discusses the anticipated outcome of the Supreme Court hearing on *Webster v. Reproductive Health Services*.

Dilanni, A. "Abortion, Liberalism and the Law," *America*, December 10, 1988, 491–494 ff.

Discusses the status of 3rd trimester abortions under the *Roe* and *Doe* decisions, and the broad interpretations permitting abortion for the sake of the mother's "psychological well-being."

Doerr, E. "Fundamental Rights in Danger." *The Humanist* 49 (May/June 1989): 39.

Expresses concern over the possible weakening of the rights provided in *Roe* by the upcoming Supreme Court decision in the *Webster* case.

Dunn, P. M., and G. M. Stirrat. "Capable of Being Born Alive?" *Lancet*, March 10, 1984, 553–555.

Recommends revision of Britain's 1929 Infant Life Preservation Act, which set fetal viability at 28 weeks. The authors recommend a limit of 22 weeks, corresponding to certain World Health Organization guidelines.

Dusky, L. "Will This Be the Year We Lose Abortion?" *Mademoiselle* 95 (May 1989): 214–215 ff.

An overview of abortion law from *Roe* to *Webster*.

Elving, Ronald D. "Abortion: Politicians' Nightmare." *Editorial Research Reports* 1 (1990): 49–64.

After the Supreme Court's *Webster* ruling in the summer of 1989, abortion may play a large role in politics in 1990, as activists in both camps gain momentum and politicians try to avoid the issue.

"Father's Rights Case Declined by High Court." *Christianity Today*, January 13, 1989, 53.

The Supreme Court declined to hear two cases involving fathers' rights in abortion situations.

Flanders, L. "Abortion: The Usable Past." *The Nation*, August 7–14, 1989, 175–177.

An amicus brief filed by 400 historians in support of the pro-choice position in the *Webster* case discusses the historical practice of and support for abortion in the United States.

Ford, M. deG. "Rocking the Roe Boat." *Commonweal*, June 2, 1989, 326–328.

Discusses the oral arguments heard by the Supreme Court in the case of *Webster v. Reproductive Health Services*.

Fowler, J. "The War Within the States." *National Review*, August 4, 1989, 35–36.

Discusses the impact of the Supreme Court's *Webster* decision on state abortion regulations.

Frame, R. "Showdown in Atlanta." *Christianity Today*, September 16, 1988, 44–45.

The founder of the pro-life group Operation Rescue is encouraging protestors to be arrested for minor offenses in connection with nonviolent demonstrations at an Atlanta abortion clinic. He hopes to thereby tie up the Atlanta legal system, to spotlight the issue of abortion.

———. "Atlanta Gets Tough." *Christianity Today*, November 4, 1988, 34–36.

Protestors with Operation Rescue, the group holding demonstrations at an Atlanta abortion clinic, filed suit against the Atlanta police, alleging that excessive force was used in arresting a demonstrator.

Fumento, M. "The H Baby Incident." *National Review*, June 24, 1988, 32–33.

Discusses the case in an Indiana court in which a father requests an injunction prohibiting his girlfriend from aborting their child.

"The Future of Federal Family-Planning Programs." *Christianity Today,* October 16, 1987, 42–43.

Interview with Nabers Cabaniss, an officer for population affairs at the U.S. Dept. of Health and Human Services. Discusses new Reagan administration regulations that separate abortion from Title X family planning programs. Also discusses the Adolescent Family Life Program.

Gallagher, Maggie. "One Step Forward . . ." *National Review.* March 13, 1987, 29–30.

A bulletin on the enforcement of a 1970 law that prohibits organizations that promote abortions from receiving federal funding.

———. "Trouble in Grove City." *National Review,* July 17, 1987, 40.

Discussion of a proposed "abortion-neutral" amendment to the Civil Rights Restoration Act, under which refusal by a university to provide abortions would not be considered gender discrimination.

Gamm, Gordon. "Abortion, Catholicism, and the Constitution." *The Humanist* 49 (July/August 1989): 24–25 ff.

Separating religion and secular law in the *Webster* case.

Gardell, Mary Ann. "June, Bioethics and the Supreme Court." *Journal of Medicine and Philosophy* 11 (August 1986): 285–290.

Discusses two U.S. Supreme Court decisions affecting policy on the care of handicapped infants and on abortion.

Gardner, William, et al. "Asserting Scientific Authority: Cognitive Development and Adolescent Legal Rights." *American Psychologist* 44 (June 1989): 895–902.

Analyzes several amicus briefs presented by the American Psychological Association to the U.S. Supreme Court in adolescent abortion rights cases.

Gest, Ted. "In the Abortion Battle, Lower Courts Are Important, Too." *U.S. News & World Report,* August 28–September 4, 1989, 30.

Abortion cases in the federal courts may eventually reverse *Roe v. Wade.*

———. "New Abortion Fights." *U.S. News & World Report.* April 24, 1989, 22–23 ff.

Discusses the forthcoming Supreme Court decision on *Webster*. Notes that historically the high court has rarely reversed itself on issues of such importance.

Glantz, Leonard H. "Limiting State Regulation of Reproductive Decisions." *American Journal of Public Health* 74 (February 1984): 168–169 ff.

Analyzes recent U.S. Supreme Court decisions in abortion-related cases to determine the Court's probable future direction on the issue. Concludes that six Justices now uphold *Roe v. Wade*, but three appear ready to overrule it.

———. "Abortion and the Supreme Court: Why Legislative Motive Matters." *American Journal of Public Health* 76 (December 1986): 1452–1455.

A review of the U.S. Supreme Court decision in *Thornburgh v. American College of Obstetricians and Gynecologists*.

———. "Abortion Is Constitutional." *Opposing Viewpoints SOURCES: Death/Dying, 1987 Annual*. St. Paul, MN: Greenhaven Press, 1987, 235–239.

Court abortion rulings are not only about the right of a woman to have control over her bearing of children, but about anyone's right to make private, personal choices without inappropriate interference by the state.

Glendon, Mary Ann. "A World Without Roe." *The New Republic*, February 20, 1989, 19–20.

Examines the pre- (and possible post-) *Roe* regulation of abortion.

Hamill, Pete. "America's Holy War." *Esquire* 112 (November 1989): 61–64.

Violent attacks on a Florida abortion clinic by fundamentalist Christians. The clinic's director says that most of the protestors are men.

Harvey, B. "The Morning After." *Mother Jones* 14 (May 1989): 27–31 ff.

Discusses the impact of the forthcoming *Webster* decision should it reverse *Roe*. The procedure would be less available, more risky, and more costly.

Heim, D. "Beyond Rights in Abortion Politics." *The Christian Century*, July 19–26, 1989, 675–676.

The clash of fetal protection with legalized abortion evidences a need for consensus legislation.

"High Court's Abortion Rulings: What They Mean." *U.S. News & World Report*, July 4, 1977, 66.

U.S. Supreme Court decisions place the responsibility on Congress and the state legislatures to provide or restrict abortion funding and facilities for the poor.

Holden, Constance. "Senate Commences Hearings on 'Human Life.' " *Science*, May 8, 1981, 648–649.

Discusses the opening hearings on Senator Jesse Helms's bill and the problems that would arise should it become law.

Holmes, Steven. "Pro-Choicers Gird for Battle." *Time*, January 23, 1989, 55.

The Supreme Court announces that it will hear *Webster*. Pro-choice groups rally.

"How Will the Abortion Ruling Affect Blacks?" *Jet*, July 24, 1989, 12–15.

In light of the *Webster* decision, a commentary by black leaders on the ruling's effect on the black community.

Isaacson, Walter. "The Battle Over Abortion." *Time*, April 6, 1981, 20–28.

Cover story focusing on the proposed Hyde-Helms Human Life bill.

James, Kay. "Abortion Should Be Illegal." *Opposing Viewpoints SOURCES: Human Sexuality, 1988 Annual*. San Diego, CA: Greenhaven Press, 1988, 99–101.

Excerpts from an interview with *American Medical News*. The fetus is a separate, viable individual. Women should not be allowed to choose abortion.

Janigan, M. "Skirting the Issue." *Maclean's*. October 17, 1988, 16.

On the Canadian Supreme Court ruling that the Criminal Code abortion provisions violate a woman's right to "life, liberty and security of the person."

Johnsen, Dawn, and Marcy J. Wilder. "Abortion Should Remain Legal." *Opposing Viewpoints SOURCES: Death/Dying, 1989 Annual*. San Diego, CA: Greenhaven Press, 1989, 1–4.

Authors argue that legal abortion has had a positive effect on the mental and physical health of women.

Kantrowitz, Barbara. "Teenagers and Abortion." *Newsweek*, October 12, 1987, 81.

Discusses the status of parental notification and consent laws and the debate over their constitutionality.

Kaplan, John. "Abortion as a Vice Crime: A What If Story." *Law and Contemporary Problems* 51 (Winter 1988): 151–179.

Examines the effect of classifying abortion as a vice crime. Explores possible effects of returning regulation of abortion to the state legislature.

Kaye, E. "The New Abortion Battle: Whose Baby Is It, Anyway?" *Mademoiselle* 94 (December 1988): 184–185 ff.

A growing number of men are trying to prevent their partners' abortions. Discusses the pros and cons of the trend.

Kelly, James R. "Winning Webster v. Reproductive Health Services: The Crisis of the Pro-Life Movement." *America*, August 12–19, 1989, 79–83.

Stresses that antiabortion groups take "pro-life" stances in such other areas as war and racism.

Kondracke, M. "The New Abortion Wars." *The New Republic*, August 28, 1989, 17–19.

The sharp rise in membership in pro-choice groups suggests that state-level battles to regulate abortion will not be an easy victory for pro-life activists.

Kort, Michele. "Domestic Terrorism: On the Front Line at an Abortion Clinic." *Ms.* 15 (May 1987): 48–53.

A suburban St. Louis abortion clinic's response to violence, threats, and arson.

Kramer, Michael. "Reagan's Backdoor War on Abortion." *U.S. News & World Report*, August 17, 1987, 14.

Discusses regulations proposed by the Reagan administration that would limit women's access to abortion as an option. Criticizes the administration's lack of straightforwardness in addressing the abortion issue.

Lacayo, Richard. "Whose Life Is It?" *Time*, May 1, 1989, 20–24.

A cover story discussing the impact of the possible weakening or overturning of *Roe* by the forthcoming *Webster* decision.

Landsberg, M. "Canada Wins Choice." *Ms.* 17 (November 1988): 86.

Discusses the legal situation of abortion in Canada since the country's abortion law was struck down.

Annotated Bibliography

Laver, R. "The Debate About Life." *Maclean's*, July 31, 1989, 20.

Advances in medicine related to reproduction and prenatal care are raising ethical questions. The Canadian government plans discussion of the necessity of new laws to respond to such advances.

"The Law on Menstrual Therapies." *Lancet*, August 21, 1982, 422–423.

Asserts the need to clarify the legality of menstrual therapies in the British Commonwealth Asian nations.

Lawton, K. A. "Could This Be the Year?" *Christianity Today*, April 7, 1989, 36–38.

A comparison of the Supreme Court's *Roe* decision and the issues raised in the upcoming *Webster* case.

———. "Confrontation's Stage Is Set." *Christianity Today*, August 18, 1989, 36–38.

In the wake of *Webster*, both pro-choice and pro-life activism has increased. Several abortion-related cases scheduled for the Supreme Court's next term may further redefine abortion law.

———. "Taking It to the States." *Christianity Today*, November 3, 1989, 36–38.

Describes the resurgence of pro-choice activism following the *Webster* decision, as the battle moves to the state legislatures.

———. "Prolife Tensions." *Christianity Today*, February 5, 1990, 49–50.

Pro-life activists are divided over strategy in the months following the Supreme Court decision in the *Webster* case.

"Legal Attack by Bishops." *The Christian Century*, October 14, 1987, 881–882.

An appeal to the U.S. Supreme Court has been made by the National Conference of Catholic Bishops, ordered by a lower court to turn over internal files to critics of the bishops' abortion stand. The lawsuit alleges the church has engaged in political activities in violation of its tax-exempt standing. The bishops claim the law allows religious groups to endorse causes and legislation.

"The Longer March." *Commonweal*, May 5, 1989, 259–260.

Societal pressures exert greater influence on a woman's abortion decision than restrictive antiabortion laws.

"Louisiana: Back to the 'Dark Ages'?" *Newsweek*, October 9, 1989, 34–35.

177

A Louisiana case in which one side hopes to reinforce the state's strict pre-*Roe* abortion laws. The case eventually may be appealed to the U.S. Supreme Court.

Lund, Caroline, and Cindy Jacquith. "The Case for Abortion." *Opposing Viewpoints SOURCES: Death/Dying*, vol. 1. St. Paul, MN: Greenhaven Press, 1984, 1–4.

Argues that abortion should be legal so that women retain the right of control over their own bodies and the number of children they bear.

McBride, J. "A Decision Entangling Church and State." *The Christian Century*, August 31–September 7, 1988, 756–758.

Describes how the Supreme Court overturned a federal court ruling that the Adolescent Family Life Act of 1981 causes entanglement of church and state. The act provides funding to agencies encouraging adolescent sexual abstinence and alternatives to abortion.

McDaniel, A. "Countdown on Abortion." *Newsweek*, January 23, 1989, 50.

The Supreme Court will hear appeal of a Missouri law limiting abortion. This is the first review of abortion law since Reagan appointees became Justices.

Machowald, Mary, and Virginia Abernethy. "When a Mentally Ill Woman Refuses Abortion." *Hastings Center Report* 15 (April 1985): 22–23.

Presents a case study in which an institutionalized schizophrenic refuses an abortion. She is considered to be incapable of responsible parenthood.

Mackey, L. "Court Fails to Block Abortion." *Christianity Today*, September 8, 1989, 65.

The Canadian Supreme Court has lifted an injunction against a woman whose former lover sought to prevent her from having an abortion. Although the woman in fact had the abortion before the ruling, the case has encouraged the Canadian government to push for new abortion legislation.

McLoughlin, Merrill. "Sandra Day O'Connor: Woman in the Middle." *Ladies' Home Journal* 106 (November 1989): 218–219 ff.

A portrait of the only woman Supreme Court justice, in light of her possible impact on abortion cases on the Court's calendar.

Mann, John Roger. "The Courts Need Not Protect the Fetus." *Opposing Viewpoints SOURCES: Death/Dying*, *1987 Annual*. St. Paul, MN: Greenhaven Press, 1987, 249–251.

In *Roe v. Wade*, the Court held that fetuses are not persons. The author argues that personhood should begin at birth, which is more easily determined than viability, although no less arbitrary.

Martz, L. "The New Pro-life Offensive." *Newsweek*, September 12, 1988, 25.

The pro-life movement has adopted nonviolent civil disobedience measures in its efforts to change national abortion legislation. The movement's most notable effort is Operation Rescue's ongoing demonstration in Atlanta.

Michelman, Kate. "Abortion Should Remain Legal." *Opposing Viewpoints SOURCES: Human Sexuality, 1988 Annual*. San Diego, CA: Greenhaven Press, 1988, 95–97.

From an interview with *American Medical News*. A woman's right to choose abortion should remain protected by law and should remain her own choice. The rights of the woman and the fetus should not be viewed as the rights of two separate individuals.

Miller, Michael K., et al. "The Effect of Legalization and Public Funding of Abortion on Neonatal Mortality." *Population Research and Policy Review* 7 (1988): 79–82.

Examines data for the United States and for two individual states to determine the effect of abortion legalization on neonatal mortality.

Nedoff, Marshall H. "Constituencies, Ideology, and the Demand for Abortion Legislation." *Public Choice* 60 (February 1989): 185–191.

Explores social and religious demographics as indicators of a state's likely political support for legalized abortion.

Nice, David C. "Abortion Clinic Bombings as Political Violence." *American Journal of Political Science* 32 (February 1988): 178–195.

Analyzes abortion clinic bombings by state, correlating occurrences to social and political characteristics.

"The Ordeal of a Divided Jury." *Time*, May 22, 1978, 24.

Describes a California jury deadlocked in the murder trial of an obstetrician whose performance of an abortion resulted in a live birth and subsequent infant death.

Parness, Jeffrey A. "The Courts Must Protect the Fetus." *Opposing Viewpoints SOURCES: Death/Dying, 1987 Annual*. St. Paul, MN: Greenhaven Press, 1987, 245–247.

The U.S. Supreme Court's *Roe v. Wade* decision recognized the legitimacy, and limitations, of the state's protective interest in human life. Further legislation is needed to protect the unborn from abuse and neglect.

Pedersen, Daniel. "The 'A-Word' in Ireland." *Newsweek*, July 31, 1989, 45.

Overseas effects of the U.S. Supreme Court's *Webster* ruling.

"Prolifers Say Civil Rights Measure Could Expand the Practice of Abortion." *Christianity Today*, April 17, 1987, 46.

Pro-life supporters are concerned that the proposed Civil Rights Restoration Act might extend antidiscrimination laws so that pro-life hospitals not controlled by religious organizations would be required to perform abortions.

Rees, Grover, and Jack Fowler. "Abortion: Law and Politics." *National Review*, August 4, 1989, 34–36.

The impact of the *Webster* decision: in terms of *Roe*, in the lower courts, and in state legislatures.

Revolutionary Worker and Workers Vanguard. "Civil Disobedience Against Abortion Is Not Heroic." *Opposing Viewpoints SOURCES: Human Sexuality, 1989 Annual*. San Diego, CA: Greenhaven Press, 1989, 75–78.

The authors argue that antiabortion demonstrators are harassing and interfering with women's right to choose abortion.

Rice, Charles E. "A Human Life Amendment Is Needed." *Opposing Viewpoints SOURCES: Death/Dying*, vol. 1. St. Paul, MN: Greenhaven Press, 1984, 29–32.

Author says a constitutional amendment defending human life is needed so that the states cannot legalize abortion.

Roberts, Stephen V. "In Search of a Compromise on Abortion." *U.S. News & World Report*, November 6, 1989, 31.

Pennsylvania makes the first post-*Webster* movement toward state-level restrictions on abortions.

"Roe on the Brink." *The Nation*, July 24–31, 1989, 112.

Although the Supreme Court's *Webster* opinion does not contravene *Roe v. Wade*, it may presage the denial to women of the freedom of choice.

Annotated Bibliography

Rosenblum, V. G. "Letting the States Set Abortion Policy." *The Christian Century*, March 8, 1989, 252–253.

Discusses positive aspects of state regulation of abortion.

Saletan, W. "If Fetuses Are People . . ." *The New Republic*, September 18–25, 1989, 18–20.

The possible legal impact of the idea that life begins at conception.

Satchell, Michael. "Abortion: Once More to the Fore." *U.S. News & World Report*, September 7, 1987, 16–17.

An assessment of the abortion issue in the final months of the Reagan presidency, focusing on the Supreme Court's ruling in a parental notification case, the possible limitation of funding to family planning clinics that provide abortion-related services, and the nomination of Judge Robert Bork to the U.S. Supreme Court.

Segers, M. C. "Semantics and Style in an Abortion Campaign." *Commonweal*, January 12, 1990, 10–13.

Uses the 1989 New Jersey gubernatorial race as an example of the impact stances on abortion may have on the outcome of an election.

Segers, Mary C. "Can Congress Settle the Abortion Issue?" *Hastings Center Report* 12 (June 1982): 20–28.

Discusses legislative hearings on the Hatch Human Life Amendment and Helms Human Life Statute.

"Sex, Not Separation." *America*, July 9–16, 1988, 27–28.

Discusses the U.S. Supreme Court ruling in *Brown v. Kendrick*, which stated that religious organizations can participate in sex counseling programs that receive government funds.

Silberner, Joanne. "When the Law and Medicine Collide." *U.S. News & World Report*, July 17, 1989, 23.

Controversy over Missouri's 20-week fetal viability legislation. Much of the medical community feels that viability varies too much from one fetus to another for a specific date to be a guarantee of the ability to survive.

Simpson, Peggy. "The Political Arena." *Ms.* 18 (July/Aug 1989): 46–47.

A preview of the impact of a possible weakening of *Roe.*

———. "Reconcilable Differences." *Ms.* 18 (October 1988): 70.

Despite differences of opinion on other issues at the summer convention of the National Organization for Women, the pro-choice coalition pulled together again to combat restrictive abortion legislation.

————. "Loony Legislator." *Ms.* 18 (November 1989): 72.

Pro-life legislators in Pennsylvania propose to ban abortion for its use in gender selection.

"Splitting Differences." *Newsweek*, February 13, 1989, 86.

The upcoming Supreme Court hearing of *Webster v. Reproductive Health Services* could reverse *Roe v. Wade*. The abortion debate should center on when sentient life begins.

Spring, Beth. "Proposed Prolife Bill Goes for the Jugular." *Christianity Today*, June 12, 1987, 48–49.

Levels of pro-life support vary for proposed Reaganite cuts in funding for abortions and abortion-related services.

Swomley, John M., Jr. "A Human Life Amendment Violates Civil Rights." *Opposing Viewpoints SOURCES: Death/Dying*, vol. 1. St. Paul, MN: Greenhaven Press, 1984, 33–36.

A constitutional amendment on this issue would nullify the separation of church and state.

Taylor, Greg W. "Bittersweet Victory." *Maclean's*, July 24, 1989, 18.

Ontario Supreme Court decides *Dodd* case in her favor.

Tedesco, T. "A Division on Abortion." *Maclean's*, August 8, 1988, 10.

After lengthy debate in the Canadian House of Commons, a proposed replacement for the now-unconstitutional 19-year-old abortion law was rejected by both pro-choice and pro-life members.

"The Thread and the Cloth: Arguments in the Supreme Court's Abortion Case." *Newsweek*, May 8, 1989, 19.

Excerpts from the arguments in *Webster v. Reproductive Health Services*.

"Toward Moderation of Abortion Law." *America*, February 4, 1989, 75.

The upcoming Supreme Court hearing on a Missouri abortion law has the potential to moderate the Court's 1973 *Roe* ruling.

Turque, Bill. "Battle of the Barricades." *Newsweek*, April 3, 1989, 26.

Militant right-to-life demonstrations are putting a burden on taxpayers, who must pay for police costs and equipment.

Annotated Bibliography

Underwood, Nora. "Abortion Deadlock." *Maclean's*, March 20, 1989, 48.

The Supreme Court of Canada refused to rule on the existence of a fetus's constitutional rights, leaving the abortion issue deadlocked. The country has been without an abortion law since January 1988, when the high court ruled the law of the time unconstitutional.

Van Dusen, Lisa. "A Unanimous View." *Maclean's*, November 27, 1989, 16.

The Canadian Supreme Court unanimously ruled that fathers cannot block a woman's decision to have an abortion, arguing that fetuses are not recognized as persons under the several legal traditions of the Canadian provinces.

Villarosa, L. "Our Bodies, Their Laws." *Essence* 20 (October 1989): 24ff.

Discusses the *Webster* decision, the subsequent surge of state legislation, and the impact of these two developments on black women.

Wallace, Bruce. "Abortion in the Courts." *Maclean's*, August 7, 1989, 14–16.

A Quebec court upholds an injunction by a former boyfriend preventing a woman from getting an abortion.

Wallace, Bruce, and Lisa Van Dusen. "Abortion Agony." *Maclean's*, August 21, 1989, 12–14.

After a Canadian Supreme Court ruling, fetal vs. maternal rights is still an issue.

"Wattleton Raps Reagan's Cut of Overseas Abortion Funds." *Jet*, August 17, 1987, 9.

Focuses on Planned Parenthood president Faye Wattleton's testimony before Congress. Wattleton criticized a Reagan administration policy she felt would impact unfairly on family planning programs in developing countries.

Whitman, David. "When Pregnant Girls Face Mom and Dad." *U.S. News & World Report*, December 4, 1989, 25–26.

State laws requiring parental notification in teenage abortions have little impact on the number of abortions performed.

"Who'll Be Hurt by New Abortion Restrictions? All of Us." *Glamour* 87 (May 1989): 184.

Abortion restrictions that may be upheld by the Supreme Court in a forthcoming decision eventually would affect the ability of all women to receive an abortion.

Williams, Dennis A. "Fresh Battle on Abortion." *Newsweek*, February 6, 1978, 32.

Assesses the climate in the United States on the abortion issue, five years after *Roe*.

Wilson, Michele, and John Lynxwiler. "Abortion Clinic Violence as Terrorism." *Terrorism* 11 (1988): 263–273.

Examines reports of violence at abortion clinics between 1982 and 1987.

Worthington, Everett L., et al. "The Benefits of Legislation Requiring Parental Involvement Prior to Adolescent Abortion." *American Psychologist* 44 (December 1989): 1542–1545.

Discusses evidence supporting the theory that legislation mandating parental notification of adolescent pregnancy is beneficial to the adolescent and her family.

"Would Roe Go?" *Time*, September 21, 1987, 14–15.

Assesses the balance of power in the Supreme Court regarding abortion should Robert Bork became a Supreme Court justice.

Yates, Susanne, and Anita J. Pliner. "Judging Maturity in the Courts: The Massachusetts Consent Statute." *American Journal of Public Health* 78 (June 1988): 646–649.

A study of Case Summary Questionnaires filed by attorneys representing minors at judicial consent for abortion hearings in Massachusetts.

MEDICAL

"Abortion as a Contraceptive." *Newsweek*, June 13, 1988, 71.

A Guttmacher Institute study of 20 Western countries from 1982 to 1986 found that one-third of all U.S. pregnancies end in abortion. One reason may be that it is more difficult to obtain contraceptives in the United States than in smaller countries.

"Abortion Without Surgery? Using Prostaglandin F2alpha." *Time*, February 9, 1970, 39–40.

Encouraging early report on prostaglandin F2alpha for abortion between the 9th and 22nd week. European researchers suggest that it may eliminate the risks of surgical techniques.

"About-Face Over an Abortion Pill." *Time*, November 7, 1988, 103.

Under order from the French minister of health following public out-
cry, the manufacturers of RU 486 returned it to distribution. It is
about 95% effective and is said to have no harmful side effects.

Alberman, Eva, et al. "Congenital Abnormalities in Legal Abortions at
20 Weeks' Gestation or Later." *Lancet*, June 2, 1984, 1226–1228.

A study of late abortions suggests that if the age at which a fetus is
legally considered viable were to be lowered, the possibility of aborting fetuses diagnosed as congenitally abnormal would be seriously affected.

American Psychological Association. "Abortion Does Not Traumatize
Women." *Opposing Viewpoints SOURCES: Death/Dying, 1989 Annual*. San
Diego, CA: Greenhaven Press, 1989, 21–23.

Lack of consensus on the variables that define post-abortion stress has
resulted in inconclusive differentiation between PAS and other disorders. There is general consensus that abortion is stressful, but many
researchers also find that the main post-abortion reaction is relief.

Andrusko, Dave. "Aborted Fetal Tissue Should Not Be Used for Transplants." *Opposing Viewpoints SOURCES: Death/Dying, 1988 Annual*. San
Diego, CA: Greenhaven Press, 1988, 117–120.

The author argues that no resulting medical good can justify the use
of tissue from aborted human fetuses.

Beardsley, Tim. "Embryonic Questions." *Scientific American* 259 (December 1988): 27ff.

Discusses the varied opinions of National Institutes of Health consul-
tants to a panel studying the acceptability of fetal tissue research.

———. "UK Pharmaceuticals: A Matter of Life." *Nature*, March 31,
1983, 367.

The British antiabortion organization Life challenged the legality of a
postcoital hormone treatment (PCHT) on the grounds that the pill is
an abortifacient, not a contraceptive.

Berkowitz, Richard L., et al. "Selective Reduction of Multifetal Pregnancies in the First Trimester." *New England Journal of Medicine*, April
21, 1988, 1043–1047.

A report on selective abortion intended to reduce the number of fetuses in multifetal pregnancies. Discusses techniques and outcomes of
12 cases, and the medical and ethical issues.

"Bitter Pill." *The Nation*, November 21, 1988, 515–516.

A discussion of RU 486, the French "abortion pill," and its possible impact on the U.S. antiabortion movement were the pill certified for sale in the United States.

Bracken, Michael B., et al. "Hospitalization for Medical-Legal and Other Abortions in the United States, 1970–77." *American Journal of Public Health* 72 (January 1982): 32–37.

Assesses the impact of *Roe v. Wade* on rates of legal and illegal abortions between 1970 and 1977. The study found that illegal procedures were replaced by legal ones during the time studied.

Brahams, Diana. "Whether Pregnancy Should Be Terminated and a Contraceptive Device Fitted to a Girl Aged 15." *Lancet*, May 22, 1982, 1194.

Presents a British case where an unmarried minor mother requested an abortion over her parents' objections. The court interpreted the Abortion Act to permit the abortion in the minor's best interests. The article raises the possibility that the court acted in violation of the Sexual Offences Act.

———. "The Postcoital Pill and Intrauterine Device: Contraceptive or Abortifacient?" *Lancet*, May 7, 1983, 1039.

Some groups contend that, if conception is defined as fertilization, the IUD and postcoital pill may be illegal under British law.

———. "Assisted Reproduction and Selective Reduction of Pregnancy." *Lancet*, December 12, 1987, 1409–1410.

Multiple pregnancies are now most commonly caused by fertility drugs and in-vitro fertilization. Reduction of the number of fetuses increases the survival chances of those remaining. The article discusses the ethics of selective reduction and circumstances that would bring it within the terms of Britain's 1967 Abortion Act.

Brazzell, Jan F., and Alan C. Acock. "Influence of Attitudes, Significant Others, and Aspirations of How Adolescents Intend to Resolve a Premarital Pregnancy." *Journal of Marriage and the Family* 50 (May 1988): 413–425.

Explores behavioral factors affecting decisions made by sexually active adolescents when faced with a premarital pregnancy.

Bulfin, Matthew J. "Legal Abortion Has Not Improved Public Health." *Opposing Viewpoints SOURCES: Death/Dying*, vol. 1. St. Paul, MN: Greenhaven Press, 1984, 43–47.

Legalization has only made abortion more available. Abortions still may be performed for irresponsible reasons, or ineptly.

Cahill, Lisa Sowle. "Abortion Pill RU 486: Ethics, Rhetoric, and Social Practice." *Hastings Center Report* 17 (October/November 1987): 5–8.

The experimental "abortion pill," RU-486, discussed in terms of fetal viability. What distinguishes contraception from early, and late, abortion? What effect does language have on our social attitudes and practices?

Campbell, A. G. M., et al. "Don't Let My Baby Be Like Me." *Hastings Center Report* 18 (August/September 1988): 25–28.

A group of international commentators discusses genetic counseling, prenatal diagnosis, and selective abortion.

Campbell, Nancy B., et al. "Abortion in Adolescence." *Adolescence* 23 (Winter 1989): 813–823.

Studies psychological differences between women who had abortions in their late teens and those who had abortions after the age of 20.

Cates, Willard, Jr. "Abortion as a Treatment for Unwanted Pregnancy: The Number Two Sexually-Transmitted Condition." *Advances in Planned Parenthood* 12 (1978): 115–121.

If unwanted pregnancy were considered an STD, it would rank second only to gonorrhea. Includes statistics on unwanted pregnancy, treatment, and safety.

———. "Legal Abortion: The Public Health Record." *Science*, March 26, 1982, 1586–1590.

Legalized abortion in the United States has reduced the rate of death among women of childbearing age and improved the development of safer surgical procedures. Indicates concern about a possible increased risk of breast cancer or complications in subsequent pregnancies.

———. "Legal Abortion Has Improved Public Health." *Opposing Viewpoints SOURCES: Death/Dying*, vol. 1. St. Paul, MN: Greenhaven Press, 1984, 37–41.

Legalization has led to a decline in deaths and complications related to pregnancy and childbirth.

Chandani, Ambika. "Abortion: Medical Practitioners' Point of View." *Journal of Sociological Studies* 8 (January 1989): 158–167.

A study of the varying attitudes toward abortion held by physicians in India. Assesses the effect of gender and type of practice (private or institutional) on the physicians' attitudes and awareness.

Chedd, Graham. "Overview: Prenatal Screening." *Opposing Viewpoints SOURCES: Death/Dying*, vol. 1. St. Paul, MN: Greenhaven Press, 1984, 49–52.

Prenatal detection of genetic flaws confronts parents with the difficult decision of whether or not to abort.

Clark, Matt. "Battle Over the Abortion Pill." *Newsweek*, November 7, 1988, 10.

In ordering the reinstatement of "abortion pill" RU-486, the French health minister said it was "for reasons of public health" and "in the interests of women."

———. "Should Medicine Use the Unborn?" *Newsweek*, September 14, 1987, 62–63.

Discusses the controversy surrounding the transplanting of tissue from aborted fetuses to treat various medical disorders.

"Clinical Procedures." *The Nation*, September 12, 1987, 217.

Discusses proposed federal regulations prohibiting federally funded family planning clinics from recommending physicians who would perform abortions. This presents an economic double standard: Poor women who are clinic users would be denied access to abortion, while more affluent women, who would use private doctors, would have ready access to the procedure.

Colson, Charles W. "Abortion Clinic Obsolescence." *Christianity Today*, February 3, 1989, 72.

Discusses the possible impact of the abortifacient RU-486 on right-to-life strategies.

Culliton, Barbara J. "Panel Backs Fetal Tissue Research." *Science*, December 23, 1988, 1625–1626.

The Human Fetal Tissue Transplantation research panel submitted a final report in support of fetal tissue research, recommending certain restrictions to protect fetuses from exploitation.

———. "White House Wants Fetal Research Ban." *Science*, September 16, 1988, 1423.

The White House is considering a ban on research involving tissue from aborted fetuses. This would have a serious impact on research on AIDS, cancer, diabetes, Alzheimer's and Parkinson's diseases, and other disorders.

Dickson, D. "Fetal Tissue Transplants Win U.K. Approval." *Science,* August 4, 1989, 464–465.

The British health ministry announced guidelines permitting the use of aborted fetal tissue in disease treatment research.

"Discarding the Females." *World Press Review* 34 (March 1987): 5.

Reports on the trend in several countries, particularly in Asia, toward amniocentesis and subsequent abortion of female fetuses.

"Do-It-Yourself Abortion Is Hazardous to Your Health." *Newsweek,* July 17, 1989, 25.

Discusses the dangers of attempting to perform "self-help" abortions.

Edwards, Janice G., et al. "Elective Termination of Chromosomally Abnormal Pregnancies: Psychosocial Effects and Experience in Genetic Counseling." *Loss, Grief & Care* 3 (1989): 21–36.

A study of couples electing abortion following amniocentesis. Focuses on the effectiveness of genetic counseling and the aftereffects of the process.

Faden, Ruth R., et al. "Prenatal Screening and Pregnant Women's Attitudes Toward the Abortion of Defective Fetuses." *American Journal of Public Health* 77 (March 1987): 288–290.

A study of the attitudes of 490 pregnant women toward the abortion of defective fetuses. The overwhelming majority believed that such an abortion would be justified.

"Fetal Flaw." *The New Republic,* January 1, 1990, 7–8.

Discusses the ongoing governmental debate about the ban on federal funds for research involving tissue from aborted fetuses.

Firestein, Stephen K. "Special Features of Grief Reactions with Reproductive Catastrophe." *Loss, Grief & Care* 3 (1989): 37–45.

Discusses cases in which mothers suffered prolonged depression after either a premarital abortion or the loss of a genetically handicapped fetus.

"The Flesh Peddlers." *The Progressive* 51 (October 1987): 9–10.

The transplanting of fetal tissue to treat disease has caused concern among right-to-lifers, who fear that abortion may be viewed as somehow humanitarian and that fetuses will become a commodity.

Fletcher, Joseph. "A Fetus Is Not Entitled to Human Rights." *Opposing Viewpoints SOURCES: Death/Dying*, vol. 1. St. Paul, MN: Greenhaven Press, 1984, 15–18.

Argues that a fetus is not a viable human being until birth, so abortion is not murder.

Fraser, Laura. "Abortion Drug RU 486 Merits Research." *Opposing Viewpoints SOURCES: Human Sexuality, 1989 Annual*. San Diego, CA: Greenhaven Press, 1989, 89–92.

U.S. pharmaceutical companies should invest in research on abortion pill RU-486, the development of which would make abortions safer.

Georgia Nurses for Life. "Abortion Traumatizes Women." *Opposing Viewpoints SOURCES: Death/Dying, 1989 Annual*. San Diego, CA: Greenhaven Press, 1989, 19–20.

Post Abortion Syndrome, a type of Post Traumatic Stress Disorder, may affect as many as 55% of women who have abortions.

Glasgow, Richard D. "Abortion Drug RU 486 Does Not Merit Research." *Opposing Viewpoints SOURCES: Human Sexuality, 1989 Annual*. San Diego, CA: Greenhaven Press, 1989, 93–94.

Pharmaceutical companies should be forbidden from researching and marketing RU-486. The author views the drug as dangerous and immoral.

Glazer, Sarah. "Birth Control: The Choices Are Limited." *Editorial Research Reports* 2 (1988): 565–580.

Faced with possible lawsuits, most U.S. pharmaceutical companies have stopped developing new methods of birth control. American women therefore have fewer contraceptive options than women in many other countries.

"The Great Pill Flip-Flop." *U.S. News & World Report*, November 7, 1988, 12.

Although France's abortifacient RU-486 has been returned to the market by order of the French government and is expected to be approved in many countries, it is expected that strong antiabortion forces in the United States will block its sale here.

Greenhouse, Steven. "A New Pill, a Fierce Battle." *The New York Times Magazine*, February 12, 1989, 22–24ff.

A chronicle of the campaign for worldwide distribution of the French "abortion pill" RU-486.

Hall, Elizabeth. "When Does Life Begin?" *Psychology Today* 23 (September 1989): 42–46.

Interview with embryologist Clifford Grobstein.

Hobbins, John C. "Selective Reduction—A Perinatal Necessity?" *New England Journal of Medicine*, April 21, 1988, 1062–1063.

Discusses selective abortion to reduce the number of fetuses in multi-fetal pregnancies. Describes the risks of fetal and maternal morbidity and mortality. Discusses ethical, legal, and clinical issues.

Holden, C. "Koop Finds Abortion Evidence 'Inconclusive.' " *Science*, February 10, 1989, 730–731.

The Surgeon General's initial response to a survey on the effects of abortion on women's health was to forbid its release, citing flaws in the research methodology.

Holder, Angela R., and Mary Sue Henifin. "Selective Termination of Pregnancy." *Hastings Center Report* 18 (February/March 1988): 21–22.

In commentaries on a case study, the authors discuss alternatives for a patient who has requested that two fetuses in a triple pregnancy be terminated.

Koop, C. Everett. "Abortion's Effects on Women Are Unknown." *Opposing Viewpoints SOURCES: Death/Dying, 1989 Annual*. San Diego, CA: Greenhaven Press, 1989, 25–26.

Too many variables are involved to determine conclusively the effect of abortion on women.

Koshland, D. E., Jr. "Fetal Tissue in Research." *Science*, September 30, 1988, 1733.

Focuses on the moral and social issues that scientists should be sensitive to in dealing with the controversy over the research uses of tissue from aborted fetuses.

Krance, M. "When Prenatal Tests Bring Bad News." *American Health* 8 (July/August 1989): 11–12.

Few support groups exist for parents who decide to abort in cases where the fetus is genetically defective.

Lawton, K. A. "Hassle-free Abortion." *Christianity Today*, December 9, 1988, 58–59ff.

Discusses debate in the United States over the French abortifacient RU-486.

Levine, Joe. "Help from the Unborn." *Time*, January 12, 1987, 62.

Discusses the growing use and importance of fetal cell transplants. Reviews ethical arguments against the use of material from aborted fetuses.

Levine, Robert J. "Fetal Research: The Underlying Issue." *Scientific American* 261 (August 1989): 112.

Emphasizes the importance of continued government support for fetal research. Attempts to allay the concerns of opponents who fear that the research will encourage abortions.

MacFarquhar, Emily. "The Case of the Reluctant Drug Maker." *U.S. News & World Report*, January 23, 1989, 54.

Controversy leads the makers of RU-486 to limit marketing.

McGowan, Jo. "In India, They Abort Females." *Newsweek*, January 30, 1989, 12.

Is abortion "selective" only if sex selection is the issue?

Mahowald, Mary B., et al. "Aborted Fetal Tissue Should Be Used for Transplants." *Opposing Viewpoints SOURCES: Death/Dying, 1988 Annual.* San Diego, CA: Greenhaven Press, 1988, 113–116.

If an aborted fetus is dead or not viable, transplanting tissue from it is morally legitimate, because fetal tissue can cure diseases in viable organisms.

"Misuse of Amniocentesis." *Lancet*, April 9, 1983, 812–813.

Sex determination by amniocentesis and selective abortion of female fetuses are widely practiced in India despite a government ban and the protests of women's groups. Many Indian gynecologists view the practice as a balance between the need for population control and the desire for sons.

"NAS Enters Human Life Bill Debate." *Science News*, May 9, 1981, 293.

The National Academy of Sciences passed a resolution, to be sent to the Senate subcommittees hearing testimony on the Helms "human life" bill, stating that the bill raises a "question to which science can provide no answer."

Neff, D. "The Human Pesticide." *Christianity Today*, December 9, 1988, 16–17.

Discusses moral issues surrounding the development of the abortion pill RU-486.

———. "Abortion-Rights Boomerang." *Christianity Today*, March 17, 1989, 16.

Discusses the issue of sex-selection abortions, which usually target female fetuses.

Neuhaus, R. "Fetal Attraction." *National Review*, December 8, 1989, 12–13.

Recommendations on the use of fetal tissue for research imply certain judgments about fetal legal status.

"NIH Approves Fetal Tissue Experiments." *Christianity Today*, October 21, 1988, 42.

A National Institutes of Health (NIH) advisory committee decided that the use of tissue from aborted fetuses for research is acceptable. The committee would not take a stand on the morality of abortion, insisting that that issue should remain separate from the issue of tissue experimentation.

Orenstein, P. "The Use of Aborted Fetal Tissue in Medical Research Is as Controversial as Abortion Itself." *Vogue* 179 (October 1989): 298ff.

Tissue from aborted fetuses has the potential to be useful in treatments for a number of diseases. Antiabortion activists fear that its use will lead to fetal exploitation.

Palca, J. "The Pill of Choice?" *Science*, September 22, 1989, 1319–1323.

A cover story on the "abortion pill" RU-486.

The Pearson Institute and Scott Keller, "Pro-Life Clinics Are Not Deceptive." *Opposing Viewpoints SOURCES: Human Sexuality, 1989 Annual*. San Diego, CA: Greenhaven Press, 1989, 81–84.

Right-to-life proponents who set up counseling clinics are saving unborn lives by educating women on alternatives to, and risks of, abortion.

Post, S. "Fetal Tissue: A 'Gift' for Transplanting?" *The Christian Century*, December 7, 1989, 1119–1120.

Discusses antiabortionists' protests against the transplanting of tissue from aborted fetuses.

Revolutionary Worker. "Legal Abortion Prevents Injury and Death." *Opposing Viewpoints SOURCES: Death/Dying, 1989 Annual*. San Diego, CA: Greenhaven Press, 1989, 13–16.

Legalized abortion has dramatically lessened the rate of abortion-related complications and deaths.

Roe, Kathleen M. "Private Troubles and Public Issues: Providing Abortion Amid Competing Definitions." *Social Science and Medicine* 29 (1989): 1191–1198.

Examines the effect of abortion workers' experiences on the formulation of definitions of abortion—for example, as part of a job, as a woman's right, as murder—and in turn the effect of such definitions on the attitude of each worker toward providing quality care.

Ruddick, William, and William Wilcox. "Operating on the Fetus." *Hastings Center Report* 12 (October 1982): 10–14.

Analyzes fetal surgery in terms of implications for the fetus's moral status, relevance to the abortion debate, and effect on the physician-patient relationship.

Sandmaier, Marian. "Is There Angst After Abortion?" *Mademoiselle* 95 (July 1989): 94ff.

Discusses the results of research that found that women's most frequent post-abortion emotions include relief and happiness. Post-abortion trauma is usually suffered by women whose pregnancies ended under stress.

Smith, E. T. "Abortion: A Vocal Minority Has Drugmakers Running Scared." *Business Week*, November 14, 1988, 59.

Vocal opposition to the French abortifacient RU-486 caused the manufacturer to take the drug off the market. The French health minister ordered it reinstated.

Smith, R. Jeffrey. "Human Life Bill Arouses More Opposition." *Science*, June 19, 1981, 1372–1373.

A petition signed by nearly 1,300 scientists and researchers from Boston area universities asserts that the claim in the "human life" bill (S. 158) that protected human life begins at conception is "a misuse and a misunderstanding" of science.

Suh, Mary. "RU Detour." *Ms.* 17 (January/February 1989): 135–136.

Discusses obstacles barring France's abortion pill, RU-486, from the U.S. market.

Sun, Marjorie. "Amniocentesis: Be Prepared." *Science*, June 12, 1981, 1253.

Assistant Secretary of Health Edward N. Brandt, Jr., favors abortion only if the mother's life is endangered, even if the pregnancy resulted from rape or incest or if amniocentesis indicates that the fetus has severe birth defects.

Thompson, Dick. "A Setback for Pro-Life Forces." *Time*, March 27, 1989, 82.

Several research reports suggest that little to no psychological damage is inflicted on women by abortion.

Tisdale, Sallie. "We Do Abortions Here: A Nurse's Story." *Harper's* 275 (October 1987): 66–70.

A former nurse in an abortion clinic describes the procedure and the reactions of patients, concluding that abortion is, paradoxically, both kind and cruel.

Toufexis, Anastasia. "Abortions Without Doctors." *Time*, August 28, 1989, 66.

Menstrual extraction, a controversial "self-help" abortion method, re-surfaces.

Weiss, R. "Panel Recommends Resuming Fetal Studies." *Science News*, September 24, 1988, 197.

A National Institutes of Health advisory panel declares that the use of cells and tissue from aborted fetuses in research is "biomedically acceptable." Fetal cell transplantation may be valuable in treating disorders such as Parkinson's disease and diabetes.

———. "Forbidding Fruits of Fetal-Cell Research." *Science News*, November 5, 1988, 296–298.

Presents the controversy over the use of fetal tissue to treat a number of disorders, such as diabetes.

"When Life Begins: Embryo Research." *Current* 292 (May 1987): 9–10.

Discusses the complex questions of abortions and embryo research. Suggests possible ceiling embryo age, after which research could not be performed.

Wickens, B. "Abortion Warfare." *Maclean's*, November 7, 1988, 51.

The Canadian viewpoint on the RU-486 controversy in France.

Wilke, J. C. "Legal Abortion Does Not Prevent Injury and Death." *Opposing Viewpoints SOURCES: Death/Dying, 1989 Annual.* San Diego, CA: Greenhaven Press, 1989, 17–18.

The dramatic decrease in maternal deaths from abortions came when penicillin was introduced, not when abortion was legalized.

Wong, Pamela Pearson. "Attracting Clients and Controversy." *Christianity Today,* September 18, 1987, 32–33.

Centers urging alternatives to abortion are increasing in number. Prochoice groups claim that such centers imply that they perform abortions, then pressure clients with pro-life "propaganda."

GOVERNMENT DOCUMENTS

Kline, Jennie. *The Role of Spontaneous Abortion Studies in Environmental Research.* Research Triangle Park, NC: Health Effects Research Laboratory, 1985.

Discusses the incorporation of spontaneous abortion studies in environmental research.

Mosher, William D., and William F. Pratt. *Fecundity, Infertility, and Reproductive Health in the United States, 1982.* Hyattsville, MD: National Center for Health Statistics, 1987.

Informational pamphlet on patterns of reproductive health in the United States.

Thornburgh, Dick, et al. *In the Supreme Court of the United States, October Term, 1985; Richard Thornburgh, et al., Appellants v. American College of Obstetricians and Gynecologists, et al.; Brief for the United States as Amicus Curiae in Support of Appellants.* Washington, DC: U.S. Supreme Court, 1985.

Text of the friend-of-the-court brief filed by the Justice Department in a major abortion case before the Supreme Court.

U.S. Congress. House. Committee on Government Operations. *The Federal Role in Determining the Medical and Psychological Impact of Abortion on Women: Tenth Report.* Washington, DC: U.S. Government Printing Office, 1988.

Research into the impact of abortion on women.

Annotated Bibliography

U.S. Congress. House. Committee on Government Operations. *Medical and Psychological Impact of Abortion: Hearing Before the Human Resources and Intergovernmental Relations Subcommittee of the Committee on Government Operations, House of Representatives.* 101st Cong., 1st sess., March 18, 1980. Washington, DC: U.S. Government Printing Office, 1980.

Panel's investigation into the medical and psychological toll of abortion on women.

U.S. Congress. House. Committee on the Judiciary. *Abortion Clinic Violence: Oversight Hearings Before the Subcommittee on Civil and Constitutional Rights of the Committee on the Judiciary, House of Representatives.* 99th Cong., 1st and 2d sess. Washington, DC: U.S. Government Printing Office, 1987.

Hearings examine organized violence directed against abortion clinics.

U.S. Congress. House. Committee on the Judiciary. *Proposed Constitutional Amendments on Abortion: Hearings Before the Subcommittee on Civil and Constitutional Rights of the Committee on the Judiciary, House of Representatives.* 94th Cong., 2nd sess. Washington, DC: U.S. Government Printing Office, 1976.

Hearings on proposed constitutional amendments to ban abortion.

U.S. Congress. Senate. Committee on the Judiciary. *Abortion Funding Restriction Act: Hearings Before the Subcommittee on the Constitution of the Committee on the Judiciary, United States Senate.* 99th Cong., 1st sess., April 2 and July 22, 1985. Washington, DC: U.S. Government Printing Office, 1986.

Considers proposed legislation to restrict federal abortion funding.

U.S. Congress. Senate. Committee on the Judiciary. *Abortion: Hearings Before the Subcommittee on Constitutional Amendments of the Committee on the Judiciary, United States Senate,* 93d Cong., 2nd sess., on S.J. Res. 110 and S.J. Res. 130. Washington, DC: U.S. Government Printing Office, 1974.

The Senate subcommittee considers proposed constitutional amendments to prohibit abortion.

U.S. Congress. Senate. Committee on the Judiciary. *Constitutional Amendments Relating to Abortion: Hearings Before the Subcommittee on the Constitution of the Committee on the Judiciary, United States Senate,* 97th Cong., 1st sess. Washington, DC: U.S. Government Printing Office, 1983.

Hearings on proposed anti-abortion amendments to the Constitution.

U.S. Congress. Senate. Committee on the Judiciary. *Fetal Pain: Hearing Before the Subcommittee on the Constitution of the Committee on the Judiciary, United States Senate*, 99th Cong., 1st sess., May 21, 1985.

Hearing considers the medical evidence concerning fetal pain during an abortion.

U.S. Congress. Senate. Committee on the Judiciary. *The Human Life Bill: Hearings Before the Subcommittee on Separation of Powers of the Committee on the Judiciary, United States Senate*, 97th Cong., 1st sess. April 23, 24, May 20, 21, June 1, 10, 12, and 18. Washington, DC: U.S. Government Printing Office, 1982.

A Senate Judiciary subcommittee considers a proposed human life bill.

U.S. Congress. Senate. Committee on the Judiciary. *The Human Life Bill S. 158: Report, Together with Additional and Minority Views to the Committee on the Judiciary, United States Senate*. Washington, DC: U.S. Government Printing Office, 1981.

The subcommittee's report to the full committee on draft Human Life legislation.

U.S. Congress. Senate. Committee on the Judiciary. *Human Life Federalism Amendment: Report of the Committee on the Judiciary, United States Senate, on Senate Joint Resolution 3*. Washington, DC: U.S. Government Printing Office, 1983.

Report of the Senate Committee examining a proposed human life amendment.

U.S. Congress. Senate. Committee on the Judiciary. *Human Life Federalism Amendment: Report Together with Additional and Minority Views of the Committee on the Judiciary, United States Senate on S.J. Res. 110*. Washington, DC: U.S. Government Printing Office, 1982.

The Committee report transmitting the Human Life Federalism Amendment to the full House.

U.S. Congress. Senate. Committee on the Judiciary. *Legal Ramifications of the Human Life Amendment: Hearings Before the Subcommittee on the Constitution of the Committee on the Judiciary, United States Senate*. 98th Cong., 1st sess., February 28 and March 7, 1983. Washington, DC: U.S. Government Printing Office, 1983.

The Senate panel weighs the projected legal impact of the Human Life Amendment.

U.S. Congress. Senate. Committee on Labor and Human Resources. *Oversight of Family Planning Programs, 1981: Hearing Before the Committee on Labor and Human Resources, United States Senate.* 97th Cong. 1st sess., March 31, 1981. Washington, DC: U.S. Government Printing Office, 1981.

Oversight hearings on the federal government's role in birth control, abortion referral, and sex education programs.

U.S. General Accounting Office. *Restrictions on Abortion and Lobbying Activities in Family Planning Programs Need Clarification: Report.* Washington, DC: U.S. Government Printing Office, 1982.

A report on the need to lay out clear guidelines on family planning activities.

U.S. Health Services Administration. *Family Planning, Contraception, Voluntary Sterilization, and Abortion: An Analysis of Laws and Policies in the United States, Each State and Jurisdiction (as of October 1, 1976 with 1978 Addenda).* Rockville, MD: Bureau of Community Health Services, 1978.

A report analyzing U.S. laws and policies on family planning, contraception, and abortion.

U.S. President George Bush. *Veto of H.R. 3810: Message from the President of the United States Transmitting His Veto of H.R. 3810. A Bill Making Appropriations for the Government of the District of Columbia . . . for the Fiscal Year Ending September 30, 1990, and for Other Purposes.* Washington, DC: U.S. Government Printing Office, 1989.

Message of President Bush's veto of federal funding for abortions in the District of Columbia.

U.S. President Ronald Reagan. *President's Pro Life Act of 1988: Message from the President of the United States Transmitting a Draft of Proposed Legislation to Prohibit the Use of Federal Funds for Abortions Except Where the Life of the Mother Would be Endangered.* Washington, DC: U.S. Government Printing Office, 1988.

President Reagan's message highlights the key points of a bill to place restrictions on federal funding of abortion.

BROCHURES AND PAMPHLETS

Abortion After Twelve Weeks. Truth About Abortion Fact Sheet Series. Washington, DC: National Abortion Federation, 1987, 2p.

Discusses the reasons for 2nd-trimester abortions and the risks involved.

Abortion: A Personal and Social Dilemma. Weymouth, MA: Life Skills Education, 1989, n.p.

A general overview, discussing key legal, moral, and ethical issues.

Abortion in the United States. New York: Alan Guttmacher Institute, 1989, 2p.

Statistics on women and abortion, including data on public funding, safety, and teenagers.

The Abortion Issue in the Political Process. Washington, DC: Catholics for a Free Choice, n.d., n.p.

Briefing for those who deal with abortion as a political issue.

Abortion: Public Opinion. Washington, DC: National Right to Life, 1987, n.p.

Assesses data from various polls on abortion.

Abortion: Some Medical Facts. Washington, DC: National Right to Life, 1987, n.p.

From a pro-life stance, defines abortion and explains procedures. Discusses physical and psychological effects of abortion.

Abortion: The Hard Cases. Washington, DC: National Right to Life, 1987, n.p.

A discussion of pregnancies that result from rape and incest, or entail genetic handicaps. Pro-life; advises against abortion.

Adamek, Raymond J. *Abortion and Public Opinion in the United States.* Washington, DC: National Right to Life, 1986. 16p.

A pro-life evaluation of the results of certain polls on abortion. Argues that Americans are less in favor of abortion than polls indicate.

After Abortion. Milwaukee: Pregnancy Aftermath Helpline, n.d. 1p.

A letter offering sympathy to a woman who has had an abortion.

Andrusko, Dave, ed. *A Passion for Justice: A Pro-life Review of 1987 and a Look Ahead to 1988.* Washington, DC: National Right to Life, 1988. 160p.

Papers on pro-life political action.

Bergel, Gary. *When You Were Formed in Secret/Abortion in America*. Washington, DC: National Right to Life, 1986, n.p.

A double booklet, explaining fetal growth on one side, abortion on the other. With antiabortion information.

Burtchaell, James Tunstead. *The Limits of the Law: Reflections on the Abortion Debate*. Chicago: Americans United for Life, 1987, 16p.

Examines early Judeo-Christian attitudes toward abortion. Evaluates court rulings on abortion, from a pro-life stance.

Can Abortion Be Justified? St. Paul, MN: Greenhaven Press, 1986, 37p.

Sets out opposing viewpoints about the economic, medical, and social factors cited to justify abortion. This is Chapter 4 from *Abortion: Opposing Viewpoints*, issued separately.

Celebrating Roe v. Wade: Dramatic Improvements in American Health. Washington, DC: National Abortion Federation, 1989, 12p.

Discusses legalized abortion's benefits to public health. Includes synopses of major U.S. Supreme Court decisions on abortion between 1973 and 1988.

A Church Divided: Catholics' Attitudes About Family Planning, Abortion and Teenage Sexuality. A Bishops Watch Report. Washington, DC: Catholics for a Free Choice, n.d., n.p.

Analyzes recent studies of Catholics' attitudes and practices.

The Church in a Democracy: Who Governs? Abortion in Good Faith Series. Washington, DC: Catholics for a Free Choice, n.d., n.p.

Examines the role of religion in government; discusses the responsibilities of Catholics.

Civil Rights Held Hostage: The United States Catholic Conference and the Civil Rights Restoration Act. A Bishops Watch Report. Washington, DC: Catholics for a Free Choice, n.d., n.p.

Discusses the efforts of Catholic bishops opposed to the Civil Rights Restoration Act. Disagrees with claim that the act should be amended to protect Catholic higher education.

A Consumer's Alert to Deception, Harassment and Medical Malpractice. New York: Planned Parenthood Federation of America, 1989, 8p.

Helps prospective clients distinguish between pregnancy counseling centers that will provide a range of options and those that are antiabortion advocates.

Cowan, Belita. *Women's Health Care: Resources, Writings, Bibliographies.* Ann Arbor, MI: Anshen, 1977, 52p.

Resource guide covering topics such as malpractice, childbirth, abortion, birth control, alcoholism, psychotherapy and rape prevention. Uses a mixed-format presentation of essays, questions and answers, recommended articles, films, and organizations.

Economics of Abortion. Truth About Abortion Fact Sheet Series. Washington, DC: National Abortion Federation, 1989, 2p.

Discusses funding for abortions. Present state-by-state circumstances in which Medicaid will finance abortion.

Eight Arguments for Keeping Government Out of Your Family's Life. New York: Planned Parenthood Federation of America, 1989, 8p.

Presents the view that parental notification laws discriminate against teenagers.

Erlien, Marla, et al. *More Than a Choice: Women Talk About Abortion.* Boston: Abortion Action Coalition, 1979, 24p.

A general pamphlet, covering economics, alternatives to abortion. Discusses sexuality and methods of birth control. Includes personal accounts.

Five Ways to Prevent Abortion—And One Way That Won't. New York: Planned Parenthood Federation of America, 1989, 12p.

Discusses reducing the number of abortions by reducing unintended pregnancies. Claims making abortion illegal will not prevent it.

The History of Abortion in the Catholic Church. Abortion in Good Faith Series. Washington, DC: Catholics for a Free Choice, n.d. n.p.

The history of Catholic thought on abortion and its relation to doctrines on ensoulment.

Horan, Dennis J., et al. *Two Ships Passing in the Night: An Interpretavist Review of the White-Stevens Colloquy on Roe v. Wade.* Chicago: Americans United for Life, 1987, 78p.

Article with a pro-life viewpoint.

Hospitals Have Essential Role in Abortion Services. Washington, DC: National Abortion Federation, 1989, 2p.

In response to *Webster*, an advocacy bulletin on the need to prevent restrictions on hospital abortions.

Annotated Bibliography

I Support You But I Can't Sign My Name. Abortion in Good Faith Series. Washington, DC: Catholics for a Free Choice, 1988, 6p.

Contains interviews with a priest, teacher, physician and nurse who have faced the abortion issue in their personal or professional lives.

Is Abortion Immoral? St. Paul, MN: Greenhaven Press, 1986, 23p.

Examines opposing viewpoints on the morality of abortion. This is Chapter 3 from *Abortion: Opposing Viewpoints,* issued separately.

Kleinman, Ronald L. *Induced Abortion.* London: International Planned Parenthood Federation, 1972, 38p.

Report by IPPF's Panel of Experts on Abortion. Includes definitions, abortion and family planning, aftereffects, and abortion legislation.

Klitsch, Michael. *RU 486: the Science and the Politics.* New York: Alan Guttmacher Institute, 1989, 21p.

Discusses the background of, and controversy surrounding, the "abortion pill."

Legal Abortion Is Safe Abortion. Washington, DC: National Abortion Federation, 1989, 2p.

An advocacy bulletin on reasons to keep abortion legal and safe.

Maguire, Daniel C. *Reflections of a Catholic Theologian on Visiting an Abortion Clinic.* Washington, DC: Catholics for a Free Choice, 1984, 12p.

Through encounters with clinic staff, patients, picketers, and embryos, the author reaches certain conclusions about Catholic theology and abortion.

Maguire, Marjorie J., and Daniel C. Maguire. *Abortion: A Guide to Making Ethical Choices.* Washington, DC: Catholics for a Free Choice, 1983, 44p.

Question-and-answer presentation of abortion-related issues from a Catholic viewpoint. Intended to help the woman develop the faculty to make an ethical decision.

"My Conscience Speaks": Catholic Women Discuss Their Abortions. Abortion in Good Faith Series. Washington, DC: Catholics for a Free Choice, 1981, 48p.

Eight Catholic women, from a range of ethnic backgrounds, discuss their abortion experiences, legal and illegal.

Nine Reasons Why Abortions Are Legal. New York: Planned Parenthood Federation of America, 198, 12p.

Reasons why abortion should be legal, safe, and accessible. Counters antichoice arguments.

Parental Notice Laws: Their Catastrophic Impact on Teenagers' Right to Abortion. New York: American Civil Liberties Union, 1986. 38p.

Information on the impact of parental notice laws and the problems resulting from denying teenagers their constitutional right to choose abortion.

Planned Parenthood Federation of America. *A Consumer's Alert to Deception, Harassment and Medical Malpractice.* New York: Planned Parenthood, 1987. n.p.

A flyer noting characteristics of anti-abortion counseling centers. Tells how to find professional pregnancy counseling centers.

Point Counterpoint. Washington, DC: Religious Coalition for Abortion Rights, 1985, 26p.

Statistics and other information on such topics as the risks of abortion, the failure of contraceptive methods, fetal development, and amniocentesis.

Preserving the Right to Choose: How to Cope with Violence and Disruption at Abortion Clinics. New York: American Civil Liberties Union, 1986. 52p.

Advice to abortion clinic workers and clients on coping with all forms of protest at clinics. Useful to antiabortion activists wanting to protest under free-speech protection.

Public Support for Abortion. Truth About Abortion Fact Sheet Series. Washington, DC: National Abortion Federation, 1989. 2p.

Discusses the results of public opinion surveys showing strong public support for legal abortion in a number of situations.

Question for the Libertarian Party on Abortion. Wheaton, MD: Libertarians for Life, 1987, n.p.

Should the Libertarian Party condone or condemn abortion? Should the state permit or prohibit abortion? Answers these and other questions.

The Road to Reversing Roe. v. Wade: Facing the Challenges of 1988. Washington, DC: National Right to Life, 1988. 28p.

Assesses pro-life efforts to overturn the landmark abortion rights ruling.

Safety of Abortion. Truth About Abortion Fact Sheet Series. Washington, DC: National Abortion Federation, 1988. 2p.

Discusses the dangers of illegal abortion, the possible complications from 1st- and mid-trimester abortions, and ways to prevent complications.

Scott, Michael J. *Abortion: The Facts.* London: Darton, Longman and Todd, 1973. 62p.

An antiabortion discussion of Britain's 1967 Abortion Act. Reviews fetal development and psychological, medical, and socioeconomic aspects.

Sedgwick, Timothy F, *Abortion: Morality and the Law.* Cincinnati: Forward Movement Publications, 1982. 14p.

A discussion of moral and legal issues, with attention to the stance of the Episcopal Church.

Should Abortion Remain a Personal Choice? St. Paul, MN: Greenhaven Press, 1986. 30p.

Presents viewpoints to be considered when choosing an abortion, including its status as a constitutional right; a woman's personal choice; and a man's involvement in the decision making. This is Chapter 2 from *Abortion: Opposing Viewpoints*, issued separately.

Should Abortion Remain Legal? St. Paul, MN: Greenhaven Press, 1986. 22p.

Outlines views on whether or not legal abortion is harmful to the public health and whether or not legal abortion is an asset to the women's rights cause. This is Chapter 5 from *Abortion: Opposing Viewpoints*, issued separately.

Teenage Women, Abortion, and the Law. Truth About Abortion Fact Sheet Series. Washington, DC: National Abortion Federation, 1988. 2p.

Discusses laws restricting teenagers' access to abortion, showing the status by state.

Walker, John. *Abortion and the Question of the Person.* Wheaton, MD: Libertarians for Life, n.d. n.p.

A leaflet giving the Libertarian opinion on when the fetus becomes a person.

———. *Children's Rights Versus Murray Rothbard's The Ethics of Liberty.* Wheaton, MD: Libertarians for Life, n.d. 2p.

Evaluates discussion in Dr. Rothbard's book on abortion and children's rights.

———. *Platform Planks and Principles: Where Do You Stand on Abortion?* Wheaton, MD: Libertarians for Life, n.d., n.p.

Description of the Libertarian Party platform on abortion.

We Affirm. Washington, DC: Religious Coalition for Abortion Rights, 1989. 8p.

A compilation of statements in support of abortion by faith groups and religious organizations.

We Are the Mainstream. Abortion in Good Faith Series. Washington, DC: Catholics for a Free Choice.

Examines dissent in the Catholic church through history; the traditional, hierarchical reaction; and eventual changes.

What Is Abortion? Truth About Abortion Fact Sheet Series. Washington, DC: National Abortion Federation, 1989. 2p.

Defines abortion and methods used in 1st- and mid-trimester procedures.

You Are Not Alone. Washington, DC: Catholics for a Free Choice.

Addressed to Catholic women making a decision about abortion, this pamphlet highlights the church's teaching on abortion, Catholic abortion statistics, and discussion by feminist liberation theologian Diann Neu.

AUDIOVISUAL MATERIALS

Abortion (First Trimester). Medfact Inc., 1977. 14 min. Video.

An objective look at vacuum abortion and its possible physical complications.

Abortion Clinic. Frontline Series. Fanlight Productions, 1983. 52 min. Video.

An Emmy-award-winning documentary about an abortion clinic in Chester, Pennsylvania. Interviews with antiabortion protestors, medical staff, and patients' friends and relatives. Includes scenes of a 1st-trimester (suction) abortion. Narrated by Jessica Savitch.

Abortion Clinic. PBS Video, 1984. 58 min. Video.

Examines abortion clinics and their clients.

Abortion: Does Anyone Really Care? Catholic Television Network of Chicago, 1977. 56 min. Video.

Theologian and writer Father John Powell examines abortion-related issues and the right-to-life movement.

The Abortion Experience. SAP Productions, 1985. 28 min. Video.

Discusses the physical and emotional aspects—both negative and positive. Includes a segment in which a physician explains the techniques and equipment used in early (suction) abortion and discusses possible complications. The film does not cover mid- or late-trimester techniques or problems.

Abortion in Adolescence. Emory Medical Television Network, 1983. 58 min. Video.

Explains the Center for Disease Control's statistics on adolescent pregnancies and abortions in the United States.

Abortion: Listen to the Woman. Planned Parenthood of Los Angeles, 1985. 50 min. Audiocassette.

Daniel Maguire discusses the factors women consider before making an abortion decision. Suggests that society should address the causes for unwanted pregnancies, such as sexism and poverty.

Abortion: Stories from North and South. The Cinema Guild, 1984. 55 min. Video.

Discusses the practice of abortion and its social, cultural, racial and religious impact around the world.

Abortion: The Divisive Issue. Video Free America, 1977. 28 min. Video.

Discusses the issue in interviews with pro-choice and pro-life leaders.

Conceived in Liberty. Keep the Faith, Inc., 1979, 59 min. Video.

A pro-life panel discussion of the graphic antiabortion film *The Silent Scream.*

Eclipse of Reason. Bernardell, Inc., 1987, 27 min. Video.

Update of *The Silent Scream* (1977). Focuses on mid- and late-trimester abortions. Shows a late abortion performed by D & E technique. Commentary by physicians opposed to abortion and two women who had abortions, each with complications.

Four Young Women. Leonard C. Schwartz. Variation Films. Perennial Education Inc., 1973. 20 min. Video.

Documentary describing four women and their widely different reasons for choosing abortion.

Holy Terror. Victoria Schultz. Cinema Guild, 1986. 58 min. Video.

Discusses the religious and political activities of the New Right, particularly in the rise of violent antiabortion protests.

"I Never Thought It Would Be Like This": Teenagers Speak Out About Being Pregnant/Being Parents. Guidance Associates, 1988. 30 min. Video.

Uses the stories of three teenagers to illustrate the social, emotional, and physical consequences of unwanted pregnancy. Highlights information that may help viewers prevent accidental pregnancy, such as the effectiveness and safety of various contraceptive methods. Suggests sources of assistance such as hot lines, clinics, and counselors.

It Happens to Us. Amalie Rothschild. New Day Films, 1974. 30 min. Video.

Women from a range of socioeconomic backgrounds discuss legal and illegal abortions.

No Alibis. Bridgestone Production Group, 1988. 30 min. Video.

A dramatic examination of fetal rights from a religious perspective.

Personal Decisions. Planned Parenthood Federation of America, Inc. The Cinema Guild, 1985. 28 min. Video.

Women of varying ages and socioeconomic backgrounds discuss the abortion decision. Dr. Kenneth Edelin emphasizes the dangers and indignities of illegal abortions. Parents and partners of women who have made the decision discuss their feelings.

Physiology of Miscarriage and Abortion. WXYZ Detroit. CRM/McGraw-Hill Films, 1977. 28 min. Video.

Discusses spontaneous and induced abortion. Part of the "Inner Woman" series.

Planned Parenthood Responses to the "Silent Scream." Planned Parenthood of Seattle and Kings County, Washington, 1985. 15 min. Video.

Physicians criticize five inaccuracies in *The Silent Scream:* altering the film speed; misstating the age of the fetus in the film; using larger models than those the age of the fetus; presenting sophisticated ultrasound images that are not readily understood; and attributing feelings and actions to the fetus that are beyond its limited brain capacity.

Silent Scream. American Portrait Films, 1977. 30 min. Video.

Bernard Nathanson, M. D., narrates this emotional antiabortion film showing ultrasound imaging of a 12-week fetus and several abortions. (See also *Planned Parenthood Response to the Silent Scream* and *Eclipse of Reason,* the 1987 update of this film.)

So Many Voices: A Look at Abortion in America. NARAL. Phoenix/BFA Films, 1982. 30 min. Video.

Examines the abortion debate in the United States. People on both sides of the issue are interviewed. Hosted by Ed Asner and Tammy Grimes.

The Waiting Room. Carousel Film and Video, 1981. 29 min. Video

Discusses both sides of the abortion debate, exploring family, religious, political, and medical issues.

What's the Common Ground on Abortion? Search for Common Ground, 1990. 30 min. Video.

A discussion of the issue by pro-life and pro-choice leaders. Focuses on efforts to find commonality despite opposing views.

Women Who Didn't Have an Abortion. Martha Stuart Communications, 1977. 29 min. Video.

A discussion of arguments against abortion, exploring the key moral, social, religious, and psychological issues.

Women Who Have Had an Abortion. Martha Stuart Communications, 1979. 29 min. Video.

A discussion of women's experiences with both illegal and legal abortions.

CHAPTER 7

───────── ■ ─────────

ORGANIZATIONS AND ASSOCIATIONS

The intense debate over abortion has resulted in the formation of numerous national, state, and local advocacy groups. Their activities range from lobbying and public awareness campaigns to picketing and other protest actions. This chapter is a listing of organizations that are a source of information and educational materials on abortion. These organizations include government agencies, professional associations, foundations, and private groups. National organizations are accompanied by a brief synopsis of their involvement in abortion issues and the types of information they make available. Similar abstracts are not provided at the state and local level as the services and activities of these organizations are subject to frequent change.

One of the leading pro-life advocacy and educational organizations, the National Abortion Rights Action League, prefers that the addresses and phone numbers of its state affiliates not be published. Readers seeking information from a state chapter are asked first to contact the national organization.

NATIONAL

Abortion Rights Mobilization
175 5th Avenue, Suite 814
New York, NY 10010
(212) 673-2040

Advocacy group for a woman's legal right to abortion. Source of information on pro-choice positions.

AD HOC Committee in Defense of Life
1187 National Press Bldg
529 14th Street N.W.
Washington, DC 20045
(202) 347-8686
Advocates the repeal of *Roe v. Wade*. Provides information and materials opposing abortion.

Alan Guttmacher Institute
111 5th Avenue
New York, NY 10003
(212) 254-5656
Conducts research on voluntary fertility control, family planning programs, and population issues. Publishes research reports and maintains statistics on the incidence and rate of abortion.

Alternatives to Abortion International
4680 Lake Underhill
Orlando, FL 32807
(407) 277-1942
Association of service groups that promote alternatives to abortion. Source of pro-life information and materials.

American Association of Pro-Life Pediatricians
11055 S. St. Louis Avenue
Chicago, IL 60655
(312) 233-8000
Composed of pediatricians who oppose abortion, the association seeks to advance its pro-life position through educational activities.

American Citizens Concerned for Life Education Fund
PO Box 179
Excelsior, MN 55331
(612) 474-0885
Advocates recognition of the humanity of the unborn. Maintains catalogs of resources and makes available audiovisual and other pro-life educational materials.

American Civil Liberties Union (ACLU)
Reproductive Freedom Project
132 W. 43rd Street
New York, NY 10036
(212) 944-9800
Legal defense and services organization that engages in pro-choice litigation. Source of information on the range of abortion-related legal issues.

American Life League
PO Box 1350
Stafford, VA 22554
(703) 659-4171
Educational and charitable organization involved in a wide range of pro-life activities. Maintains an extensive library and provides information on abortion issues. Publishes and disseminates books, brochures, information packets, and other materials.

American Life Lobby
PO Box 490
Stafford, VA 22554
(703) 659-4171
Organization that lobbies on behalf of pro-life causes and issues. Source of information on legislative and government activities pertaining to abortion.

Americans United For Life
343 S. Dearborn, Suite 1804
Chicago, IL 60604
(312) 786-9494
Pro-life legal and educational group. Maintains resource center of information on abortion-related legal issues.

Association of Reproductive Health Professionals
409 12th Street S.W.
Washington, DC 20024
(202) 863-2475
Pro-choice professional association that promotes the establishment of family planning services. Source of information on reproductive health care.

Birthright, United States of America
686 N. Broad Street
Woodbury, NJ 08096
(609) 848-1819
Pro-life association of groups that assist pregnant women in finding alternatives to abortion.

Catholics for a Free Choice
1436 U Street N.W.
Washington, DC 20009
(202) 638-1706
Organization of Roman Catholics who endorse the right to abortion. Conducts public education and publishes literature reconciling Catholicism with pro-choice views.

Catholics United for Life
New Hope, KY 40052
(502) 325-3061
Disseminates information on Catholic teachings regarding abortion and the value of human life. Maintains library on theology, history, papal teachings, and related topics.

Center for Population Options
1012 14th Street N.W. Suite 1200
Washington, DC 20005
(202) 347-5700
Engages in advocacy and educational activities to reduce the number of unintended teenage pregnancies and to assure minors access to family planning services. Provides information on sex education and other adolescent fertility-related issues.

Centers for Disease Control
1600 Clifton Street N.E.
Atlanta, GA 30333
(404) 329-3311
Agency of the Public Health Service. Maintains statistical information on the rate and incidence of abortion.

213

CHOICE
125 S. 9th Street, Suite 603
Philadelphia, PA 19107
(212) 592-7644
Pro-choice organization that supports providing reproductive health services to people at every economic level. Operates resource information center.

Christian Action Council
701 W. Broad Street, Suite 405
Falls Church, VA 22046
(703) 237-2100
Conservative Christian organization committed to the sanctity of life. Publishes brochures and other materials.

Family Life Information Exchange
PO Box 10716
Rockville, MD 20850
(301) 770-3362
Agency of the Department of Health and Human Services. Collects and disseminates information on family planning, reproductive health, contraception, teenage pregnancy, and related topics.

Feminists for Life of America
811 E. 47th Street
Kansas City, MO 64110
(816) 561-1365
Feminist organization that endorses the right to life from conception to natural death. Source of information on abortion and feminism.

FORLIFE
PO Drawer 1279
Tryon, NC 28782
(704) 859-5392
Distributes pro-life materials including audiovisual items, plays, stories, books, pamphlets, and monographs.

Human Life Foundation
150 E. 35th Street
New York, NY 10016
(212) 685-5210
Publishes and distributes books, pamphlets, and informational materials on abortion, bioethics, and family issues.

Human Life International
7845-E Airpark Road
Gaithersburg, MD 20879
(301) 670-7884
Research, education, and service organization that advocates pro-life and family values. Prepares and distributes reference materials.

International Life Services, Inc
2606 1/2 W. Eighth Street
Los Angeles, CA 90057
(213) 382-2156
Research and educational association that opposes abortion from a Judeo-Christian perspective. Publishes and distributes brochures, educational materials, and audiovisual items.

Lutherans for Life
275 N. Syndicate
St. Paul, MN 55104
(612) 645-5444
Lutheran organization opposed to abortion. Provides information and resources on pro-life issues.

Michael Fund
(International Foundation for Genetic Research)
400 Penn Center Blvd., Suite 721
Pittsburgh, PA 15235
(412) 823-6380
Conducts scientific research on genetic disorders. Based on a pro-life philosophy, opposes the abortion of the defective unborn. Provides research findings and related information.

National Abortion Federation
1436 U St., N.W.
Washington, DC 20009
(202) 667-5881
National professional forum of abortion service providers and others involved in related pro-choice activities. Maintains library of information on abortion, contraception, reproductive health care, and related subjects.

National Abortion Rights Action League (NARAL)
1101 14th Street N.W.
Washington, DC 20005
(202) 371-0779
Pro-choice advocacy group that seeks to maintain the right to legal abortion. Source of information on legislation in particular and abortion issues in general.

National Conference of Catholic Bishops
United States Catholic Conference
1312 Massachusetts Avenue N.W.
Washington, DC 20005
(202) 659-6673
Provides information on the Roman Catholic Church's opposition to abortion and its belief in the sanctity of life.

National Family Planning and Reproductive Health Association
122 C Street N.W.
Washington, DC 20001
(202) 685-3535
Association of health professionals and others involved in reproductive health issues. Operates network for information on family planning services and reproductive health care.

National Health Lawyers Association
1620 Eye Street N.W.
Washington, DC 20006
(202) 833-1100
Professional association of lawyers involved in health issues. Serves as an information clearinghouse on health law.

National Organization for Women
1401 New York Avenue N.W.
Washington, DC 20005
(202) 347-2279
Supports the preservation of legal abortion services. Source of information on women's issues.

National Organization of Episcopalians for Life
10523 Main Street, Suite 35
Fairfax, VA 23030
(703) 591-6635
Episcopalian organization committed to the sanctity of life. Publishes and disseminates religious, ethical, and scientific information.

National Right to Life Committee
419 7th Street N.W.
Washington, DC 20004
(202) 626-8800
Antiabortion organization involved in the major pro-life movement issues. Prepares and distributes information and materials.

National Women's Health Network
1325 G Street N.W.
Washington, DC 20005
(202) 347-1140
Advocacy organization that supports legalized abortion. Acts as an information clearinghouse on women's health issues.

National Women's Political Caucus
1275 K Street N.W.
Washington, DC 20005
(202) 898-1100
Pro-life political organization that provides information on proposed constitutional amendments related to abortion.

National Youth Pro-Life Coalition
Jackson Avenue
Hastings-On-Hudson, NY 10706
(914) 478-0103
Pro-life organization for young adults. Operates an educational foundation that develops audiovisual and other resources.

People for Life
3375 N. Dousman
Milwaukee, WI 53223
(414) 332-3423
Pro-life organization that focuses on adoption issues. Publishes postabortion, postadoption, and general information materials.

Physicians for Choice
810 7th Avenue
New York, NY 10019
(212) 541-7880
Engages in activities to educate the public on the health benefits of reproductive freedom.

Planned Parenthood Federation of America
810 7th Avenue
New York, NY 10019
(212) 541-7800
Engages in widespread activities to make contraception, abortion, sterilization, and infertility services available and accessible to all. Operates more than 800 centers that provide family planning services and educational programs.

Population Renewal Office
36 W. 59th Street
Kansas City, MO 64113
(816) 363-6980
Research group that advocates population growth and consequently opposes abortion. Supplies research findings and statistics.

Pro-Choice Defense League
131 Fulton Avenue
Hempstead, NY 11550
(516) 538-2626
Serves as a forum for information on reproductive rights and related legal issues.

Pro-Life Action League
6160 N Cicero, #600
Chicago, IL 60646
(312) 777-2900
Engages in lobbying, demonstrations, picketing, and other activities designed to halt abortions. Maintains, publishes, and distributes information resources.

Pro-Life Direct Action League
PO Box 35044
St. Louis, MO 63135
(314) 863-1022
Opposes abortion and promotes reverence for the sanctity of life based on Christian beliefs. Provides brochures, films, and other materials.

Pro-Life Nonviolent Action Project
PO Box 2193
Gaithersburg, MD 20879
(301) 774-4043
Seeks to prevent abortions through nonviolent direct action. Publishes and distributes brochures, pamphlets, and handouts.

Religious Coalition for Abortion Rights
100 Maryland Avenue N.E., Suite 307
Washington, DC 20002
(202) 543-7032
Publishes and distributes pamphlets, booklets, and other materials in support of the legal right to abortion.

Save A Baby
PO Box 101
Orinda, CA 94563
(415) 758-1117
Sponsors antiabortion programs and services. Distributes tapes of pro-life speeches and messages and other materials.

U.S. Coalition for Life
Box 315
Export, PA 15632
(412) 327-7379
Pro-life research and information clearinghouse on population control activities. Maintains international reprint service and publishes monographs and reports.

Women Exploited by Abortion
24823 Nogal
Moreno Valley, CA 92388
(714) 924-4164
Organization with Christian focus of women who regret having had abortions. Seeks to educate society about abortion and its impact on women.

Zero Population Growth
1400 16th Street N.W.
Washington, DC 20036
(202) 332-2200
Promotes population stabilization policies and women's access to abortion services. Source of information on population issues.

STATE AND LOCAL

ALABAMA

Alabama Citizens for Life
PO Box 184
Montgomery, AL 36101
(205) 434-3488

Alabama Civil Liberties Union
PO Box 447
Montgomery, AL 36101
(205) 265-2754

ALASKA

ACLU of Alaska
PO Box 201844
Anchorage, AK 99520-1844
(907) 276-2258

Alaska Right to Life
PO Box 772449
Eagle River, AK 99577
(907) 522-1550

ARIZONA

Arizona Civil Liberties Union
2021 N. Central #301
Phoenix, AZ 85004
(602) 254-3339

Arizona Right to Life
PO Box 3148
Tempe, AZ 85280
(602) 244-1102

ARKANSAS

ACLU of Arkansas
209 W. Capitol #214
Little Rock, AR 72201
(501) 374-2660

Arkansas Right to Life
PO Box 1697
Little Rock, AR 72203
(501) 374-0445

CALIFORNIA

ACLU of Northern California
1663 Mission Street #460
San Francisco, CA 94103
(415) 621-2488

California Pro-Life Council
926 J Street, Suite 1100
Sacramento, CA 95814
(916) 442-8315

ACLU of Southern California
633 South Shatto Place

Planned Parenthood Affiliates of
California

Los Angeles, CA 90005
(213) 487-1720

ACLU/San Diego
1202 Kettner Boulevard, Suite
6220
San Diego, CA 92101-3533
(619) 232-2121

1317-A 15th Street
Sacramento, CA 95814
(916) 446-5247

Planned Parenthood Regional
Office
333 Broadway
San Francisco, CA 94133
(415) 956-8856

COLORADO

ACLU of Colorado
815 E. 22nd Avenue
Denver, CO 80205
(303) 861-2258

Colorado Right to Life Committee
2500 Curtis, #108
Denver, CO 80205
(303) 753-9394

CONNECTICUT

Connecticut Civil Liberties Union
32 Grand Street
Hartford, CT 06106
(203) 247-9823

Pro-Life Council of Connecticut
411 Townsend Avenue
New Haven, CT 06512
(203) 469-9185

DELAWARE

ACLU of Delaware
702 King Street, Suite 600A
Wilmington, DE 19801
(302) 654-3966

Delaware Citizens for Life
PO Box 210
Rockland, DE 19732
(302) 651-0932

DISTRICT OF COLUMBIA

ACLU of the National Capitol
Area
1400 20 Street N.W., #119
Washington, DC 20036
(202) 457-0800

D.C. Right to Life
PO Box 90360
Washington, DC 20090
(202) 547-6721

Planned Parenthood Federation of America
2010 Massachusetts Avenue N.W., Suite 500
Washington, DC 20036
(202) 785-3351

FLORIDA

ACLU of Florida
225 N.E. 34 Street, #208
Miami, FL 33137
(305) 576-2336

Florida Association of Planned
  Parenthood Affiliates
1704 Thomasville Road, Suite 209
Tallahassee, FL 32303
(904) 386-1494

Florida Right to Life
PO Box 794
Cassleberry, FL 32707
(407) 834-9699

GEORGIA

ACLU of Georgia
233 Mitchell Street S.W., #200
Atlanta, GA 30303
(404) 523-5398

Georgia Right to Life
PO Box 81474
Atlanta, GA 30366
(404) 454-7612

Planned Parenthood Regional Office
Tower Place
3340 Peachtree Road N.E., Suite 1620
Atlanta, Ga 30026
(404) 262-1128

HAWAII

ACLU of Hawaii
PO Box 3410
Honolulu, HI 96801
(808) 545-1722

Hawaii Right to Life
1019 University Avenue
Honolulu, HI 96826
(808) 943-1595

IDAHO

Right to Life of Idaho
1425 S. Mountainview Road
Moscow, ID 83843
(208) 853-6103

ILLINOIS

ACLU of Illinois
20 East Jackson
Chicago, IL 60604
(312) 427-7330

Illinois Planned Parenthood
  Council
527 E. Capitol Avenue, Suite 113
Springfield, IL 62701
(217) 522-6776

Illinois Federation Right to Life
412 Langdon
Alton, IL 62002
(618) 465-7655

Planned Parenthood Regional
  Office
2625 Butterfield Road
Oak Brook, IL 60521
(312) 574-9270

INDIANA

ACLU of Indiana
445 N. Pennsylvania Street, #911
Indianapolis, IN 46204
(317) 635-4056

Indiana Planned Parenthood
  Affiliates Association
3209 N. Meridian
Indianapolis, IN 46208
(317) 926-4662

Indiana Right to Life
127 E. Michigan Street
Indianapolis, IN 46204
(317) 637-2722

IOWA

Iowa Civil Liberties Union
446 Insurance Exchange Building
Des Moines, IA 50309
(515) 243-3988

Iowa Right to Life Committee
6000 Douglas Avenue
Des Moines, IA 50322
(515) 270-6655

KANSAS

ACLU of Kansas and Western
Missouri
106 E. 31st Terrace
Kansas City, MO 64111
(816) 531-7121

Kansas for Life
3202 W. 13th, Suite 1-A
Wichita, KS 67203
(816) 945-9291

KENTUCKY

Kentucky Civil Liberties Union
425 W. Muhammad Ali
  Boulevard, #230
Louisville, KY 40202
(502) 581-1181

Kentucky Right to Life
  Association
134 Breckenridge Lane
Louisville, KY 40207
(502) 895-5959

LOUISIANA

ACLU of Louisiana
921 Canal Street, Suite 1237
New Orleans, LA 70112
(504) 522-0618

Louisiana Right to Life Federation
PO Box 8807
Metairie, LA 70011
(318) 893-1515

MAINE

Maine Civil Liberties Union
97A Exchange Street
Portland, ME 04101
(207) 774-5444

Maine Right to Life Committee
9 Densmore Court
Hallowell, ME 04347
(207) 622-3837

MARYLAND

ACLU of Maryland
2219 St. Paul Street
Baltimore, MD 21218
(301) 576-1103

Maryland Right to Life
PO Box 115
Kensington, MD 20895
(301) 933-1933

MASSACHUSETTS

ACLU of Massachusetts
19 Temple Place
Boston, MA 02111
(617) 482-3170

Massachusetts Citizens for Life
529 Main Street
Boston, MA 02129
(617) 242-4199

MICHIGAN

ACLU of Michigan
1553 Woodward Avenue,
 #1701
Detroit, MI 48226-2003
(313) 961-4662

Planned Parenthood Affiliates of
 Michigan
PO Box 19104
Lansing, MI 48901
(517) 482-1080

Right to Life of Michigan
920 Cherry S.E.
Grand Rapids, MI 49506
(616) 451-0601

MINNESOTA

Minnesota Citizens Concerned
 for Life
4249 Nicollet Avenue
Minneapolis, MN 55409
(612) 825-6831

Minnesota Civil Liberties Union
1021 W. Broadway
Minneapolis, MN 55411-2503
(612) 522-2423

MISSISSIPPI

ACLU of Mississippi
921 N. Congress Street
Jackson, MS 39202
(601) 355-6464

Mississippi Right to Life
RR 3, Box 205C
Vicksburg, MS 39180
(601) 634-1304

MISSOURI

ACLU of Eastern Missouri
4557 Laclede Avenue
St. Louis, MO 63108
(314) 361-2111

ACLU of Western Missouri
106 E. 31 Terrace
Kansas City, MO 64111
(816) 531-7121

Missouri Citizens for Life
PO Box 651
Jefferson City, MO 65102
(314) 635-5110

Planned Parenthood Affiliates of
Missouri
129 E. High Street, Suite B
Jefferson City, MO 65101
(314) 634-2761

MONTANA

ACLU of Montana
104 N. Broadway, Room 335
Billings, MT 59103
(406) 668-7789

Montana Right to Life Association
2139 Broadwater Avenue
Billings, MT 59102
(406) 443-0827

NEBRASKA

ACLU of Nebraska
633 S. 9th Street, #LL10
Lincoln, NE 68508
(402) 476-8091

Nebraska Coalition for Life
5561 S. 48th Street
Lincoln, NE 68516
(402) 477-3993

NEVADA

ACLU of Nevada
557 E. Sahara Avenue, Suite 222
Las Vegas, NV 89104
(702) 796-8558

Nevada Right to Life Committee
1600 E. Desert Inn Road
Las Vegas, NV 89109
(702) 871-9693

NEW HAMPSHIRE

New Hampshire Civil Liberties
Union
11 S. Main Street
Concord, NH 03301
(603) 225-3080

New Hampshire Right to Life
PO Box 421
Merrimack, NH 03054
(603) 225-6866

NEW JERSEY

ACLU of New Jersey
2 Washington Place
Newark, NJ 07102
(201) 642-2084

New Jersey Right to Life
102 Walnut Street
Cranford, NJ 07016
(201) 276-6620

Planned Parenthood Affiliates of NJ
132 W. State Street
Trenton, NJ 08608
(609) 393-8423

NEW MEXICO

ACLU of New Mexico
130 Alvarado Drive N.E.
Albuquerque, NM 87108
(505) 266-5915

Planned Parenthood Association
of New Mexico Affiliates
4084 Dietz Farm Circle N.W.
Albuquerque, NM 87107
(505) 345-6012

Right to Life Committee of New Mexico
2800 San Mateo Boulevard N.E.
Albuquerque, NM 87110
(505) 881-4563

NEW YORK

Family Planning Advocates of
New York State
17 Elk Street
Albany, NY 11207
(518) 436-8408

New York Civil Liberties Union
132 W. 43 Street
New York, NY 10036
(212) 382-0557

New York State Right to Life
41 State Street
Albany, NY 12207
(518) 434-1293

NORTH CAROLINA

North Carolina Civil Liberties
Union
PO Box 28004
Raleigh, NC 27611
(919) 834-3390

North Carolina Right to Life
PO Box 9282
Greensboro, NC 27429
(919) 274-LIFE

NORTH DAKOTA

North Dakota Right to Life
115 N. Second Street
Bismarck, ND 58502
(701) 258-3811

OHIO

ACLU of Ohio
1223 W. Sixth Street
Cleveland, OH 44113
(216) 781-6276

Ohio Right to Life
718 S. High Street
Columbus, OH 43206
(614) 445-8369

Planned Parenthood Affiliates of Ohio
16 E. Broad Street, Room 915
Columbus, OH 43215
(614) 224-0761

OKLAHOMA

ACLU of Oklahoma
1411 Classen, Suite 318
Oklahoma City, OK 73106
(405) 524-8511

Oklahomans for Life
3150 E. 41st Street
Tulsa, OK 74105
(918) 749-5022

OREGON

ACLU of Oregon
310 S.W. 4th Avenue, #705
Portland, OR 97204
(503) 227-3186

Family Planning Advocates of
Oregon
3231 S.E. 50th Avenue
Portland, OR 97206
(503) 775-3918

Oregon Right to Life
11220 S.E. Stark, #6
Portland, OR 97216
(503) 254-3107

PENNSYLVANIA

ACLU of Pennsylvania
PO Box 1161
Philadelphia, PA 19105
(215) 923-4357

Pennsylvania Pro-Life Federation
1801 Investment Building
Pittsburgh, PA 15222
(717) 963-0301

Planned Parenthood of Pennsylvania
227 State Street
Harrisburg, PA 17102
(717) 234-3024

RHODE ISLAND

Rhode Island Civil Liberties
  Union
212 Union Street, #211
Providence, RI 02903
(401) 831-7171

Rhode Island Right to Life
  Committee
27 Marcy Street
Cranston, RI 02905
(401) 521-1860

SOUTH CAROLINA

ACLU of South Carolina
533-B Harden Street
Columbia, SC 29205
(803) 799-5151

South Carolina Citizens for Life
PO Box 50622
Columbia, SC 29250
(803) 252-LIFE

SOUTH DAKOTA

ACLU of South Dakota
623 W. 11th
Sioux Falls, SD 57104
(303) 753-1214 (Regional Office)

South Dakota Right to Life
366 1/2 S. Pierre Street
Pierre, SD 57501
(605) 224-9181

TENNESSEE

ACLU of Tennessee
PO Box 120160
Nashville, TN 37212
(615) 320-7142

Tennessee Association of Planned
  Parenthood Affiliates
PO Box 121736
Nashville, TN 37212
(615) 385-3979

Tennessee Volunteers for Life
8005 E. Church Street
Brentwood, TN 37027
(615) 370-0027

TEXAS

ACLU/Houston Chapter
1236 W. Gray
Houston, TX 77019
(713) 524-5925

Texas Family Planning
  Association
905-A W. Oltorf, Suite A
Austin, TX 78704
(512) 448-4857

ACLU of Texas
1611 E. First Street
Austin, TX 78702-4455
(512) 477-5849

Texas Right to Life Committee
7011 Southwest Freeway
Houston, TX 77074
(713) 772-LIFE

UTAH

ACLU of Utah
#9 Exchange Place, #701
Salt Lake City, UT 84111
(801) 521-9289

Right to Life of Utah
95 N. 575 W
Layton, UT 84041
(801) 544-1050

VERMONT

ACLU of Vermont
100 State Street
Montpelier, VT 05602
(802) 223-6304

Vermont Right to Life Committee
PO Box 1079
Montpelier, VT 05602
(802) 229-4885

VIRGINIA

ACLU of Virginia
6 N. 6th Street, #2
Richmond, VA 23219-2419
(804) 644-8022

Association of Virginia Planned
Parenthood Affiliates
PO Box 1651
Richmond, VA 23213
(804) 783-7719

Virginia Society for Human Life
1214 Westover Hills Boulevard
Richmond, VA 23225
(804) 233-LIFE

WASHINGTON

ACLU of Washington
1720 Smith Tower
Seattle, WA 98104
(206) 624-2180

Human Life/Washington
2725 152nd Avenue N.E.
Redmond, WA 98052
(206) 882-4397

Planned Parenthood Affiliates of Washington
Capitol Park Building
1063 S. Capitol Way, #217
Olympia, WA 98501
(206) 754-6784

WEST VIRGINIA

West Virginians for Life
227 Chestnut Street
Morgantown, WV 26505
(304) 293-3402

WISCONSIN

Wisconsin Civil Liberties Union
207 E. Buffalo Street, #325
Milwaukee, WI 53202
(414) 272-4032

Wisconsin Right to Life
4840 Fond du Lac
Milwaukee, WI 53216
(414) 447-8333

WYOMING

Right to Life of Wyoming
PO Box 1601
Glenrock, WY 82637
(307) 436-8202

APPENDIX

Appendix A

ACRONYMS

ABA	American Bar Association
ACLU	American Civil Liberties Union
AGI	Alan Guttmacher Institute
ALI	American Law Institute
AMA	American Medical Association
CDC	Centers for Disease Control
CUL	Catholics United for Life
HEW	(U.S. Department of) Health Education and Welfare
HHS	(U.S. Department of) Health and Human Services
HLA	Human Life Amendment
HLFA	Human Life Federalism Amendment
MPC	Model Penal Code
NAF	National Abortion Federation
NARAL	National Abortion Rights Action League
NCCB	National Conference of Catholic Bishops
NIH	National Institutes of Health
NOW	National Organization for Women
NRLC	National Right to Life Committee
WEBA	Women Exploited by Abortion

APPENDIX B

STATUS OF PUBLIC FUNDING BY STATE

No restrictions

In cases of rape, incest or to save woman's life

To save life of woman

Other (See notes)

N.H.
VT.
N.Y.
PA.
W. VA.
VA.
N.C.
S.C.
GA.
FLA.
ME.
MASS.
R.I.
CONN.
N.J.
DEL.
MD.
D.C.

MICH.
OHIO
IND.
KY.
TENN.
ALA.
MISS.
LA.
ILL.
WIS.
MINN.
MO.
ARK.

IOWA
N.D.
S.D.
NEB.
KAN.
OKLA.
TEX.

MONT.
WYO.
IDAHO
UTAH
COLO.
N.M.
ARIZ.
NEV.

WASH.
ORE.
CALIF.

ALASKA
HAWAII

Iowa
In cases of rape or incest, grave health threats or to save woman's life

Virginia
In cases of rape, incest or severe fetal abnormality

Copyright © 1989, The New York Times; Reprinted with permission.

APPENDIX C

STATUS OF CONSENT AND NOTIFICATION LAWS BY STATE

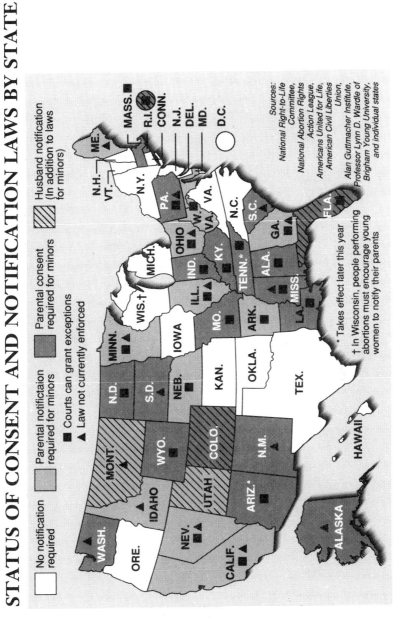

□ No notification required

▨ Parental notificaation required for minors

▨ Parental consent required for minors

■ Courts can grant exceptions

▲ Law not currently enforced

▨ Husband notification (In addition to laws for minors)

* Takes effect later this year

† In Wisconsin, people performing abortions must encourage young women to notify their parents

Sources:
National Right-to-Life Committee,
National Abortion Rights Action League,
Americans United for Life,
American Civil Liberties Union,
Alan Guttmacher Institute,
Professor Lynn D. Wardle of Brigham Young University,
and individual states

INDEX

237

238

Index

239

Index

241